W9-AEE-421

WITHDRAWN

WRITING THE SOCIAL:
CRITIQUE, THEORY, AND INVESTIGATIONS

This collection of essays, written by Dorothy Smith over the past eight years, is a long-awaited treasure by one of the world's foremost social thinkers. In it, Smith turns her wit and common sense on the prevailing discourses of sociology, political economy, philosophy, and popular culture, at the same time redefining her own sociological and feminist theory and practice.

Shedding the idiom of the sociologist, Smith inquires directly into the actualities of people's lives. Her critical investigations of postmodernism, political correctness, university politics, and the Standard North American Family (SNAF) draw on metaphors and examples from a stimulating range of autobiographical, theoretical, historical, and political resources. Out of an abstract encounter with Bakhtin, for example, comes an analysis of a child learning to name a bird, and a new way of seeing the story of Helen Keller. In introducing a radically innovative approach to the sociology of discourse, even the most difficult points are addressed through scenes of everyday life.

Smith's engaged, rebel sociology throws light on a remarkable range of issues and authors, forever changing the way the reader experiences the world. This, her signature work, will inspire a wide and varied audience, and enliven university courses for years to come.

DOROTHY E. SMITH is Professor in Sociology at the Ontario Institute of Studies in Education/University of Toronto. She is the author of *The Everyday World as Problematic: A Feminist Sociology* and *The Conceptual Practices of Power.*

DOROTHY E. SMITH

Writing the Social: Critique, Theory, and Investigations

UNIVERSITY OF TORONTO PRESS
Toronto Buffalo London

© University of Toronto Press Incorporated 1999
Toronto Buffalo London
Printed in Canada

ISBN 0-8020-4307-0 (cloth)
ISBN 0-8020-8135-5 (paper)

Canadian Cataloguing in Publication Data

Smith, Dorothy E., 1926–
    Writing the social : critique, theory, and investigations

    Includes bibliographical references and index.
    ISBN 0-8020-4307-0 (bound)   ISBN 0-8020-8135-5 (pbk.)

    1. Sociology – Philosophy.   2. Feminist theory.   I. Title.

    HM24.S542 1999   301'.01   C98-931426-X

University of Toronto Press acknowledges the financial assistance to its publishing
program of the Canada Council for the Arts and the Ontario Arts Council.

For George W. Smith
1935–1994

Good friend

Contents

WRITING THE SOCIAL

1

Introduction

This book is made up of papers written over a period of eight years. I have divided them into three categories – critique, theory, and investigations – though the distinctions between them are not as sharp as the categories suggest. All of them have something of the character of investigations and have come about in rather similar ways. They are unlike other research I have done; for example, with Alison Griffith, studying the work that mothers do in relation to their children's schooling (Griffith 1995; Griffith and Smith 1987, 1990; Smith 1989, 1998 [forthcoming]; Smith and Griffith 1990); or, with Paula Bourne and Liza McCoy (Smith, McCoy, and Bourne 1995), on what girls think about their schooling. The latter studies, while adopting a standpoint in women's or girls' lives, followed a more traditional path. A definite project, questions, and methods of investigation were developed; bibliographies were prepared; applications were made for funding; individual or focus-group interviews, addressing predefined topics, created a body of data that became the basis of reports, papers, and so on. The various papers incorporated in this volume have originated very differently. They might be described as originating in the intertextuality of my own experience as a reader. All of them have begun with some sensation of disquiet, a political discomfort that directed attention to a problem that I could not, at that stage, make explicit.

All the papers are, in one way or another, preoccupied with what I have come to call the 'ruling relations' (see chapter 5). In my earliest writing from women's standpoint, I located a break in my own consciousness: on the one hand, my being as mother and housewife, at home, with two small children; and, on the other, my work in relation to the university as a sociologist. The latter had this strange character, when I looked at it from the point of view of a woman located in the actualities of her every-day/everynight living, of being put together so that the subject partici-pated in objectified relations organized beyond the local particularities of her domestic consciousness. Women's standpoint as a place to begin an inquiry into the social locates the knower in her body and as active in her work in relation to particular others. In a sense it *discovers* the ruling rela-tions. They come into view from where she is in the actualities of her bodily existence, as relations that transcend the limitations of the embod-ied knower. To explore them from women's standpoint is to recognize them as they enter her/my own experience and in her/my own practices as a knower, reader, and thinker. These papers, in their varieties, have as a consistent focus that of examining problems in my own participation in the ruling relations, in the hope and expectation that such an explora-tion has something to say about those relations and how they are at work in our consciousnesses.

Writing the Social

In working towards a method of writing the social from women's stand-point, I am conscious of participating in, and learning from, many dia-logues, among them the critical theoretical work of feminist theorists such as Sandra Harding (1986) or Joan Scott (1992). But perhaps most important in shaping these studies has been my work as a teacher. To teach, I have had to find out how to make explicit much that I *just knew*. It is this that has given a special sense to the notion of writing the social. I have had to try to make plain just what it is that differentiates this way of doing sociology from what I call 'established sociology,' the sociology in which I was trained.

Social scientific inquiry ordinarily begins from a standpoint in a text-mediated discourse or organization; it operates to claim a piece of the actual for the ruling relations of which it is part; it proceeds from a con-cept or theory expressing those relations, and it operates selectively in assembling observations of the world that are ordered discursively. The standpoint of women proposes a different *point d'appui*. It begins one step back before the Cartesian shift that forgets the body. The body isn't for-gotten; hence, the actual local site of the body isn't forgotten. Inquiry starts with the knower who is actually located; she is active; she is at work; she is connected up with particular other people in various ways; she thinks, eats, sleeps, laughs, desires, sorrows, sings, curses, loves, just here; she reads here; she watches television. She sits at her computer playing solitaire, analysing data, sending e-mail messages to friends, writing a paper. Activities, feelings, and experiences hook her into extended social relations, linking her activities to others and in ways beyond her knowing. While a standpoint beginning in text-mediated discourse begins with the concepts or schema of that discourse and turns towards the actual to find its object, the standpoint of women never leaves the actual. The knowing subject is always located in a particular spatial and temporal site, a particular configuration of the everyday/everynight world. Inquiry is directed towards exploring and explicating what s/he does not know – the social relations and organization pervading her or his world but invisible in it.

Central to this sociology (since it cannot be gender-restricted, it should, perhaps, be called a sociology for people) is a method of inquiry. The notion of a standpoint of women doesn't stand by itself as a theoretical construct. It is a place to begin inquiry. Proceeding (and I emphasize the activity here) according to established methods of inquiry in sociology, beginning in discourse with *its* concepts, and relying on standard good social scientific methodologies, produces people as objects. This is an effect of its methods of thinking and inquiry. It is not an effect of sociologists' intentions. Sociologists' intentions may be as oppositional and progressive as any of us could wish, but if they work with standard methods of thinking and inquiry, they import the ruling relations into the texts they produce (this is *not* an issue of quantitative versus qualitative method). In making an alternative sociology, its method of inquiry is central.

A Method of Inquiry

Here is a brief characterization of the method of inquiry I have made use of in writing the social into the papers collected here.

1. The subject/knower of inquiry is not a transcendent subject, but situated in the actualities of her own living, in relations with others. I don't give the term 'actual' content because I want it to function like the arrow you see on maps of malls that tells you 'you are here!' I want the term 'actual' to be always directing us back to the 'outside the text' in which living goes on and in which the text is being read or written. Of course, the text is always in the actual, though we seem to feel that we can escape through the text, riding it like the magic carpet of legend. The term 'actual' remains undefined to remind us of the carpet we are riding, of us too who are riding it, and of the ground below. 'Actual' points outside the text to the reader and her or his site of reading within which the text is activated, becomes a text.

Established sociology's stylistic conventions, some of which are examined and criticized in chapers 3 and 4, constitute subject positions locating the reader/inquirer outside the social world in which the text is read or written and in which she does her work, lives her life, cares or does not care about the people she investigates. They create for sociology a 'layer' of discursive entities subsuming and displacing actual activities and actual people, installing the social as a topic, as the subject and object of sentences, without having to engage with or problematize how what is thus referenced is actually being brought into being[1] 'out there' where it all goes on. By contrast, the situated knower is always also a participant in the social she is discovering. Her inquiry is developed as a form of that participation. Her experiencing is always active as a way of knowing, whether or not she makes it an explicit resource.

2. In this method, we're talking about the actual ongoing practices of actual individuals as they go forward in just the everyday/everynight sites in which they happen and in the time they perdure. This ontology originates in Marx and Engels's (1976) formulation in *The German Ideology*. But we're not just concerned with what individuals do. That would return us to sociologies grounded in the individual, which leave us with the insuperable problem of the gulf between individual and society and the fallback position of postulating social systems or social structures to capture the substance of the social. The sociology I'm proposing conceives of the social, that is, sociology's business or focus, as *the ongoing concerting and coordinating of individuals' activities.* Here is 'the social' as the discursively constituted object of sociology's inquiry. Established sociology's ordinary possibility of doing ethnography, description, or generalization, let alone the ordinary intelligibility of notions such as 'institutions,' 'formal organization,' and so on, presuppose people's ever-to-be-renewed coordinating of their activities.

The social, therefore, is not conceived as an entity separable from the actual people and the activities in which we find it. It is not demarcated as a determinate order of phenomena – as Walter Wallace's (1988) '*interorganism behavior regularity,*'[2] for example. Rather, the concept of the social directs a focusing of sociological attention on how people's activities are coordinated. It is a specialization of attention that produces for this sociology its discursive object. Topically, an investigation of the social could range from the most intimate of interplays, between mother and suckling child, between lovers, in dancing, all the way to the dynamic of relations of exchange or the circulation of capital. There are many other ways in which what people are doing, thinking, and feeling in the actualities of their everyday/everynight living could be written. The sociologist (practising this sociology) chooses to direct her gaze towards the social as the ongoing concerting of people's actual activities; her only restriction is a commitment not to reduce the social to properties of individuals or to reconstitute it as a supra-individual blob.

3. For this sociology, concepts such as social organization and social relations become central. Of course, it's important not to hypostasize either. It's particularly important to avoid conceptualizations that lift phenomena out of time and place, constituting them as discursive entities in the peculiar timelessness of established sociology's discourse.

Terms such as 'social relations,' 'social organization,' and 'socially organized' are used in the studies included in this collection to recover those forms of concerting people's activities that are regularly reproduced. 'Social relations' does not refer to relationships such as instructor-student, between lovers, parent-child, and so on. *Rather, it directs attention to, and takes up analytically, how what people are doing and experiencing in a given local site is hooked into sequences of action implicating and coordinating multiple local sites where others are active* (Smith 1990b: 93–6; G.W. Smith 1995). A social 'relation is not a thing to be looked for in carrying out research, rather, it is what is used to do the looking' (G.W. Smith 1995: 24). It is a practical realization of the commitment to the discursive problematic of the everyday/everynight world (Smith 1987).

4. Learning how to address concepts, beliefs, ideology, and other categories of thought or mind as people's actual practices in the local settings of their everyday lives has become central to this sociological project. The traditional theory/practice split is avoided. Taking up women's standpoint as a place to begin locates the knower in her body, in a lived world in which both theory and practice go on, in which theory is itself a practice. The course of writing the social into these papers is one of finding out how to make active, present, and observable the theoretical, conceptual, ideological, and other forms of thought.

5. I have come to see the text in its material as well as in its symbolic aspect as the bridge between the eveyday/everynight local actualities of our living and the ruling relations (see chapter 5). The text is a material object that brings into actual contexts of reading a standardized form of words or images that can be and may be read/seen/heard in many other settings by many others at the same or other times. It creates something like an escape hatch out of the actual and is foundational to any possibility of abstraction of whatever kind, including this one written here. Writing the social exploits the power of writing and of the text to analyse and

isolate dimensions of organization that are fully embedded in the actualities of living. It is the text that confronts that writing with the challenge of standardization across settings and of wrestling with preserving the presence of actual individuals in deploying a technology that displaces them.

6. The politics of the project are foundational. Opening inquiry by beginning in the actualities of people's lives as they experience them does not mean making them the objects of research. The aim is not to explain people's behaviour but to be able to explain to them/ourselves the socially organized powers in which their/our lives are embedded and to which their/our activities contribute.

Inquiry is in and of the same world as people live in. Hence this sociology is self-consciously attentive to the social relational dimensions of its own practice, a critical attention that is, of course, never perfected. It is always also about ourselves as inquirers, not just our personal selves, but our selves as participants in the social relations we explore. In discovering dimensions of the social that come into view when we begin inquiry from the actualities of people's lives and experience, we discover the lineaments of social relations in which our own lives are embedded. For this sociology, there is no outside, no Archimedean point from which a positionless account can be written. Writing the social is always from where people are. Discovery is of the relations that generate multiple sites of diverging experience. It is from those multiple and diverse sites that their dimensions, organization, and organizing powers can be brought into view.

These Studies

The studies that make up the collection as a whole, whether they are what I have called investigations or not, have all come about in similar ways. I have contrasted them earlier in this chapter with other research I have been doing that has been more conventional in its format. These studies have started very differently, with a feeling of uneasiness or problem in some aspect of my working life as a participant in various discourses, reading journals, and eclectically in books, newspapers, and political magazines, as well as in sociology.

Writing the social has been integral to every one of the critical investigations that it records. Every paper has been a discovering of the social in what has been part of my textual engagement with the ruling relations. Investigation was largely in the process of writing. It has been supplemented in some instances by research beyond the texts with which I have engaged, but I have not started writing on the basis of research data.

Rather, I have started with a sense of problem, of something going on, some disquiet, and of something there that could be explicated.

Writing the social profits from the dialogue between what we mean to say and what we discover we have said, and, of course, the work of rewriting to embrace what we find we have said that is beyond or other than our intentions. So when I started to write about feminism in the academy, I knew in my own life that the academy had somehow come to reorganize the original project of making a sociology from women's standpoint that I had so happily joined. In chapter 2, I explore a hidden political ground that enters into our work without announcing itself, hindering the connectedness of an academic intelligentsia with the social movements of the community. Writing this paper was a process of discovering barriers that have been built historically into universities to inhibit the interconnections of academy and 'community' (doubtful term) with which this phase of the women's movement began.

I held a number of pieces in my hands when I started, some of them part of my life experience, others drawn from reading, and yet others discovered as I sampled historical writing on this century of the North American university. The connections I have drawn are not very firmly developed in terms of their historical documentation – that would take a good deal more research than I had time to commit to the project – but it was the process of writing that discovered the interconnectedness of the pieces with which I started. You might say, I just had 'this feeling' there was something there and wanted to be able to make it clear for myself.

The feelings, the uneasinesses, in which these papers originated register something that is at work in the relations in which I am active. In committing myself to investigation, I am taking up something like a piece of the fabric and examining it to make plain, as far as I am able, just how the warp and weft have been laid down and the pile knotted into them. If you've ever looked at books on 'Persian' rugs and carpets and their making, you can find examples of just what I mean. For example, here are descriptions of two different techniques:

The vase-carpet technique: Three shoots of weft lie between each row of knots, and when the outer ones are pulled tight the warp is forced to lie on two planes. The symmetrical knot, used principally in Turkey, the Caucasus, and Turkestan: The cut ends of the knot emerge in the middle of the two warps around which it has been tied. (Marko 1994: 17)

The descriptions are accompanied by diagrams. Neither is fully intelligible without the other, and together they are not intelligible independently of the actual carpets whose making they describe. If you spent time examining carpets in a museum or even a carpet store, you could begin to distinguish the different methods. I envisage writing the social as rather like whatever it takes to begin to make such a description. I start work with a piece of the weave, wherever it may be, whatever has caught my attention, and try to explicate the way in which it is put together. What is it about universities that impels the academicization of feminism? I have a sense that somehow political economy (examined in chapter 3), as well as established sociological ontologies (chapter 4), replicate a standpoint that excludes that of women as well as other marginalized groups. How can I find out just what actual practices of discourse produce such exclusions? Of course, I want to change them, to do things differently, to be able to tell others what they look like, which means being able to explicate them as definite and identifiable practices.

The papers included in the section on 'theory' have been written in a rather similar way. Chapter 5 locates the emergence of women's standpoint dialectically with the expanding trajectory of the ruling relations in Western Europe. I have thought further, than I have in this introduction, the divide/conjuncture between the everyday/everynight world of living that comes into view from women's standpoint and relations organized extra-locally. The sketch of the ruling relations I have drawn represents them as the objectified form of social consciousness, parallel to the objectified relations of dependence (the economy) on which Marx's investigations were focused. By recognizing the double-faced character of standardized texts, macro-social relations and organization can be made investigatable as actual forms of coordinating people's activities in the multiple local sites of people's everyday/everynight living.

Chapter 6, 'Telling the Truth after Postmodernism,' is a paper that has given me more pleasure to write than any other. When I finally had to send it off for publication, I mourned the passing of the space I had inhabited. Again, when I started, I had only a vague idea of how this piece of the social I had hold of was knotted, but I thought I could see which way the threads lay. In writing it, I discovered progressively how to specify what was emerging into view. I could see there was a problem in formulating the knower as an individuated subject that postmodernism had in common with the modernism it rejected. Finding out how to explicate referencing as a sequence *in time and among people* came about in one of those strange moments when you just see something happening that almost speaks to you – learn from this! As did my watching Karen on the sunny sidewalk of Albany Avenue in Toronto calling her mother's attention to the black cat grooming itself just in front of me. I don't know how such moments single themselves out. Perhaps the writing has come to where a kind of space has been created, rather in the way the shape of a particular missing piece in a jigsaw puzzle becomes defined as the other pieces are put in place. The moment in question just happens to fit this space, this hole, that the writing has delineated. Finding that piece enabled me to crystallize my sense of the dialogic character of anything we might call representation and hence to extend that to the reading of a map that I used as a metaphor for the sociological project.

The investigations that are called 'Investigations' attempt to map a particular piece of the ruling relations with which I have been, for various reasons, engaged; or maybe I could say, having discovered my new metaphor of the knotting of a Persian rug, they are attempts to explicate just how a particular piece of the social is woven. Because they have emerged out of the intertextual engagements of my life, they are not systematic. I have been writing the social as analyses of the ruling relations *as I've participated in them as local practices*. I should emphasize, however, that I do not view what I have explicated in these studies as merely idiosyncratic. Participating in these relations means entering their practices as subject and agent, competent in the stylistics, the theoretical practices, the categories, the social organization carried by the speech genre (Bakhtin 1986 and chapter 7), and so on that standardize the forms of ruling across local sites of people's living. They are not mine alone, but *of* the relations of ruling as we bring them into being in our activities as individuals. So my writing of the social in each instance discovers and explicates a particular piece of the fabric of ruling that I have taken hold of.

Though these investigations are fragmentary, I am working towards a method of writing the social in these regions, one that conforms to principles such as those written above and the modifications of them that I discover as I proceed. In the four papers making up this section, I try out different things, each a way of looking at sociology: the first (chapter 7) takes off from Bakhtin's (1981) theory of the novel, arguing that sociology (any kind) is essentially dialogic, and goes on to describe observations of reading sociological theory as a local practice regulating that dialogue; the two investigations in chapters 8 and 9 examine forms of coordinating different institutional sites *within* the ruling relations, which I call 'ideological codes,' imitating the notion of genetic codes with their capacity to replicate themselves; the fourth (chapter 10) explores, as a sequence of texts, the regulatory operation of juridical discourse and its repressive effects on the raising of chilly climate issues by women in a university context.

Though this collection does not include all the work I have done in the past few years, it has a modest coherence which I have tried to express in this introduction. As with other work I have done, it represents developing work in which I am learning as I go along. There are repetitions, but not, I hope, too many. Later work goes further in some ways than earlier work. A sociology organized as inquiry does not, cannot, begin with an exhaustively developed and comprehensive theory. It goes forward as a work of discovery among an increasing number of sociologists[3] in which we find out how to write the social, learning from the course of inquiry, from each other, and from the discipline of teaching.

Part One:
Critique

2

Contradictions for Feminist Social Scientists[1]

Universities, Women, and the Ruling Relations

I am unreservedly committed to securing for women the resources institutionalized in the academy that create knowledge, build and transmit
intellectual tradition, house and foster debate, and sustain continuities
across generations. We have lacked these, and in the past twenty years or
so we have begun to secure them. But there is a cost. Twentieth-century
North American universities have never been directly subjected to state
control. Nevertheless, buried historically in their foundations is a powerful politics. It is a politics that, at crucial periods during the 1930s and
1950s, and again today, has sought to isolate the university bases of the
intelligentsia from local and regional connections, from linkages with the
working class and the activism of the trade union movement, and from
organization identified with oppressed and marginalized groups. This
politics is institutionalized in the university system. Most of the time it is
taken for granted. It only comes into view when it has to be enforced.
Freedom of thought and speech, and the pursuit of knowledge, however
imperfectly realized in the university system, create an endemic pressure
threatening to authority. When it breaks out of bounds, as it did during
the early 1950s and the 1960s and 1970s, it is actively repressed, though
repression may not always appear very directly. Discourse – the across–
time and space conversation of the intelligentsia – builds in the boundaries of the institutional order, adopting its standpoint and incorporating
its relevances and interests. So long as it observes the class boundaries
imposed by that order and does not serve the need to know of the people
that order subordinates, it is not exposed to repressive political pressure.

The work of the social sciences sediments the logic of these controls.

The sociology we have works within institutional boundaries. It is hooked up dialogically to the institutional order at multiple points. Sometimes the latter's categories and concepts are directly incorporated into its discourse; invariably its standpoint is located in the ruling relations. Its research methodologies harvest information, data, and other forms of knowledge derived in various ways from people and what they have to say, and bring them home to the text-base discourses housed in universities. In general, social scientific knowledge represents the world from a standpoint in the ruling relations, not from the standpoint of those who are ruled.

The ruling relations are far from monolithic. Multiple and diverse interests and voices are at work in them. Nonetheless, generally their terrain is never conceded to, or opened up to use and influence by, those people who are exploited, marginalized, or subordinated by the relations of contemporary capitalism. As a system of control, the ruling relations have been particularly effective in ensuring that, in the main, whatever knowledge is produced is not oriented to the needs and interests of the mass of people, but to the needs and interests of ruling. When loopholes are found and leakages occur, they are stopped; when those privileged with access desert and go over to the other side, their access is cut off. Breached during the 1960s, this system of control has been re-formed and tightened.

The women's movement has its distinctive history within, and its distinctive struggle against, the ruling relations because these relations enacted the gender hierarchy we call 'patriarchy.' Its critique of patriarchy has often been also a critique of the ruling relations, proposing radically alternative forms of organizing the social relations of knowledge and communication. It revealed, for many women, the taken-for-granted class, gender, and racial subtexts of academic institutions – the hidden boundaries, exclusions, and positionings on which the texts and practices of ruling rely.

The women's movement has struggled to make women's voices heard in universities and colleges, and within academic disciplines. Those of us who were active in universities and colleges were, in the early stages of this struggle, activists in the women's movement outside as well; what we worked for in the academy was inseparable from what we were working for outside it. We wanted the immense resources vested in the university and college systems to sustain the development of thought, knowledge, and culture by women and for women. We had discovered – were and are discovering – an intellectual and political world to which women were marginal, if present at all. The intellectual, cultural, and political achievements of our foremothers had been for their own time only – if at all. The academy has never vested its resources in preserving and advancing their thought and work. If there was no ongoing intellectual tradition among women, no conversation extending from the past into the present, it was in part because the resources of the academy were never dedicated to this project.

The Women's Movement outside, in, and against the Academy

To remind us that the women's movement didn't begin with us, we have called this a new phase or wave of the North American and European women's movement. But this phase has been and is distinctive in making us conscious of the complex of power relations we have named 'patriarchy' and of developing strategies to transform it. Whatever that term might mean when subjected to refined definition, it showed us the institutionalized barriers and exclusions that we had for so many hundreds of years taken for granted. And though women are everywhere in the society, established channels of communication – academic discourses and universities, book publishing, the mass media of television and newspapers, and even women's magazines – were not for us, as women, to use in organizing among women, speaking and writing as women for women, developing issues, innovating expression, and remaking academic and professional discourses from women's standpoint (they are still resistant).

A radical critique speaking from the experience of women has been integral to the politics of the women's movement. Insisting on women's right to speak from the actualities of our experience is always potentially disruptive; there is always something new to be heard; there is always rethinking of established positions and representations to be done. The 'we' of the women's movement has been open; hence settled positions in it are always subject to challenge. The perspectives and relevances of white heterosexual middle-class women built into the definition of women's issues have been disrupted by working-class, lesbian, and non-white women opposing that hegemony. Elsewhere women of the 'Third World' were and are evolving a women's movement or women's movements independent of and in many respects more radical than those of North America and Europe.

New bases of organization were constantly emerging; rifts and rows resulted in new activism, realigning and expanding the women's move-

ment's system of communication. We published newspapers and news-
letters, created new publishing houses, established bookstores. And, of
course, we also tried to convert the established structures for women,
most often by creating within them a shell, such as a women's caucus or
committee, or in universities and colleges, a women's studies course, even
a program. We took seriously in practice and in theory the universality
lent our project by the category 'women.' Though established exclusions
and barriers of race, class, politics, and imperialism were implicit in
women's movement practice, they were, and are, always subject to confrontation and disruption. The very claim to speak *as women* and *for women*
creates its own instability as the speaker is found not to be speaking for
me, for you, for her, for us.

Today women like myself working in the academy most often learn of
other women's experience in the disembodiments of the text, wherein
they appear only as 'voices.' But in the early days of the women's movement, we were also connected in multiple ways through organization and
activism. Of course, these may have been the peculiarities of my own
experience growing up as a feminist in the women's movement in Vancouver, Canada, a city then of some one and a half million, sharing (at
that time) the strong radical traditions of the northwest coastal regions.
The women's movement of those times was a many-headed organization,
a hydra of contending groups. Yet despite contention, or perhaps
because of it, there was an interlacing of multiple relationships cross-
cutting factional differences.

Our challenges to the ruling relations weren't only voices. They were
challenges created by activism and experience acquired in activism; issues
of gender and class were raised, not as a matter of theory, but as a matter
of political practice (much more rarely at that time were challenges
raised concerning issues of race). The activism and debates of the
women's movement were embedded in, and responsive to, other forms of
activism and organization of the time – the openings created by the
movements of the 1960s, the idealization of the Chinese Revolution, the
renewal of Marxism-Leninism. The dogmatisms and sectarian forms of
organization were hooked into a foot-loose women's movement whose
participants moved in and out of organizations, quarrelled, made friends
and enemies, debated positions, and created new organization out of dissatisfaction with what was already in existence or from newly recognizing
a gap where action was called for.

The splitting, trashing, passionate quarrels, and debates out of which
opposing sides came resolving never to speak again to former friends and

allies, were the dynamic of a movement that was grounded in multiple ways in the society. What had seemed a first a simplicity of our sisterhood, what we confronted as patriarchy, what we found as the bases of our oppression in the control of our bodies, for example, turned out to be magnificent but untenable simplifications. Because women were everywhere in the society and because the forms of what we named patriarchy turned out to be multiple and various, the women's movement came to take up issues, not as a generality cross-cutting such divisions, but based in particularities of experiences in paid employment, in the home, in the community, in relation to children, in political organization, of racism – wherever the social relations organizing our daily/nightly lives, including the complex intersecting discourses of the society, located us as subjects.

Differentiation did not mean separation. Arguments and debates were intense and passionate; they engaged others in opposition as well as in agreement. In them, positions became defined, were given theoretical formulation, dissolved, and reformed. The debates, alignments, conflicts, and shared experiences and issues linked women across institutional barriers. The connections were *active*, partly in and through the media of the women's movement, partly in organization around issues of shared concern, and partly just in informal support and discussion.

Women taking up the women's movement in the academy were part of this connectedness. We participated with women outside the university, attempting to create linkages that broke with its traditional isolation and its traditional claims to authority. Certainly this was my experience. And I found that the institutional barriers that detach the university from the local community had two sides: on the one hand, there was nothing in the university that supported making connections outside. If anything it made difficulties. On the other hand, as we became active in off-campus organizations, we found that the women we worked with were antagonistic to the implied superiority of knowledge derived from the institutional dominance of the academy. We were under constant critical pressure in this encounter, constantly challenged by thinking and theories originating outside academic discourse, and by being confronted with bases of knowing grounded in experiences other and beyond our own.

In universities and colleges, we sought alternatives to institutional connections, and we sought to use *for* women the skills and resources the academy commands. The women's studies courses that we established also relied on experience and understandings grounded outside the academy. Since there was little or nothing in the way of books or articles that we could teach from in more orthodox styles, we didn't speak in our classes from an established discourse that we were trying to pass on to our students. Rather, we encouraged and evoked their and our speaking from our experience as women, beyond the comprehension of the academic discourses as they were then.

Institutional Disconnections: The Hidden Work of Class within the Academy

In these twenty or twenty-five years since that time, we have achieved extraordinary things in the academy. Of course, we do well to take nothing for granted, but women's studies are now part of the normal course of business in many if not most universities and colleges of English-speaking North America. We now have resources that we did not have before. We have rich and brilliant achievements. The contrast between the early days of teaching women's studies and today is very marked. Then we had extraordinarily little material to learn and teach from. Now the wealth of women's scholarly, cultural, and political writing is vast. It is powerfully enriched by the progressive displacement of white women from the centre and the advent of the authoritative presences of Hispanic, Afro–North American, Asian, and Native women. Whereas once each individual could think she could know it all – read a little later at night, get up a little earlier in the morning – we now know that is impossible. And for better or for worse, we now have specializations, sub-disciplines, schools, academic factions, hierarchies.

We have been successful, I do believe, in vesting some at least of the institutional resources of the academy in preserving, transmitting, and advancing knowledge of and for women. We have also been somewhat successful in breaking down the radically one-sided character of the male-dominated discourses of the disciplines and sciences, particularly in the humanities and social sciences. If we have not succeeded altogether in overturning the claims to generality based on gender partiality, we have at least succeeded in creating a richness of critique and alternatives that is astonishing given the relatively brief period of our 'renaissance.'

But there is a cost. There are powers operating at a less visible level in the university that pull our feminist work in unseen ways. In establishing ourselves in the academy, in making a place for women and women's experience in social science and the humanities, to a modest degree in law and the life sciences, and, at least marginally, in medicine, we have also become increasingly detached from our former linkages with activism and organization outside the academy. This is partly a result, no doubt, of the changing organization of the women's movement itself, of the growth and advances that have meant more specialization, and less place for the multi-connected activism of the earlier movement. In the academy, it has meant a progressive conforming of the discourses of women's studies and feminist theorizing to the institutional boundaries of the university. Once the production of knowledge for women became fully embedded in the academy, the ties that hooked its characteristic forms and directions of development with the concerns of women outside the academy became increasingly attenuated. Not that such knowledge production has not continued; this is particularly true for Afro–North American and Hispanic women with ongoing activist ties outside the academy. Euro–North American women have also continued to do work that serves women, but the pull these earlier forms of activism and organization exercised over our minds, imaginations, energies, and loyalties has been attenuated. Increasingly, feminists working in the academy with ties to activism beyond it are hooked into the ruling relations – professions, public service, political life, scholarly careers, and so on. As our own thinking becomes more articulated to disciplines sedimenting the hidden political ground of the academy, we become increasingly detached from independent sources of resistance and from the profoundly different take on the world they represent. Our feminism becomes professionalized.

And there *is* a hidden political ground. It has a history that is part of the developing organization of class in North America. The recurrent politicization of university campuses, each time stimulating alternative approaches to teaching and research, has always encountered, sooner or later, repressive political responses. The pressure may come via boards of governors, representing very directly the interests of a regional ruling class; or from university administrators and organizations of administrators; or from within the academic community itself; or from external and indirect pressures from the media or politicians. Clyde Barrow's study of the 'reconstruction' of American higher education during the early years of the twentieth century describes a major political shift from control by the faculty to control by administrators and boards of governors. He details the specific practices, now institutionalized in universities, by which that control was secured; in particular, over the freedom of faculty to develop knowledge independent of the interests of business (Barrow 1990: 250-9). Capacities established then have come into play during the recurrent waves of campus political activism since that time. Here is a recent example from the United States:

Throughout this protracted struggle [for a Chicana/o studies department], a student-community alliance matured and campus mobilizations at UCLA [University of California at Los Angeles] began to take the shape of a crucial community struggle. Equally important, as the movement gained concessions from a resistant administration, Chicana/o student-faculty relations were strengthened by the presence of seasoned community organizers who mediated disputes and challenged all parties to keep the goal of the department at the heart of each action. This resulted in several key philosophical victories. Chief among these was a faculty pledge to include students and community people in the governance of Chicana/o Studies. Faculty were also pushed to develop curriculum focusing on current problems of the Latina/o community. Finally, faculty members were challenged to reaffirm through concrete action the basic aims of Chicana/o Studies – the development of an informed and community-minded leadership among our college youth. (Lizardo 1993: 13)

Though the above example was unusually well organized, struggles of this kind, aimed at connecting the intellectual resources of the university with the needs of people in a local community, are an endemic feature of campus activism. This kind of activism invites repressive moves. By contrast, theorizing revolution or an activism dedicated to causes elsewhere in the world is much less threatening, as it does not directly jeopardize the monopoly control of intellectual resources and 'production' by the class or classes that dominate in contemporary capitalism. Hence the carefully crafted controls that have been built into the academy and the discourses it sustains, and, in North America, the progressive shift of intellectual resources into organizations such as 'think-tanks' that can be more directly and consistently regulated.

One major intervention focused on bringing the North American intelligentsia back into line was 'McCarthyism.' The public target of McCarthyism was the Communist party, but its effective, perhaps intended, aim was the broader-based political activism of students and faculty after the Second World War (Schrecker 1986: 84–5). Student organizations created linkages with labour, took up civil rights issues, proposed foreign relations radically opposed to 'cold war' thinking, and were involved with left-wing presidential politics. Earlier campus radicalism in the 1940s had been repressed. The 1950s attack on radicalism, now identified with McCarthyism, confronted and repressed a new and more general political activism on campus. The attack on communism has been called a witch-hunt because merely to come under suspicion was to become the object of persecution. Faculty were frightened, particularly liberal faculty.

They might not change their views, but they were afraid to act on them. In some instances, political activism on campus was prohibited altogether – the issue that eventually, in the 1960s, sparked the free speech movement on the Berkeley campus of the University of California.

Emphasis on the ideological dimensions of campus radicalism tends to obscure the extent to which it breached a class-enclosure institutionalized as the effect of various repressive moves. I've sometimes thought that faculty could be as radical as they wished in their writing and in the classroom so long as radicalism did not lead to an activism that built relationships between a university-based intelligentsia and a society's marginalized and exploited people. Writing of the early decades of this century, Barrow (1990) describes the repression of individual faculty who undertook research in the interests of local communities and against those of 'big business.' An agricultural chemist, for example, was penalized for bringing evidence to a state legislature about the damage done to local crops by copper-smelting (Barrow 1990: 241). The notion of the scholarly and academic as detached from concerns and interests external to discourse itself is constructed and reconstructed recurrently in the context of an endemic campus activism. Writing of the post-1970s period, Paul Diesing describes how administrative and budgetary powers of university administrations and boards were used to tame radical faculty:

... we found faculty resolutions ignored by the university administration and tenure recommendations overruled; library budgets cut and class sizes increased; tenured professors fired with three months' notice or less; educational policy and resources shifted without consulting us ... Our illusions crumbled; we began soberly to face our real conditions of life ... (Diesing 1982: 262)

Political repression had its effects in social scientific thinking. The sharp divorce during the McCarthy period between intellectual activity and what it might imply in terms of the society at large can be traced in sociology's shifts away from the influences of Marxism or traditions of radicalism indigenous to North America, such as those embodied in C. Wright Mills's work. The 'systems' thinking of Talcott Parsons, in which issues of class and racial oppression disappear, assumed a dominant role (Diesing 1982). 'Mass society' theory was briefly popular, perhaps because it offered a striking redefinition of the intelligentsia's relationship to the masses, proposing that an elite's ability to sustain democratic values could only be effective as it preserved its detachment from the people. Marxist conceptions of class and class struggle were displaced by, and sublated in, the new politically purified notion of 'social stratification.' Durkheim's devices for converting the world of actual people into a subjectless phenomenal universe became standard practice (see chapter 4). The popular methodological artifice of the Archimedean point constituted a discursive space for sociology outside class relations; race was an object but lacked subjects; and gender was not yet even a whisper. The artifices of objectified discourse concealed the real subtexts of race, class, and gender oppressions.

In the contemporary context, postmodernism has written the constitution that eliminates from the phenomenal domain of social and cultural thinking the bases of oppression that Marxism had brought into view, replacing them with a self-reflexive critique of discourse within discourse. Feminist postmodernism is feminism's own variant of the post-McCarthy redesigning of sociological discourse that stripped social science of its relation to political activism beyond the academy. It insists on the subject as existing only in discourse, creating a discursive seclusion that restricts speakers and speech, writers and writing, to discourse's objects and conventions (Butler and Scott 1992; Smith 1993a). It repudiates the speaking from experience that was so powerful in the beginnings of this phase of our women's movement and that has been so powerful in the disruptions and displacements of white middle-class heterosexual hegemony in feminism. At an earlier period, women would speak up from and for the margins that had been created by the focus of a conference or meeting. They could speak from their own realities, and that had its own authority; others might not agree or believe, but had to attend to what was said and take it seriously. But the conventions of postmodernist feminism, for all its denial of the unitary subject of modernism, set up barriers to such speech by denying the validity and originality of speaking from experience and insisting on a solipsistic confinement to discourse.

I emphasize that this isn't a matter of individual responsibility or guilt. It is a matter of the social relations in which our work comes to be embedded, who its readers are, how it is funded (and let's not pretend that we can go on forever doing work on shoestrings and night oil), and how it is recognized for purposes of publication and hence how it serves not only our survival in the academy (and I don't trivialize the issue of survival) but also as our means of reaching others through our work. The political ordering of the academy is less significant in our choice of subject matter than it is in ensuring that we write from a standpoint that fits our work within the dialogic parameters of the ruling relations.

Our Problem and Problematic

Here is our difficulty, our problem and problematic. On one side, there's the problem of how to write a sociology that speaks in and of the world as it is in women's, in people's, actual experience. If we are to be writing a sociology that serves people, we have to create a knowledge of society that provides maps or diagrams of the dynamic of macro-social powers and processes from the standpoint of people's everyday/everynight experience. We want to create a systematically extended consciousness of society from women's, indeed from people's, standpoint, and therefore we want more than short-run applications of our sociological skills. We also need to advance the technicalities of such a knowledge so that our research can be responsible in terms of 'truth,' accuracy, and relevance. And we have to contend with the jungle created by the in-text organization of sociology's object world, so that we can put in place a sociology or sociologies oriented to exploring the extended social relations of people's lives. Such a sociology or sociologies would recognize that, as Marx saw, the social comes into being only as the doings of actual people under definite material conditions and that we enter into social relations beyond our control that our own activities bring into being. Thus our own powers contribute to powers that stand over against us and 'overpower our lives' (Marx and Engels 1973: 90).

On the other side is the problem of connecting such a sociology to those for whom it might be useful and who might use it. There must be real and equal interchange. Solving this problem is essential to how such a knowledge can be developed; knowledge is not abstract but is embedded in a discourse or discourses. How could a knowledge of the kind sketched in the previous paragraph develop if it were embedded in discourses wholly within the academic circuits of sociological and feminist theory? My own experience has been telling in this respect, for I started work on a sociology for women in the very practical contexts of a women's research centre that was oriented, outside the university context, to working *for* women in the community. My thinking was pulled by the exigencies of doing this kind of research properly and finding that the sociology I knew would not do. But as my thinking on a sociology for women became known in academic contexts, and I was invited to speak (at first, largely at American) universities to audiences of women scholars who were interested in issues of theory and epistemology, I became a participant in discourses of quite a different order. These were discourses that were framed within the academy and were determined more by a feminist dialogue with established disciplines than by one with activists. My thinking began to orient towards these debates and, in consequence, more than functionally towards the theoretical and epistemological frames of academic discourses. My work was certainly strengthened in this process; if the other term of the relationship had continued to be as strongly present as it was when I started on this line of inquiry, my work could only have benefitted from being pulled more immediately and vitally into relevance to women outside the academy. The effect was to redirect my energies and thinking – and time – towards a theoretical discourse that it had not intended originally. I could feel how my focus began to shift, a process that was progressive as the great political impetus originating in the 1960s faltered and was repressed.

Any work and its development becomes what it is and will do in discursive settings. Discursive settings that are insulated from activism produce research and theorizing that is oriented elsewhere than activism. The theory may still be 'radical,' but nonetheless it is withdrawn from its anchorage with the actualities of people's lives, as we see with contemporary Marxist theorizing. There are no easy solutions here. Since it's not a matter of an individual's intentions, or individual guilt, it is also not something that can be changed simply by an act of will. The implicit political organization of the ivory tower university is still effective. It is not easy to go against it, though we can sometimes get things done within its scope. Indeed, the recent attack on what is described by its opponents as the 'political correctness' movement on North American campuses suggests that we have been more successful than perhaps we'd realized.

But this isn't the only isolation. The disciplinary norms to which we are subject sediment the politics of the ivory tower. They were put into place during the 1950s and 1960s in the process of moving sociology away from its earlier dubious connections with class struggle, and the suspect ties of the North American intelligentsia of the '40s and '50s to the working class. The academy creeps up on us. How do we get to keep our jobs? By writing papers that will be published in academic journals. To get our papers published, we have to conform to procedural and methodological canons that have no relationship to what might be conceived of as the canons of relevance of women activists. Of course, we have made and preserve our openings into the relationships in which so much of what we have done as feminists originates; we are ingenious. But it becomes increasingly difficult, and increasingly difficult as new feminist theories are established, even popularized, that conform to the class contours of the academy, the more so now that universities themselves are being increasingly pulled into direct subservience to the requirements of a global capitalism.

The academy is not seamless. I've shown earlier how repressions have followed on initiatives among students and faculty opposing injustices, oppressions, and suffering in the society. Universities bear, I believe, the hidden radicalism of the Enlightenment and, in teaching, in talk, and in the access to stored knowledges, become, every now and again, reconnected to this long historical project. Here, for feminism, is our distinctive project in the academy. It is one in which, in fact, many of us are involved. I propose that we become more conscious of it and of each other.

The idea of developing a social science *for* women, which has been my own project, is not, of course, exclusively mine. There are women in the academy all over North America who in different ways are also engaged. We can change the way sociology knows the world because it is still a site of debate; because the academy is changing; because we know that there's desperation in society, and our social sciences don't know how to know this new and frightening world; and because we know as women that we have the power and capacity to change and to create a social science that serves people rather than servicing their ruling. We can indeed create a knowledge of the social that does not bind so readily with the ruling relations as does established social science. We can teach, and I have come to see that as a more important dimension of activism in the academy than I used to do, particularly as other critical sources in the mass media and elsewhere dry up or are put out of business. But the problem remains of how to create active linkages with women working in sites outside the academy and to establish dialogue between the intra- and extra-academic.

No intellectual enterprise can subsist in a social vacuum. Every such enterprise participates in something we could call, perhaps euphemistically, a community. Because we are working with texts, reading and writing texts, the existence and significance of that community are often invisible to us. Yet it is always implicit in what we write. How, then, are we to defend and intensify connections beyond the academy against the multiple ways it inhibits them? In the session at the annual meetings of the Society for the Study of Social Problems at which the ideas of this paper were originally presented, a woman activist spoke of her dismay in finding how distant the sociology she had been hearing at the meetings was from the concerns and interests of activists and the women they represented. We had no answer then. This paper has no answer. But it has a diagnosis.

It does not locate the issue in the individual intentions of women sociologists, nor in 'careerism.' The issue is not a matter of individual guilt. Rather, it is to be located in the social relations embedding a politics at a level of the organization of the academy, where it is not visible as such. Making it visible is a first step in addressing how we can overcome, bypass, and, as a minimum, avoid consciously replicating and reaffirming a politics which is neither for women nor for people in general.

3

Feminist Reflections on Political Economy[1]

Beginning in Our Lives

These reflections on feminism and political economy originate in my experience as activist and academic in the women's movement. They arise from my efforts to translate into a political and scholarly practice the discoveries of the power relations organizing the personal and domestic as feminists have experienced and analysed them. These reflections bear the traces of those extended conflicts, challenges, and debates that feminists have brought to Marxism and political economy. Indeed, they are intended to bring to bear upon these last some of what I have learned in this dialogue for the development of a feminist politics of epistemology.

Rethinking how we work as social scientists began for me with a problem which came into view in relation to political practice. A group of feminists, most, but not all, of us socialists, got together in Vancouver some years ago to found a women's research centre. We thought we would reverse the normal flow of information and inquiry that transfers knowledge about people to the institutions which produce knowledge for the ruling of society, namely, to universities and academic discourses. We thought of a women's research centre as a means of producing knowledge for women, making the stored-up knowledge and skills of academe serve the people who are usually their objects. We set up a research centre outside the university, and, in constant difficulty with funding, we went to work.

My experience of that work was concurrent with another kind of discovery. I had been teaching women's studies at the University of British Columbia and was becoming more and more sharply aware of the full implications of our (women's) exclusion from the making of the social forms of consciousness (the knowledge and culture) of our kind of society. What had seemed at first merely a problem of absence, to be remedied by including women as topics in appropriate sites, had come to be seen as a deeper and virtually total gender warping of culture and intellectual life. It became clear that remedies must be much more radical; that there were problems about the relationship of social science to those who became its objects; about conceptual and theoretical practices that incorporated one-sided assumptions based on one class, race, and gender standpoint; about the exclusion of the standpoint of experience from social scientific versions of the world.

The emphasis on women's experience as a primary site and source of knowing originates in this dilemma. The political logic of consciousness-raising extended into the realms of culture and intellectual life. The very grounds of knowledge were being called into question. As it has for many other feminists in the social sciences, this issue, the grounds of objectified knowledge of society and social relations, has remained for me a major preoccupation.

Working with the women's research centre posed such issues in a different way. We saw them at first, I think, as problems arising from the fact that we wrote and talked in a specialized language, mystifying the ordinary events of people's lives and the power relations organizing them. But they were not, I came to see, merely problems of the unhappy and often clumsy abstractions of social scientific discourse. The problems would not be solved by finding ways of making social scientific discourse ordinarily understandable. There was something else. The whole method of thinking, how social science addresses the world, creates a very peculiar relationship between women and our experience. Rather than beginning in our own actual situations and with our own good knowledge of the practicalities and organization of our everyday and everynight worlds, social science's methods of writing its texts create a standpoint from which the reader reflects on her life as if she stood outside it; taking up the relevancies and focus built into the conceptual structures of the discourse. She becomes an object to herself. Popularization makes no difference; the conceptual structures are recursively present. As a practical problem, we found in the women's movement that texts written in social scientific terms would not do the kind of job to which we were committed, which was to expand women's knowledge of what was going on from where they were in real, as contrasted with textual, life.

This problem has been a major object of my interest. I thought I would rewrite sociological methods of thinking, writing texts, and constructing knowledge to make a feminist method; we should have more, I thought, than a sociology in which women had a place and had become, however belatedly, the objects of sociological interest. We needed a sociology able to create an account or accounts, analysis or analyses, of how societies were put together so that the worlds of our everyday/everynight experience happened to us as they did. Then we would have a knowledge from our standpoint, making claims to comprehend a scope of history and society equal with those that have been made by men. We would be capable of analyses and of developing knowledge relevant to women's struggles. It would be a knowledge and an analytic capacity written to be read or heard from the standpoint of women, a standpoint which is outside the textually mediated conversations of the relations of ruling (embodied in established social science), and situated in the particularities of the local everyday and everynight worlds of our immediate experience.

Objectifying Consciousness

I am emphasizing the experiential grounds of this thinking because they are ordinarily excluded as merely 'subjective.' They have been central to the organizing and politics of the women's movement. They are also central to the feminist challenge to academic discourse, at least in the social sciences. The latter maintain a sharp division between people's experiential knowledge and the objectified and authoritative knowledge of the expert. Experiential knowledge isn't recognized *as* knowledge in the terrain of professional, scientific, and other academic discourses. I distinctly remember learning the peculiar practices of a sociology which purported to speak of the same world as the one in which I lived, and yet required me to exclude from classroom or term paper any reference to a knowledge which I had acquired on bases other than its authorized texts. This was an observation that had a later relevance as I slowly discovered methods of doing a social science to which such conventions did not apply. Indeed, on the contrary.

As I began to see the objectified methods of thinking and writing texts characteristic of the social sciences, I also began to see them as integral to that great complex of ruling relations operating in contemporary society at a level abstracted from the everyday/everynight particularities of our local worlds. In this context, the social sciences appeared as a systematically constructed consciousness of society which creates a synthetic standpoint, locating the reading subject outside the actual time and place in which she reads, and in a conceptual space isomorphic with that of the

abstracted, extra-local relations of ruling of contemporary capitalist societies. A number of observations fell into place: Why was it that sociology (at
least when I was in graduate school in the United States) was a required
course in community colleges? Why was it that when people thought about
themselves sociologically, they seemed to disintegrate into a multiplicity of
selves, each located in a role, or, in the contemporary version, a multiplicity of subjects, each located in a different discourse? Why was it that the
ordinary observations of experience were not admissible to thought as
part of a discourse purporting to analyse and explain the same world as
that which we inhabited? Why was it that politically active graduate students had such an alarming tendency to want to study the movements in
which they were active? Why was it that the social sciences wanted to *explain*
people's behaviour (to whom?), rather than, say, to explain the behaviour
of the economy, or the society, or the political process to people, particularly as these enter into, organize, and disorganize people's lives?[2]

We saw gender bias as an imperfection of processes that were properly
gender neutral. More recently we have come to see gender as pervading
all social relations.[3] The earlier accounts of patriarchy as vested not only
in the interpersonal relationships between women and men, but also in
the massive organization of masculine power in the state (and in its mobi-
lization of violence to regulate and impose its will), and in the legal, cultural, scientific, and professional establishments, can be seen as attending
to the same organization of power which is characterized in other discursive settings as rational, impersonal, and universal.

From the traditional sites of women's work and consciousness, oriented
towards particular others and situated in local contexts of action, the ruling relations appear as abstracted systems, hooking up local events with
extra-local organizational forms. The emergence of bureaucracy, objective systems of management, professional discourse, and analogous forms
of control and organization can be traced as it occurs in multiple independent sites. The late-nineteenth-century transition from forms of capitalist enterprise identified with individual owners to the corporate forms
of monopoly capital provided the basis for the development of systematic
approaches to management.[4] In the early twentieth century, transitions
from the forms of local organization vested in a local class structure to
relations vested in new administrative forms of management in municipal
affairs, education, public health, and so forth are initiated. The same
period sees, particularly in North America, the very rapid development of
professions as an institutionalized form standardizing skills, knowledge,
and practices in the many actual local sites of professional practice.[5]

Correlatively, the organization of 'higher learning' breaks free from local organization.[6] There is a progressive organization of academic discourse at national and international levels; news media evolve away from a position embedded in local interests and struggles, in which they have an active role, to an organization at extra-local levels. This shift entails new practices of 'objectivity,' essentially concerned with avoiding the identification of news stories with any one side.[7] Academic, professional, political, and cultural discourses evolve as coordinators of the actual local sites in which life and work must always actually proceed. These and related developments in state administrative organization at national, provincial, and municipal levels create a new level of organization in society. Organization, execution, and regulation are progressively leached out of local settings and particularized relations. They are transferred to this new level of organization in which communication, control, and organization become differentiated and specialized functions, creating a layer of relations governing and coordinating local sites.

The complex of the ruling relations is mediated by texts, that is, by written, printed, or otherwise inscribed words and images (on television and movie screens, on the computer monitor). Those who inhabit them (as do most of us in this business, as a matter of our work, indeed almost of our being) take their textual ground for granted as a basis for what we know in an ordinary way about the world. Our knowledge, our practices of thinking and theorizing, and our images of the world are textually grounded and grounded in the ruling relations. The 'knowledge-power' relationship that Foucault (1980) has proposed is a metaphor for this reality, an organization of power mediated textually. And, of course, we can't do without it. Societies, the global economy itself, would disintegrate if some magical or extraterrestrial power were to obliterate every text (computer hackers' vandalism of corporate records gives us some notion of what this might mean, but it's still only a taste).

Class in *The Communist Manifesto* and Contemporary Marxist Theory

There is a standpoint, then, in the ruling relations appearing through the varieties of disciplines, focuses, relevancies, interests, specializations, textual technologies, and the like. It is a standpoint which objectifies society, social relations, and what people do. It is a standpoint evident in texts that conceal in their methods of telling that world, a subject, an 'I,' a 'we,' outside what is looked at; it is a standpoint producing a consciousness of society as if she who reads and speaks can stand outside it;[8] it is the celebrated Archimedean position so long and fruitlessly desired by sociologists. ('You can't have that wish, Little Bear!' says Mother Bear.)[9]

When I was teaching a course on women and class a few years ago, I had the following experience. We had done a critical review of some of the major contemporary Marxist theorists of class, Olin Wright, Poulantzas, Carchedi, and so forth. Then we read Marx and Engels's *The Communist Manifesto*. There was a startling difference. The latter locates the reader in the movement of history; classes are not mapped out as a structure consisting of categories of persons or positions; the reading subject is located at a moment between a past, in which classes have arisen that subjected society to their conditions of appropriation, and a future, in which the proletariat abolishes previous conditions of appropriation and thereby appropriation itself. Readers are placed pronominally; the bourgeoisie is directly addressed as Other, in opposition to the 'we' situated on this, our, side of the struggle. You are horrified, Marx and Engels write to that other subject, 'at our intending to do away with private property.' 'You reproach us with intending to do away with your property,' and 'that is just what we intend.' The irony is heavy here. The 'you' and 'yours' are the bourgeoisie, addressed directly. 'We' are the communists, whose position is stated in the manifesto by the communist authors; 'we' creates a position for a subject in the text that is home for whoever takes our side; 'we' are placed by this textual act in class struggle.

The text places the reader historically; class struggle is going on, and we are in the middle of it. The sides are drawn up in the text itself as subjects are directly summoned and addressed. We can enter ourselves directly into its drama. Class is not objectified in the text as it is in the elaborate theoretical constructs of the contemporary Marxist theorists, needing rather careful fitting to the actualities of contemporary social relations. Rather, class emerges as a great historical process of struggle in which the pamphlet and its analysis are situated, and it draws us into it. The time of the text is just exactly that hinge where the past turns on a present that will be the making of the future. This is where you, as reading subject, are placed by the pamphlet. This also is where you live. The polemic of the text is a call on you to act at precisely this juncture. But the temporal siting of reading and writing subjects in an historical trajectory of which the text itself is part isn't just a polemical effect. Though the reader isn't always being called on to act as he (I use the pronoun advisedly) is here, Marx's and Engels's analyses have generally this historically situated character; the time of the text isn't separate from the historical time of which it speaks.[10]

Contemporary Marxist texts on class locate the reading subject very differently. Characteristically they take advantage of the elaborate textual devices developed in the social sciences since Marx and Engels wrote. These constitute social and economic relations as if they went forward without the presence of actual subjects; characteristically they construct a temporal order that does not situate the reader in an historical trajectory from past to future; nor does it situate her in the time and place of her living; characteristically the reading and writing subjects, if they are explicitly present, are external to the phenomenon of which the texts speak. Class is a theoretically constituted entity that will classify positions or individuals. To use the language of class to speak of the everyday/everynight world that we experience directly involves entering ourselves into discursive space and interpreting our own lives, friends, and political associates from its standpoint. Such practices of objectification are constitutive of modes of organization in the ruling relations, creating forms of consciousness that are properties of organization and discourse rather than of individuals.

I'm suggesting that it is the emergence of the ruling relations as a standpoint, as institutionalized practices of knowing within texts, that makes possible the objectification of processes known, lived, and experienced only from within. Sociology has attempted to deal with this in its critique of positivism, but its interpretive substitutes preserve the same relation to actualities. Political economy appears never to have seriously addressed such issues. Perhaps it borrows from economics its confidence in the reality of the entities, objects, and relations given presence in its discourse. But such discourse is deeply rooted in and deeply dependent upon the elaborately evolved texture of texts mediating the ruling relations. The intertextuality of our work as social scientists is wholly taken for granted in how we proceed.

Take the notion of 'position,' for example, which is so central to contemporary Marxist theorizing of class. Its force and intelligibility are grounded in multiple, textually mediated sites in the organization and management of ruling in state and capitalist enterprise. For example, the occupational categories of the *Canadian Classified Dictionary of Occupations* are a constituent of state accounting that are part of the management of a labour force;[11] systems of job description and formally designated positions are formal properties of the organization of large-scale corporations and government bureaucracies. Positions arise in an organization of management through texts. Categories such as 'skill,' 'occupation,' 'industry,' and so forth are constituted in textually concerted organization lodged in the ruling relations.[12] Contemporary Marxist conceptions of class, grounded in forms of knowledge generated by the relations of ruling, contain and conceal a basis in an organization of class (in state and management) that they are incapable of explicating. The entities incorporated as taken-for-granted presences in the discourses of political economy evidence their intertextual embedding in the ruling relations. The relevancies and conceptual frameworks, as well as the informational bases, of political economic discourse are profoundly dependent upon the textually coordinated processes of ruling.

At the same time, an institutionalized discourse such as political economy comes to constitute its own relevancies, concepts, entities, critical standards, and so forth. A textually contained world comes into being. '[G]roups of texts, types of texts, even textual genres, acquire mass, density, and referential power among themselves and thereafter in the culture at large' (Said 1979). A sphere of work and inquiry is created with its own internal logic, its agreed upon objects and categories, its recognized authorities and referents. These constitute it as political economy; an object world is created which members of the discourse have in common; the actualities of social, economic, and political process are interpreted through this prism. A textually contained world is created, standing as object, external to the writing and reading subject; the lived world is to be interpreted through the medium of the textually contained.

Such structuring isn't just a matter of will and intention; it is a matter of how our work gets taken up, who responds to it within discursive or organizational processes, and hence of the part it comes to play within the division of the labour of ruling. Discourse establishes canons of relevance and validity, reproduces judgments and values, and incorporates experiences and perceptions introduced by its participants as themes and topics that have become properties of discourse institutionalized in ruling relations. We come to reflect on the world in terms of such relevancies, through the interpretive practices it provides, and indeed the constituents of the world we recognize as such are given to us by its categories. Most important of all, we come to be related to the world in which we are politically active (in whatever way) in its terms; thus class is constituted as external to us, an object to be investigated; political questions as to who are the working class arise as problems of the relation between a theoretically constituted entity and finding how to build its textual correlates through a selective investigation of the already textual (census and department of labour statistics, economic reports of task forces, commissions, think-tanks, and so forth) and the extra-textual world mediated by interviews, observation, and personal reports.

Feminism, Political Economy, and the 'Main Business' of Ruling

Feminism has made important inroads on political economy. There have been very substantial achievements. At the same time there are barriers to our further advance. As the discursive domain of political economy has been institutionalized in the ruling relations, it has acquired their relevancies. It depends upon their habits of thought and conceptual organization through the unexplicated incorporation into its discourse of the categories institutionalizing the 'main business' of ruling: to facilitate the self-expanding dynamic of capital.[13]

The feminist critique of political economy clearly marks the boundaries of the agenda comprising the 'main business' of ruling. Important theoretical work has established women's place in political economic discourse; the domestic labour debate wrote women into the classical categories of political economy – surplus value, exchange value, and use value. And even though the debate has been inconclusive, it has created an official door to a range of topics concerning the household and its organization that had not formerly been received as a legitimate discursive presence. The gendered organization of political economic processes has been insisted upon; issues of biological reproduction and of sexuality have been incorporated; important studies of women's paid work, women in the trade union movement, and of the development of state management of women's domestic lives have been done. The insertion of such topics into political economy (as evidenced, for example, by two Canadian anthologies, one edited by Heather Jon Maroney and Meg Luxton [1987], the other by Michele Barrett and Roberta Hamilton [1987]) marks, through the absences and gaps they highlight in traditional political economic discourse, the contours of its relevancies.

The traditional relevancies are shaped, I suggest, less by 'sexist' practices than by a deeper relationship between the gendered organization of the ruling relations and the central and centripetal effects in them of the 'main business' of a capitalist economy. Embedded in the textual mediations of the ruling relations, and therefore built on the textual forms integral to the governing of the society in relation to its 'main business,' the discourse of political economy operates within their parameters. The 'main business' defines the central position from which topics introduced by feminism are marginalized. The topics of feminism inscribe the contours of the 'main business' by marking what is excluded.

This exclusion corresponds to that divide introduced by capitalism into the productive organization of society. In the earliest pre-capitalist societies there is no separation between 'production' and 'reproduction.' Producing food, shelter, tools, and so forth produces the subsistence and provides for the child-bearing and child-rearing of those who do the work of production. There is no economic organization that is not also an organization of gender. Indeed to speak of economic organization is to make an abstraction unwarranted in simpler social forms. Capitalism breaks the integration of production and reproduction. Production no longer produces the subsistence of those who do the work; nor does it provide for child-bearing and child-rearing; production is governed by the relations of capital accumulation; those who can earn a wage by selling to capital their capacity to labour may buy the commodities on which household members, including children, can subsist. The direct relationship between production, producers, and reproduction has been ruptured. What we call the 'economy' emerges thus as a differentiated order of activity. Indeed what is commonly known in political economy as 'the capitalist mode of production' is constituted as an internally driven sphere of dynamic relations mediated by money and commodities. Subsistence enters this sphere only insofar as it is given economic presence by the uses of the wage to buy commodities and hence also as 'consumption.' The other dimensions of household work and of child-rearing, on which feminist political economists have insisted, don't become visible.

The central relevancies of political economy are the 'main business' of ruling, servicing, regulating, planning, criticizing, managing, and organizing the process of capital accumulation. It is a mistake to see the 'main business' as having to be constantly enforced by a ruling class. Over time, the 'main business' has become thoroughly built into the division of labour within the ruling relations concerting it. It is institutionalized. Let me give one example. Sylvia Ann Hewlett (1986) is an economist who worked for the Economic Policy Council in the United States. During the 1980s, she tried to set up a committee to study problems of women's work, family, and daycare with a view to making recommendations to the President and to Congress on this topic. She had, however, the utmost difficulty in establishing the committee, for while both women and men were willing to work on committees investigating such topics as the World Bank, childcare and family were clearly topics that were peripheral to the 'main business.' Participation would not lead to career opportunities or appropriate and advantageous connections, nor would it enhance a participant's professional reputation, and so forth. Hewlett writes of this episode thus:

... when I attempted to convene my panel in the spring and summer of 1983, I got a rude awakening. Most of my distinguished male members were simply not interested; they either yawned or raised their eyebrows when I insisted on explaining to them why they should get involved. After listening to my pitch, one eminent banker looked embarrassed and told me rather lamely that he was not 'up to speed' in this policy area, and couldn't he join one of our other panels? I should point out that these men were not, in general, shrinking violets and had no problems in speaking out on Japanese defense policy or third world debt even when they had no fine-grained expertise in the area. Somehow issues like maternity leave and child care made them very nervous. But it was not just nerves; I could have overcome an attack of nerves. When pushed, they revealed another reason behind their reluctance to get involved: Family policy had no standing in their world. Being involved in this project would get them no brownie points in boardrooms or at cocktail parties. It seemed clear that while they might sacrifice precious time getting up to speed on Japanese defense policy, they were not prepared to do so for 'women's stuff' – as one member called it.

If the male reaction was bad, the female reaction was even more difficult to take. I discovered that most of my distinguished women members weren't interested either. I remember feeling almost numb when one woman, a senior vice-president at a major manufacturing corporation, excused herself on the ground that she could not afford to become identified with this panel. She explained, 'It has taken me fifteen years to get a hard-nosed reputation, and I just daren't risk it. If I were to get involved in these messy women's issues, it could do me a lot of harm in the company.' (Hewlett 1986: 369–70) [14]

Childcare and family are not articulated to the 'main business' organizing jobs, let alone a career process, in government and economy. The interests and relevancies institutionalized in the ruling relations marginalize topics such as childcare and family. Marginalized politically, they are correspondingly marginalized in academic settings. The pull of academic status is towards the categories identified with the institutions sustaining the 'main business.' Even a critical discourse such as political economy has its agenda set by 'the main business.'

The 'main business' is built into the categories and concepts organizing what we treat as 'information,' news, statistical data of all kinds, and so forth – these are integral to getting the 'main business' done and are, of course, shaped to its uses. [15] It is built into the categories and concepts that are the working currency of discourse. The centripetal effect of discourse around the 'main business' is sustained by academic practices restricting the ways in which knowledge can be developed as a service to those who may participate as subjects but not as agents in the ruling relations. The institutionalized practices restricting the access of the ruled, the marginal, the excluded, to knowledge are deeply built into the ordinary working practices of academia, and are, for the most part, below the level of consciousness. They include the normal methodological procedures of sociology, indeed precisely those that my experience with a women's research centre called into question. They also become visible in the requirements imposed on those seeking research funding, less as a matter of topic than of the methodological and evaluative criteria reproducing the objectifying practices of academic, professional, and state discourse.

The institutions of ruling are themselves taken for granted as the ground on which political economy operates, and women have been marginal to these. Thus the topics of political economy have marginalized women not only as an effect of sexism, but as an effect of how the discourse has built itself upon the textual accounting and information practices of 'the main business' and thereby taken over its parameters and its bounding assumptions. Issues concerning women don't seem somehow to be there when general topics are undertaken. For example, Göran Therborn's 'Classes and States: Welfare State Developments, 1881–1981' (1984) is a comparative account of welfare state development. It is concerned with the question of what labour movements have contributed to the making of the welfare state. The venue of struggle is the political process of the state. Class analysis is rendered into the perspectives of business and trade unions. Women are absent. Therborn recognizes the gendered nature of the working class but justifies their exclusion in terms of male dominance of working-class organization. Thus he justifies his masculinist version of class. The actors and entities on his stage – state, trade unions, the political process, business, and so forth – are the players summoned by the 'main business' of capitalism. His formulation adopts the contours of the latter in its marginalizing of the work that has been traditionally women's.

But suppose we shift to a standpoint from which women's experience becomes visible. New actors, institutions, and organization come into view: the extensive charitable and voluntary work of women of the middle and upper classes in the later nineteenth and early twentieth centuries was the organizational foundation for social services later integrated into the welfare state. Here systems of managing the domestic and reproductive lives of working-class women were developed. On this basis, professions essential to the welfare state, such as social work and public health nursing, were built. Class relations among women were redefined. Such aspects are missing when the procedures for collecting historical instances are governed by the institutional forms central to the 'main business.' An undertaking, such as that made at one time by the journal *Studies in Political Economy* to incorporate women's issues in general papers, turns out to be awkward and difficult to adhere to, because it's hard to see how to fit them in when the very presuppositions of discourse have already denied them presence.

One aspect of the problem is the tendency to identify class struggle with trade union organization. This too marginalizes women and, in particular, women's distinctive experiences of work outside and inside the home. I recognize, of course, the important changes in trade union policies which women trade unionists have been able to bring about as well as the significant shift in organizing policies impelled by the changing proportions of the manufacturing and service industries in the economy. Nonetheless, women's workforce situations can't be cut off from their special relationship to childcare and child-rearing as well as housework. To treat 'trade unions' as a textual stand-in for class is an illustration of the kind of centripetal pull of the 'main business' and its marginalization of women that I'm explicating here.[16] Though the political economist may recognize class as gendered, in practice, when the point of production is treated as the exclusive site of class and class struggle, major dimensions of women's lives are dropped from view.

The site from which issues relevant to women have been brought into view is at the margins and not at the centre. Feminist corrections to the discursive relevancies of political economy struggle within, more rarely against,[17] existing contours. Women's issues are organized in terms of an agenda defined from that centre. Assertions of women's presence in class, of the significance of domestic labour in economic relations, let alone of the need for representation within political economy of the neglected areas of sexuality and motherhood, have not yet succeeded in shifting the central determination of the focus of political economy from the 'main business' dominating the relations of ruling.

A Standpoint outside the Ruling Relations

The central relevancies, assumptions, methods, and conceptual practices of political economic discourse remain largely unchanged by attempts to embed feminist topics in the discourse. The contours of the discursive barrier are perhaps most strikingly displayed in our failure as feminists working within the political economic tradition to come to terms with a racism implicit in our practices and arising less from attitudes we hold as individuals as from the ways that we participate in and practice the discursive assumptions and the structuring of the 'main business' within the ruling relations. As we latch our feminist work to the discourse of political economy, we latch it to the structures organizing and managing class and race as well as gender. Edward Said's *Orientalism* (1979) describes the development of a body of knowledge and scholarly study the apparent objectivity of which conceals its profound structuring from a centre inside the Western capitalist powers and their imperialist enterprise, constituting the Orient and Oriental as Other. '[P]olitical imperialism governs an entire field of study, imagination, and scholarly institutions – in such a way as to make its avoidance an intellectual and historical impossibility.' The disciplines organized from this centre claim to stand outside such effects but do not.

The parallels are obvious here. Indeed the structures are the same. The ruling relations constitute other Others than the Orient and Oriental – of class, of gender, and of race. This statement is to be taken quite literally. The divisions between gender, class, and race don't exist at the level of the everyday/everynight world of people's actual lives; to be black, a woman, and working-class are not three different and distinctive experiences. Himani Bannerji has dissected the constitution of gender, class, and race as realized abstractions as follows:

In this method of operating, the abstraction is created when the different social moments which constitute the 'concrete' being of any social organization and existence are pulled apart, and each part assumed to have a substantive, self-regulating structure. This becomes apparent when we see gender, race and class each considered as a separate issue – as ground for separate oppressions. The social whole – albeit fraught with contradictions – is then constructed by an aggregative exercise. According to this, I, as a South Asian woman, then have a double oppression to deal with, first on the count of gender, and second on the count of race. I am thus segmented into different social moments, made a victim of discrete determinations. So it is with the moment of gender, when it is seen as a piece by itself, rupturing its constitutive relationship with race and class. Needless to say, race and class could also be meted the same treatment. What this does is to empty gender relations of their general social context, content and dynamism. This, along with the primacy that gender gains (since the primary social determinant is perceived as patriarchy), subsumes all other social relations, indeed renders them often invisible. (Bannerji 1987: 12)

The objectified and objectifying practices constituting the systematically developed forms of social consciousness of contemporary society – among them political economy – conceal the 'subject-other' relationships structuring the centre from which that consciousness 'looks' out. As political economic discourse participates in and is intertextually engaged with the ruling relations, it stands on the same ground and walks the same circumference. So do our feminist riders to the theorems of political economy.

Issues of racism confront, I believe, the same barrier, a barrier confining thinking and analyses to the racist tracks of the ruling of contemporary capitalism. The problem isn't to make women of colour a topic within a feminist political economy, nor yet to invite women of colour to speak in this zone of discourse. Of course, they have already seized that initiative. The problem I am explicating is of a different kind; it is a problem of the concealed standpoint, the position in the ruling relations that is taken for granted in how we speak and that bounds and constrains how a political economy of women can speak to women, let alone to Third World women. It is a problem of the invisible centre that is concealed in the objectifications of discourse, seeming to speak of the world dispassionately, objectively, as it is. For women of colour, nothing is gained by being entered *as topics* into white, male- or female-grounded, discourse. The theoretical expansions of political economy introduced by white women have merely rewritten the boundaries. The centre still remains; the standpoint within ruling is stably if invisibly present. Nothing will serve but the dissolution of objectified discourse, the decentring of standpoint and the discovery of another consciousness of society systematically developed from the standpoint of women of colour and exploring the relations of political economy or sociology from a ground in that experience.

The logic of the feminist critique, as I understand it, opens up not only the issue of women's absence or the agenda of the 'main business,' but also the making of a political economy from standpoints outside the ruling relations. Back, then, to the issue of how *The Communist Manifesto* relates the reader to the world in which she lives and reads. Obviously we cannot reconstruct the relations characteristic of an earlier stage of capitalism, when the emergence of what I'm calling apparatuses and relations of ruling was only in its infancy.[18] We can't return to that relatively pristine state (so far as political economy is concerned).[19] But we want, I want, a political economy exploring the world in which I live, in which we live, and exploring it in ways that do not objectify it or relate us to it through the medium of ruling. I want a political economy that explicates and analyses just how our lives are caught up in political economic processes, including, of course, the ruling relations in which our own work as social scientists is embedded.

This, as I see it, is the next step in the feminist critique. It calls for methods of thinking, of writing texts, and of investigation that expand and extend our knowledge of how our everyday/everynight worlds are put together, determined and shaped as they are by forces and powers beyond our practical and direct knowledge. It calls for an openness to the multiple sites of experience in contemporary capitalism and the evolution of a systematically developed social consciousness (a political economy, a sociology) that does not depend upon collapsing them into a single overriding standpoint. Taking up the standpoint of subjects outside the ruling relations means evolving a political economy not confined to the 'main business,' and that does not assume a single standpoint, nor that the relations and forces of capital, including those of ruling, are going to look the same from every standpoint. Different sites, different experiences, provide different perspectives and propose different strategies of exploration; they enhance and expand our capacity to grasp the nature of the beast.

This doesn't mean an endless relativism of perspective, a multiplicity of 'truths,' for we are addressing relations, practices, powers, and forces which are actual, have consequences, need exploration, can be discovered, are there. But we are addressing that complex from the sites and standpoints it has constructed. In exploring how we are related through its determinations, the concept of class has an essential role as a method of analysing and explicating the actual organization of relations in which our lives and struggles are embedded. Our concept of class can't be identical to that of Marx and Engels, for the analytic capacity of such concepts is firmly articulated to the social relations of their time. Nonetheless, as we have inherited the tradition of analysis they founded, only entering at a later stage the same historical trajectory, and as we are caught up in the same historical struggles that they charted, their work is the original and the model for ours. We want the analytic powers of a concept of class that will display our site in a trajectory of struggle in which we are necessarily already implicated and already act. Women's struggles for liberation and equality are already deeply embedded in these relations; we need a political economy that will explore and display the properties and movement of the complex of powers, forces, and relations that are at work in our everyday/everynight worlds.

4

Sociological Theory: Methods of Writing Patriarchy into Feminist Texts[1]

As I was going up the stair
I met a man who wasn't there
He wasn't there again today
I wish to god he'd go away.

Anonymous

I have emphasized in my work a distinctive standpoint for women, not necessarily as a general attribute of women as a class of persons, but as a mode of experience that is distinctive to women and in important ways has marked us off from men and still continues to do so (Smith 1987). This is an experience of work around particular individuals, especially children; it is an experience grounded in a biological difference – our bodies give birth and men's do not – but through complex institutional mediations organized as caring and serving work directed towards particular others or groups of others. Locating the knowing subject of a sociology in this site locates a subject outside the textually mediated discourse[2] of sociology: it locates her in her own life, in her self as a unitary being, as a body active, imagining, thinking, as a subject situated in her local and particular actualities.

Designing a sociology for a knower situated in the everyday/everynight world of her actual lived experience means proceeding differently than in the standard practice of sociology. It means, among other things, turning the established enterprise on its head: rather than explaining how and why people act (or behave) as they do, we would seek from particular experience situated in the matrix of the everyday/everynight world to explore and display the relations, powers, and forces that organize and shape it.

Many women have been developing sociologies based on women's experience (DeVault 1986, 1987; Collins 1990; Kasper 1986; Oakley 1981; Paget 1987; Reinharz 1983; Stacey 1988; Stanley and Wise 1983). There has been great unanimity on this score. Though we have worked from this beginning in different ways, we share this critical stance. Here I am concerned with a problem arising when we try to carry this enterprise beyond the careful and loving listening with which women sociologists have been attending to what women have to tell us of their lives.

A central problem for a feminist sociology is the continual and powerful translation back of our beginnings in women's experience, whether our own or others, into the textual forms of the discourse placing the reading (and writing) subject outside the experience from which she starts. I hold this to be a major issue for feminists. For while we have developed methods of working with women that are fully consultative and open, a moment comes after talk has been inscribed as texts and becomes data when it must be worked up as sociology.

This chapter explores and unfolds this contradiction. It suggests that a feminist critical consciousness, grounded in experiencing and insisting on knowing from where women are, is redirected into the older paths of a patriarchal organization of knowledge as we work within the conventions of sociological discourse. So long as we work within the objectifying frame that organizes the discursive consciousness, we will find ourselves reinscribing the moment of discovery of women's experience, as women talk with women, into the conceptual order that locates the reader's and writer's consciousness outside the experience of that talk.[3]

The objectified and objectifying modes of organizing the systematic consciousness of society developed by sociology (and other social sciences) set up a standpoint within ruling relations that have class, gender, and racial subtexts. Objectivity in the social sciences is a form of social organization in and through which those who rule transliterate the relevancies, experiences, and dialogues going on among them into the universalized forms required by the relations of ruling. I will argue here that conventions of objectivity have been laid down as constitutive conventions of sociology, that is, as methods of writing the social into texts, making them recognizable to readers as sociology, and generating the phenomenal worlds that organize the multiple theoretical enclaves of the discourse.

I'm not addressing the issue of positivism or the related issue of quantitative versus qualitative methods in sociology. The constitutive conventions I am addressing in this chapter are more general and pervasive in the discipline than these special sites. They present special problems for feminists trying to find ways of working from women's experience for two reasons: first, they remorselessly undo our attempts to write a sociology from a standpoint in actual women's experience so that imperceptibly we are returned to just that way of looking we have tried to avoid; second, they organize the construction of a phenomenal world, as the world known to sociology, according to conventions that return us to the standpoint of the ruling relations that they carry and transmit, much as a gene carries and transmits particular properties from one generation to the next.

The particular version of the standpoint of women that I've worked with comes out of my own experience. Feminism taught me the freedom to see the significance of working in two worlds for developing an alternative consciousness of society than that I had practised. When my children were small, I was working at the University of California at Berkeley. I went back and forth between doing the work of mothering in all its particularities and demands, and the sociological world-in-texts that I taught and contributed to in my research. Becoming a feminist taught me to see the latter as an integral part of the abstracted, extra-local ruling relations, so characteristic of the extraordinary societies we live. The work of mothering gave me a site of knowing prior to those relations; it located a knowing within the actualities, the particularities, of our being, where knowing is always embodied and where the lifting-up that the abstracted organization of ruling requires is itself a material, actual, work organization, carried on in particular sites, by particular actual people. And, of course, having myself been for several years a secretary, I could add to my understanding of a knowing situated in the actualities of people's worlds my experience of being among those workers who directly produced for others, for men, the abstract character of texts as mere meaning, purified from the dross of their materiality by the gender boundary that assigned the embodiment of meaning to she who took down the master's words in shorthand (in those days) and did the typing that embodied his words/ thoughts in a form that others could read.

In learning feminism; not as a discourse, but as a personal practice, I discovered that I had to discard a practice of situating myself as subject in the objectified discourses and relations that I now identify as the ruling relations. I realized slowly that as a member of a department and a university I had participated in decisions and upheld practices that often I had either no personal interest in or at some other level loathed. I had learned to be 'responsible.'[4] I became conscious that I had learned how to be a subject alienated in an objectified mode. I had learned how to teach sociology as it was embodied in the texts of the discourse and to teach the different perspectives and theories as they were written and authorized. Sociological discourse was something outside me that it was my business to reproduce for students, and I did that pretty well. But feminism called that into question because it called into question the ways in which I had become simply a means through which these objectified modes of ruling were passed on, through which, therefore, ruling got done. I was the medium through which a systematically developed consciousness of society governed by formulations developed at the imperial centre was transmitted to the provinces whole and unmarred.

The critical consciousness of feminism was more than the perception that women were not part of this; it was also a search for a consciousness in myself that had been present (in the anxieties, the tension, the headaches, the feelings of nausea accompanying my work, departmental meetings, trying to write sociology, and so forth) but impotent. It was the learning of how to be a subject in my body, in the actualities of my life, and working from a grounding in experience and an ongoing sensitivity to 'where I am.' It was the learning and practice of a subject to whom the alienated practice of a subject in the ruling relations was no longer tolerable.

Of course, this meant doing sociology differently; and it meant, too, a desire to explore how the ruling relations were put together, how our lives were shaped and determined from outside us. These have indeed turned out to be aspects of the same enterprise, for to explore alternatives is also to explore how normal sociology is done; and exploring normal sociology has led me to an exploration of the social organization of knowledge in the ruling relations of which sociology is part. This enterprise has been ruled by a commitment to taking the standpoint of women as I've spelled it out above. This doesn't mean trying to find an experience that is general to all women and setting that up to govern our relevancies. It does mean that the knower is always situated in the particular actualities of her everyday/everynight world; it means that she's always embodied. That constrains the method of inquiry and analysis. It declares that from a particular standpoint, generalizing relations, objectified knowledge, universalized forms, and so forth are always to be made problematic. There is always a question about how the knower thus situated can transcend the particular site of her knowing to enter an objectified realm. How does she do it? What are the actual practices of the social organization and relations that she herself knows how to do, and does? What are the material conditions enabling her to neglect her particular local existence, as Alfred Schutz (1962) tells us we must do, to enter the cognitive domain of scientific theory?

I am making use here of just that approach I have been developing elsewhere in my work as a feminist sociologist. It proposes an insider's sociology, that is, a systematically developed consciousness of society from within, renouncing the artifice that stands us outside what we can never stand outside of. Beginning from where the subject is actually located returns us to a social world arising in and known in and through the ongoing actual activities of actual people. Here there is no contrast between thought and practice. Thought, the social forms of consciousness, belief, knowledge, ideology, are as much actual socially organized practices as cutting the grass in the front yard,[5] taking place in real time and in real places, and using definite material means under definite material conditions.

This doesn't mean working subjectively; rather, it means working from that site of knowing that is prior to the differentiation of subjective and objective. It means an explication of the actual practices in which we are active. It means attending to the primary materiality of the text as an essential moment in the transition from the locally embodied to the discursive. Hence, in exploring how sociology is assembled and organized as actual practices in which we too participate and by which our practices too are organized, we are also engaged in a reflexive examination and critique of what we know how to do and do.

The Objectified Organization of Ruling

By the 'ruling relations,' I mean that internally coordinated complex of administrative, managerial, professional, and discursive organization that regulates, organizes, governs, and otherwise controls our societies. It is not yet monolithic, but it is pervasive and pervasively interconnected. It is a mode of organizing society that is truly new for it is organized in abstraction from local settings, extra-locally, and its textually mediated character is essential (it couldn't operate without texts, whether written, printed, televised, or computerized) and characteristic (its distinctive forms of organizing and its capacity to create relations both independent and regulative of local setting depend on texts). This is a world we enter every day when we go to work as sociologists: we enter this world organized in and through texts as we sit down to the computer to write, as we work our way through a stack of papers to grade, as we roam the bookstore looking for ideas for teaching an old course in a new way, as we wrestle with problems of data analysis, as we write a memo to the administration, complaining about the arbitrary and unjust intervention they have made into our affairs. We don't even think of it as a world of relations and ourselves as insiders, as its practitioners. It has an ordinary existence for us, the ordinary existence that the means, objects, and practices of our coordinated work creates. It has a kind of thickness, a solidity, a taken-for-grantedness, for us that is surprising when we consider its primarily textual ground. There properties are created as we participate with others in the work that orients to and actively accomplishes the features of that reality.

An objectified world-in-common vested in texts is the essential coordinator of activities, decisions, policies, and plans produced by actual subjects as the acts, decisions, policies, and plans of large-scale organizations of various kinds. The primary mode of action and decision in the superstructures of business, government, the professions, and the scientific, professional, literary, and artistic discourses is symbolic and on paper or in computers. The realities to which action and decision are oriented are symbolically constructed virtual realities, accomplished in distinctive practices of reading and writing. Their objectification creates the necessary separations between what we know as individuals, located in our particular places in the world, and what we come to know as trained readers of the textual realities (Smith 1990a), actively implicated in the constitution of a textual world as the same for us as for any other trained reader, a world-in-common and hence a world.

Let me clarify with an example the difference between knowing, arising directly in local historical experience of a subject, and a factual account, a property of the externalized and objectified relations. In 1968, in Berkeley, California, there was a confrontation between police and street people (Smith 1990b). An account of what one witness to the events saw was published in the form of a letter in an underground newspaper. It accused the police of trying to provoke a reaction from the crowd that would justify harassing and arresting them. The story is told from the perspective of someone who was there. It begins when he comes on the scene, ends when he leaves, and is told in terms of what he could see from where he was.

The second story is a rebuttal. It was published from the mayor's office and contains the story as told to the mayor by the chief of police after an internal investigation. The mayor's story, of course, denies the accusation of improper police behaviour. But what is of relevance here is that the standpoint built into the mayor's story is quite different from that as told by the witness to the events. The second account is represented as the product of an official inquiry. It is produced in an institutional process, using its distinctive methodologies for producing an objectified account. It is not located in the perspective and experience of any particular individual: police officers – presumably the source of the account – appear as interchangeable with one another and have no narrative continuity. Which individual saw what, and was involved in what, cannot be determined.

The reading subject is placed quite differently with respect to the original events by the two accounts. The witness is enraged; he seeks to enliven the reader's anger by sharing his experience with her. The mayor's account, in its objectification, sets us at a distance, detaches us from the immediacy of the events; it has a different temporal structure, setting the events in an institutional order. The methodology of the positionless account[6] relates us differently to what happened than the engaged, involved account given by the witness.

Further, the positionless account both depends upon and transmits the institutional order in which it originates. The witness's account describes one young man being roughly searched by the police and then sent on up the street. The mayor's version is put together quite differently. It is not bounded by the situation of observation. We are told that the young man is a 'juvenile' already known to the police. We are told that, far from being sent on up the street, the young man was arrested and later pleaded guilty to the charge of being a minor in possession of alcoholic beverages. A complex division of labour among police, court-probation officers, and the law and legal process provides for the possibility of a description of events beyond the present of observation in which the young man has been charged and found guilty.

Such a social organization of knowledge is integral and essential to the organization of large-scale enterprise, government, and profession and to the organization of a discourse. Objectified worlds-known-in-common are also integral to the organization of sociology as a discourse. It is argued here that the methods of accomplishing its worlds-known-in common are conventions originating in sociological theories that have had a constitutive force in the organization of the discourse. The conventions provide general procedures for 'transliterating' the interests and experience of readers and writers of sociological discourse located in particular social relational sites into the objectified forms that entitle them to treatment as presences in the textual world-in-common of sociological discourse (and hence subduing individual subjectivity to the authority of the objectified). They provide methods of writing (and reading) the social as external to the particularities of people's lives, organizing in that mode relations among reading subjects and of reading subjects to those others of whom the text does – or, as we shall see, does not – speak.

The Objectification of Society in the Sociological Text

Shoshana Felman, in her marvellous explication of Jacques Lacan, makes use of Austin's (1962) notion of 'performative' to contrast the making of statements with writing (or talk) that organizes relations (Felman 1987). Here we are adopting a similar strategy. It is to attend to (some) theoretical texts of sociology, but not with respect to their content or substance as theoretical statements, nor in terms of what they have to say about 'society' or the 'social'; rather, we will focus here on theories as organizers of the relationship between the textual world created by such methods in the text and the actualities of the lived world where the reader reads the sociological text.[7] At least some types of sociological theory provide the ground rules or conventions for generating the virtual realities of sociological discourse.

From the distinctive site of women's consciousness in the place of our bodies and in the actualities of our lives, the text is not disembodied meaning as it is in the theorizing of contemporary literary and philosophical theorists of the text. The text is an actual material presence; it is the book, the pixilated letters that come up on my computer screen, the paper, or whatever form in which it enters the actual present site of my reading. The text occurs in the actual local historical settings of our reading and writing. Sitting just where we are, we enter through the text into relations of a different order, the relations mediated by texts that organize our participation as we read. We are raised, in our reading, from the narrow localities of lived actuality into the textual world with its marvellous capacity to launch us as subjects into looking-glass land. From where we are at a particular moment of reading (sitting as I am now in a midsummer cafe under a colourful umbrella), we haven't already entered the magic of time-space freedom that entry to the textual world gives us; we haven't stepped outside time or outside ourselves. So taking up the material text and reading (or sitting down at the keyboard with the monitor before us and writing) is an actual practice, something I do, you do, and know how to. The text is there as given; it defines a subject or subjects; it calls for and enables methods of reading. We know how, we know partially how, or we may not know how. But, in any case, our reading is a practical activity in time, and, as in conversation, we are not the same at the end as we were at the beginning. Even though text enables us to escape the local historical constraints of lived actuality, it does so as an ongoing sequence of living in that very actuality. Reading, too, is living and lived; reading, too, is practical activity: escaping the constraints of local time and place as lived is a practical activity located in a particular time and place, accomplished by a particular subject.

So here I am, and there you are, my reader. Here I am writing this in a third-floor room, looking out at the large old maple tree (now dying from the effects of acid rain) that shades my attic in summer and half hearing in the background on the radio the latest figures on unemployment in the United States. The linear text conceals my transition from cafe lunch to workroom. And you, wherever you are, are reading. There is a movement in time: I writing now, and you reading then; I writing then, and you reading now. The text lies between us, organizing our relation.

This is the sense of the text I want to hang on to. I want somehow to move away from the notion of texts as existing as meaning, and to see them instead as occurrences in time (partly captured in Derrida's notion of *différance*) and as organizing, through time, relations between people considered as sequences of action in which more than one is involved.

In Alfred Schutz's paper 'On Multiple Realities,' he writes of different cognitive domains. To each such domain, or 'reality,' corresponds a specific tension of consciousness, a specific *attention à la vie*. In the domain of scientific theorizing, the subject (knower) sets aside (brackets) his personal life, his pragmatic relevancies, the localized time-space coordinates that exist for him as body. He enters as subject the temporal/spatial order of the domain of scientific theorizing, according it, during his occupancy, the 'accent of reality' (Schutz 1962b). But Schutz's ethnography of consciousness sees the process from one side only. He does not see the essential complement to this work of consciousness, the social organization of that domain, nor its character as a discourse or its essential textuality. For if Schutz's knower is to set aside his personal and local life, what is it about the world he enters that enables that forgetting, that gives him a mode of being and activity in which his personal and local existence has no place, that takes him out of himself? This separation, unproblematic perhaps in the context of natural science, comes to have a peculiar extension in the context of sociology, for it constitutes there a separation between the subject's actual life and the textually mediated discourse that claims to speak of the same world she lives.

Reading sociology, we are reading about a world we are part of and active in, a world that situates exactly the actualities that we live. We are also, of course, reading in that world and being related to the same world as that in which our reading is going on. Sociology, then, has this peculiarity: it organizes our relations not only to other members of the sociological discourse but also to ourselves and others known and unknown.

What, then, are the characteristic ways in which sociological texts organize those relations, entering us through them into relations that stand us outside the actualities in which we read, locating us in the objectified modes of the ruling relations? How do the texts of sociology organize relations between subjects reading and the others of whom they speak, do not speak, or speak only by indirection? In examining these questions, we are examining the properties of what I shall call, for short, 'the sociological relation' to emphasize again that analytic attention here is on sociological texts as organizers of reader/writer relations rather than on the substantive propositions of theory. The constitutional theories of sociology have provided methods of writing society into texts. The conventions established construct an objectified standpoint situating their readers and writers in the ruling relations and subduing particular local positions, perspectives, and experiences. This is an organization of relations that we enter in reading.

Designing Objectivity: Emile Durkheim and Others

(Some) sociological theories have been constitutional for the discourse in providing rules and conventions organizing a standpoint within-the-text detaching the social-in-the-text from society as it is lived and experienced.[8] Such methods of writing and reading texts create positionless accounts (White 1976), versions of the world in which subjects are relegated to no place in particular and before which, therefore, all subjects are equal and equally absent. The construction of an absence of position both enables and is constituted by the writing of accounts of society as if it could be embraced in its totality; the writing of a social system as if indeed there were a position outside, a no place in which totality could be brought into view. At one time, I thought of such positionless accounts as a bird's-eye view, but indeed there is no bird, no place in flight from which a city appears laid out before the subject. The great imaginary constructions are brought before us as if we could participate in that odd mode of knowing that has been attributed to God alone, the capacity to see all aspects at once without taking a particular view or perspective upon them. We can roam, then, through the corridors and hallways of the text untrammelled by constraints of space and time. There is no now or then; there is no distance, nearness.

Such organization is realized in the textual practice accomplishing the appropriate, proper formation of discursive entities and objects (Foucault 1972), the proper attributions of capacities such as subject, agency, causal efficacy, and so forth, and hence the proper calling of syntactic relations among discursive entities. Sociological theories providing 'constitutional' rules and conventions can be thought of as governing these textual practices, selecting language forms and syntax in the writing of society into the text.[9]

In exploring theory as an organization of sociological discourse, I turn first to the rules of sociological method developed by Emile Durkheim. These, of course, have been subsequently challenged, improved upon, modified, and discarded. I shall suggest, however, that they are of particular significance because they enunciate conventions that have become standard, normal practices of writing sociological texts. I am not making an historical argument here, in the sense of what or who came first. I am making the claim that these, among other early sociological texts, were foundational and that in them we can identify a set of constitutive conventions that, stripped of their vulgar positivism, can be identified as normal practices of writing sociological texts and hence of producing the world in texts organizing sociology as discourse.

In Durkheim's *The Rules of Sociological Method*, the rules are designed cumulatively. He goes through a series of steps, each building upon its predecessor and enabling its successor. These steps (1) suspend the presence of the subject; (2) posit social phenomena (or social facts) as existing externally to particular individuals; (3) reattribute agency from subject to social phenomena; (4) require explanations of social phenomena to be in terms of social phenomena (without reference to phenomenal domains defined by other 'life science' discourses such as biology or psychology); and (5) substitute for goals, purposes, and so on the conception of function as a procedure for expressing relations among social phenomena. We try, then, to see these steps in the performative mode, that is, imagining how the reader learns *from* the text a practice of thinking society *into* texts.

Durkheim's first step is teaching us to 'see' an objectified order of presence that is independent of particular subjectivities:

There is in every society a certain group of phenomena which may be differentiated from those studied by the other natural sciences. When I fulfil my obliga-
tions as brother, husband, or citizen, when I execute my contracts, I perform
duties which are defined, externally to myself and my acts, in law and in custom.
Even if they conform to my own sentiments and I feel their reality subjectively,
such reality is still objective, for I did not create them; I merely inherited them
through my education. (Durkheim 1964: 1)

We learn the externality of law and custom in learning to ignore the
testimony of experience. The issue here is not the social efficacy of law
and custom; rather, it is the procedure the reader learns from this text,
which is to exclude what subjects might feel of duty, guilt, or the like as a
component of the social-in-the-text. What subjects feel or think is
declared as simply irrelevant to the constitution of the sociological phenomenon. The objectification of law or custom is to be accomplished by
following a procedure something like this: find ways of writing about law
or custom (or norm) to exclude reference to subjectivities.

And having been instructed in a preliminary, simple procedure for
constructing social facts, agency can be transferred from actual subjects
to the virtual entities of the sociological text:

These types of conduct or thought are not only external to the individual but are,
moreover, endowed with coercive power, by virtue of which they impose themselves upon him, independent of his individual will. Of course, when I fully con-
sent and conform to them, this constraint is felt only slightly, if at all, and is
therefore unnecessary. But it is, nonetheless, an intrinsic characteristic of these
facts, the proof thereof being that it asserts itself as soon as I attempt to resist it. If
I attempt to violate the law, it reacts against me so as to prevent my act before its
accomplishment, or to nullify my violation by restoring the damage, if it is accomplished and reparable, or to make me expiate it if it cannot be compensated for
otherwise. (Durkheim 1964: 2)

The first step that objectifies has already laid the basis entitling us to ascribe
agency to law or custom. Law assumes the function of agent: 'it' reacts.

This ground achieved, Durkheim is able to make a move that would otherwise be incredible. Thinking and feeling can now be treated as objectified agents acting on and controlling individuals: 'Here, then, is a category
of facts with very distinctive characteristics: it consists of ways of acting,
thinking, and feeling, external to the individual, and endowed with a
power of coercion, by reason of which they control' (Durkheim 1964: 4).

Through steps such as these, Durkheim sets up procedures for constituting an object world that is the proper object of sociology. It is a self-
contained world, explicitly independent of biology and psychology. A
new variety of phenomena is constituted, and it is to this exclusively that
the term 'social' ought to be applied (Durkheim 1964: 3).

The introduction of functional reasoning is the final step: '*When, then,
the explanation of a social phenomenon is undertaken, we must seek separately the
efficient cause which produces it and the function it fulfils*' (Durkheim 1964: 95;
emphasis in original).

This has two effects: one is the introduction of a final cause that
grounds and governs the attribution of agency to 'social facts,' transfer-
ring telos from subjects to society;[10] more important is the creation of a
self-contained explanatory space in which social facts are explained
socially (in Durkheim, with reference to a reified conception of society).
Sociology is thereby insulated from the claims of other disciplines to its
empirical domain.

We could, I think, trace the history of these constitutive conventions as
they are rewritten and modified, and as their awkward and sometimes
incoherent postulates are refined and even discarded. But, of course, that
isn't possible or indeed relevant here. The interest here is in isolating
some of the steps that have brought us to the conventions with which we
now work. Here the constitutional work of Talcott Parsons has been of
major significance. He does away with the *prima facie* problems arising
from Durkheim's impetuous and unconvincing elimination of the subject. He overcomes the problem of Durkheim's declaration-by-fiat of the
externality of a normative and representational order vis-à-vis the individual by, first, building his theoretical structure upon an abstraction of the
actor, disembodied and assigned just those properties that are concordant with the theoretical order (Parsons 1968);[11] and, second, by adapting psychoanalysis as a theory of the internalization of social norms,
values, and symbolic systems (Parsons 1982) so that subjects are in effect
treated as expressions of a socio-cultural system.

Equally important is Parsons's establishment of conceptual procedures
in which the virtual reality of society, as an essential organizing constituent
of the emerging discourse, is vested. He set up an array of concepts defining the parameters of the field: role, role-expectations, social system,
norms, values, order, and so forth. As procedures for ordering translitera-
tions from actuality to sociological text, they hold and carry, in a fashion
analogous to the transmission of 'genetic' material, the objectification of
the social. They govern the narrative practices of sociology, producing

society as an emergent that can be stripped away from individual actors, who can then be reconstituted in the text as 'bearers'[12] of structure or system. The actualities of a world created in the actual activities of actual individuals are transliterated to a textual order from which those actualities can be read as properties of system or structure (other such terms with a different provenance are class, stratification, status, power, and so forth).

As concepts such as these become ordinary sociological currency, they vest objectifying practices in the discourse. We don't have to go back to Durkheim any longer or even to Parsons to find out how to accomplish the proper objectifications of sociology; we learn to use its concepts.

Subsequent developments have stripped sociology of the global theorizing that characterized the foundational work of theorists such as Durkheim and Parsons. But the framework organizing the discourse that their and similar work founded has remained. Subsequent steps have detached the principles and conventions organizing an objectification of the same world that sociologists live from inside. The founding theories are no longer needed. Robert Merton argued for 'theories of the middle-range,' in contrast to the global theorizing of his predecessors (Merton 1967). In proposing a strategy of building cumulatively towards theoretical synthesis, he in effect stripped away the grand theoretical enterprise while preserving the 'logic' of the relations grand theory had put in place. Discarding functionalism on the grand scale, he preserved it as a device for isolating sociological knowledge from what anyone might know by distinguishing between manifest and latent function, between functions of which people are or may be aware and that may indeed be planfully organized and produced, and latent functions, the unseen interrelations of social phenomena. Later Kingsley Davis declared the demise of functionalism, arguing that the interrelations among elements of social structure were now fully established as normal sociological practice (Davis 1967). Davis was announcing publicly a shift that had already taken place in sociological practice. *Ad hoc* 'theorizing' of the relations among variables, increasingly sophisticated methods of theorizing variables and of developing and testing hypotheses, and technically sophisticated methods of sampling, of developing 'instruments,' and of measurement had given practical substance to Durkheim's and Parsons's constitutional formulations.

Such methods operate within and give technical substance to the parameters of the discursive space organized by the founding fathers. They realize as sociological practice (1) a discursive universe vis-à-vis which the reading subject is positionless – she cannot locate its presences in relation to the actual site and situation of her reading; (2) the suppression of the presence of subjects as others whose presence defines the reader, who are related to the reader in and through the text; (3) the constitution of boundaries demarcating sociology from other disciplines and establishing an internally referential universe of entities; (4) the constitution of a self-contained discursive world that does not require (let alone insist on) a reflexive grounding in actualities for its sense[13] nor, while dependent on actual individuals to produce what it recognizes as phenomena, require that their active presence be registered in the text.

Ordinary Sociological Practices of Objectification

The world as we know it in our everyday/everynight experience of it doesn't 'naturally' yield up the properties and organization of the virtual realities of sociological discourse. The founding constitutional conventions of sociology provide a general set of instructions for selecting and shaping concepts and categories, grammatical forms expressing relations among them, and methods of representation.[14] Here are examples of how they work in practice.

Suspending the Presence of the Subject

Positing social phenomena (or social facts) as existing externally to particular individuals has been developed through specialized conceptual and categorial forms that operate as objectifying devices. Characteristic are methods of representing people's activities, talk, relations, and thinking without the subjects who act, talk, relate, and think. A common practice is the use of nominalization, wherein a verb expressing the action of a subject is given the form of a noun. For example: aggression, depression, suicide, family violence. Related are terms construing subjective states of individuals as entities in and of themselves, capable of entering into relations with other such entities. Examples include the following terms: attitude, opinion (as in opinion poll), motivation, belief, alienation, interests; as well as terms originating in institutional forms such as law, education, and medicine.

Reattributing Agency from Subject to Social Phenomena

Once nominalized social phenomena are constructed, agency can be attributed to them rather than to people. Here is an example. There's a considerable body of studies focusing on the relations among family, class, and school achievement. Here is a passage from Maurice Craft's introduction to a British collection of papers on the topic:

> Demographic calculations tell us little of the subcultural processes (social class attitudes), or of the more intricate psychosocial processes of the individual family which together provide the motivation to excel and the implementary values which can turn school achievement into career success. (Craft 1970a: 7)

This passage is almost overloaded with nominalizations constitutive of social phenomena shifting agency from people to the sociologically constituted entities. Behind the veil of such formulations are women and men whose work in the home is directly oriented towards a child's work in school. People take time, think and plan, and work under definite material conditions within constraints placed on them by the exigencies of providing the economic basis of the family. They also work within constraints and under standards imposed on them by the schools, over which, for the most part, they have little control. The term 'intricate psychosocial processes' collects the work and thought of actual people into a sociological entity that becomes the agent in the text, providing 'the motivation to excel and the implementary values,' which, in turn, are the agents turning school achievement to career success. In an analogous version, homes provide varying levels and kinds of the cultural capital that determines school achievement (Bourdieu and Passeron 1977).

The relations among sociologically constituted phenomena explain sociologically constituted phenomena. The drama of sociological texts is the active relations among phenomena (dependent variables ruled by independent variables, structures ruling history, culture ruling consciousness) transliterated from human lives and activities.

Detaching the Sociological from the Actual

Various methodological moves have deprived the dominant sociological discourse of accountability to the actual. Parsons's conception of the analytic status of theory, categories, and concepts vis-à-vis the actual removes theory from the requirement that it recover properties or features of the actualities of people's lives or conform to the ordering or organization that people are themselves producing:

> Analytical theory in the sense in which I mean the term here, is a body of logically

interrelated generalized concepts (logical universals) the specific facts corresponding to which (particulars) constitute statements describing empirical phenomena. (Parsons 1982a: 72)

Facts themselves are conceptually ordered. It is a procedure that privileges the order of the discourse over the order of the actual. Analysis, for Parsons, isn't dissection or exploring the anatomy of a social world; it's the conceptual carving out from 'the concrete phenomena'' (Parsons 1982a: 73) those aspects constituting (and constituted by) the values of variables. Such thinking has been foundational to the later positivism of quantitative research, developments to which the philosophical positivism of Carl Hempel (1966) has written the conceptual architecture. Contemporary theoretical moves such as 'rational choice' theory perpetuate these effects.

In different ways, these theoretical moves privilege the textual order of discourse and its textually constituted realities as the object of sociological work. A peculiar distance between the discursive world and the actual world is created. Theories, concepts, and categories of discourse aren't accountable to the actual; theories may be tested through hypotheses generated from them, but the existence and privileging of the discursive world itself is never called into question. The universe created within sociological texts by such methods realizes, in its research practices, the actual as an expression of the discursive. It is a peculiarity of sociological discourse that *its constitutional procedures deny it any common ground outside the text to which sociologists can refer in settling disputes.* Common ground must be constructed within the text and is always held in place by prior agreement about and commitment to the conventions that sustain it.

Reconstructing Subjects as Figments of Discourse

The practices evolved from constitutional principles privilege sociological interpretations. It is normal practice to treat our interpretations as the attributes, properties, and interpretations of subjects of study. The originals are entered into the sociological texts as pseudo-subjects, categories of personages, such as parents and children, to whom the objectified attributes and properties can be assigned, sometimes producing the appearance of action, but action fully regulated by the sociological theorizing of relations. Here is a story about how the school performance of children is influenced by the attitudes of parents:

The middle-class parents take more interest in their children's progress at school than the normal working-class parents do and they become relatively more interested as their children grow older. They visit the schools more frequently to find out how their children are getting on with their work and when they do so are more likely to ask to see the Head as well as the class teacher, whereas the manual working-class parents are usually content to see the class teacher only. (Douglas 1970: 152)

Actual subjects are entered into the text as actors in the sociologist's narrative. Social relations are attributed to individuals. Whatever may be going on between school and parent in differing class settings is transposed into different attributes of individual parents, using methodologies that rely on counting individuals as expressions of social variables. Concepts such as parental attitudes or interests make use of pre-existing theoretical work enabling the treatment of subjective states as objectified entities. In using such concepts to organize inquiry, sociologists develop indicators treating what respondents interviewed have said or what the school records of individual children show as expressions of the discursively constructed entity. The actual then becomes an indicator of the discursively constructed phenomenon, giving it a local habitation. For example, numbers of parental visits to school and to school principal are used as an indicator of 'parental interest' (Musgrove 1970).

Such elaborate technical and artful practices produce from the actualities of people's lives readings that are expressed in terms that are not theirs and from a standpoint that conceals its positioning in the relations of ruling while appearing to be that of nowhere in particular. They enable properties of the social organization and relations in which people are active to be attributed to the figmental personages of the sociologist's narrative. Even interpretive sociologies insisting that our interpretations conform to those of our subjects entitle the sociologist to take away what people have told her and remake it in the terms of our discourse, creating in the text the subjects who bear our interpretations as theirs.[15]

How Constitutive Conventions Subvert the Feminist Enterprise

Feminists, myself among them, have criticized the overriding of women's local experience by the interpretive hegemony of sociology and have sought solutions that preserve the voices and interpretations of women we have talked with. We have made a specifically feminist critique of sociology's objectifying practices. Judith Stacey writes:

Feminist scholars evince widespread disenchantment with the dualisms, abstractions, and detachment of positivism, rejecting the separations between subject and object, thought and feeling, knower and known, and political and personal as well as their reflections in the arbitrary boundaries of traditional academic discipline. Instead most feminist scholars advocate an integrative trans-disciplinary approach to knowledge which grounds theory contextually in the concrete realm of women's everyday lives. (Stacey 1988: 23)

This critique cannot be reduced, as it sometimes is, to a critique of positivism or to calling for traditional qualitative methods. Rather it searches for a sociology related quite differently to its subjects, denying the separations that refuse to admit to discursive presence subjects in the fullness of their feeling, thought, and knowing.

But in seeking an alternative, we all too often find ourselves caught in a trap created by the constitutive conventions of our discipline. We begin with attempting to establish relations with subjects that don't produce them as research objects. Shulamit Reinharz (1983), for example, has developed a conception of experiential analysis, recommending that sociologist and subjects work out interpretations together as a joint product, rather than interpretations simply being imposed upon subjects. Stacey (1988) sought consciously to work with her respondents by treating them as full subjects, getting to know them well, even developing friendships. Ann Oakley (1981) sought an approach that involved an interchange between herself and those she interviewed. These are only some of the many innovative approaches to the feminist researcher's relation to her respondents. The problem does not lie here, but at the next stage.

Both Reinharz and Stacey locate problems of disjuncture in the process of producing the research product. Reinharz locates these in the historical process that breaks apart the developments in the local setting and the agreed-on framework. Stacey attends to a more fundamental difficulty, one that I would like to suggest is 'symptomatic' of the organizing power of the sociological relation built into discourse over the years:

A major area of contradiction between feminist principles and ethnographic method involves the dissonance between fieldwork practice and ethnographic product. Despite the aspects of intervention and exploitation I have described, ethnographic method appears to (and often does) place the researcher and her informants in a collaborative, reciprocal quest for understanding, but the research product is ultimately that of the researcher, however modified or influenced by informants. With very rare exceptions it is the researcher who narrates, who authors the ethnography. In the last instance an ethnography is a written document structured primarily by a researcher's purposes, offering a researcher's interpretations, registered in a researcher's voice. (Stacey 1988: 23)

Stacey individualizes the dilemma. But the protagonist of her story is a researcher producing a research product. The relations of the discourse (or discourses) within which research is conceived are already implicated. The research product will be located in the ongoing textually mediated conversation of sociology. It will, I suggest, be in some way organized by the sociological relation, even when the researcher is committed to work from the viewpoint of subjects. Even working collaboratively with subjects on the production of the interpretation of their talk does not as such exorcize the presence and power of the founding conventions of the discourse.

Ann Oakley describes an instance of the emergence of this contradiction at the juncture between 'interviewing' and the sociological product. In her paper 'Interviewing Women: A Contradiction in Terms' (1981), referred to above, she analyses a 'lack of fit' between the proper sociological practice of interviewing, as the textbooks prescribe it, and what happens when a feminist interviews women. She describes her own experience of doing a study of women's experience of pregnancy and childbirth. It was, she found, ridiculous, if not impossible, to avoid personal involvement. The women she talked to asked her questions and were interested in her own experience. She saw no reason not to engage with them fully as a person, and did so, answering their questions, responding to their interest, getting to know many of them, some as friends or long-term acquaintances.

Yet turning to an analysis of some of the interview material, we find that the switch engineered by the constitutive conventions has gone through. With Hilary Graham, Oakley wrote a paper called 'Competing Ideologies of Reproduction: Medical and Maternal Perspectives on Pregnancy' (Graham and Oakley 1981). The title itself is indicative of the power of the founding conventions. The paper, using a wealth of interview material, describes two different 'perspectives' on childbirth, that of obstetrician and that of women in childbirth. The two perspectives conflict:

Specifically, our data suggest that mothers and doctors disagree on whether pregnancy is a natural or a medical process and whether as a consequence, pregnancy should be abstracted from the woman's life-experiences and treated as an isolated medical event. (Graham and Oakley 1981: 52)

We've still got people here, but they are now framed as instances or expressions of a conflict that is located in ideology. The actualities explored in interviews and observation become *illustrations* of the two frames of reference. Graham and Oakley write, for example, of 'some of the ways in which the differences between them [the two frames of reference] are displayed in antenatal consultations and women's experience of having a baby' (ibid., 52). There is a characteristic, although undramatic, shift of agency. They ask: 'How do the conflicts ... between medical and maternal frames of reference manifest themselves?' (ibid., 56). The conflicts are not conflicts directly between doctors and patients. They are between 'frames of reference.' The conception of two ideologies orders a selection of passages from interviews contrasting what women in childbirth say with what obstetricians say. The conflict is a dramatic production scripted by the sociologists to create the virtual reality of the text.

The convention of explaining social phenomena in terms of social phenomena is also found, although in a relatively weak form, as conflicts between the 'two perspectives' are 'explained' 'by rooting [them] in the particular frames of reference employed by the providers and users of maternity care.' The displacement from subjects to discourse is characteristic. Although multiple citations from interview material are used and no causal attributions are made, the 'constitutional' move shifts agency from people to discursively constructed entities. The relationships are not between pregnant women and doctors but (as the title indicates) between medical and maternal perspectives.

My second example is not a feminist text.[16] I came across it in investigating the ways in which the constitutive conventions can be seen to be at work in qualitative sociologies and use it because it exemplifies the contradiction between commitment to the viewpoint of subjects and the capacity of the constitutive conventions to subvert it. In this instance, the researchers were explicit in intending to work from the subjects' point of view. A work by Peter March, Elizabeth Rosser, and Rom Harré, *The Rules of Disorder* (1978), claims to be a study that expresses the standpoint of young men involved in the notorious football gangs of British soccer:

We have come to see it through the eyes of the people who take part in it [what is happening]. They see their social life as a struggle for personal dignity in a general social framework that daily denies them this dignity. Far from valuing disorder, they are engaged in the genesis of significance for their lives and an order in their action that is their own. The struggle begins when they see many of the things that seem routine to the rest of us as ways of devaluing them. (March et al. 1978: 2)

However the researchers may have begun their project, in the analysis and writing they create a structure that subdues the voices of those with whom they talked to just that organization of relations in the text that I am exploring. They begin with a critical view of how these young men and their activities are presented in the press and in the pronouncements of a British intelligentsia. Their own strategy will diverge; they will work differently: they will look at things 'through the eyes of the people who take part in [them].' They are also specifically critical of Parsons's theorizing of school as integrating young people into the larger social order. From the point of view of the playground, they argue, school is to be seen as generating an alternative order in the playground, deviant in terms of the official norms. Notions of order, deviance, and so on are, of course, familiar vesting devices entering the constitutive conventions of sociology into the text. Inverting the standard application of these concepts doesn't change the standpoint built into them; the latter is carried in the concepts like a virus hidden in computer software.

The researchers' interviewing and analysis are organized by the notion of rule. Rule has become one of those 'vesting' concepts referred to above in my discussion of Parsons. For these researchers, 'rule' will bridge the 'view through their [informants'] eyes' and the sociologists' interpretation of these young men as participating in an alternative order. The concept of rule runs a line through the interviews and other ethnographic material linking artfully selected passages as expressions of the sociologically known. Working within the constitutive conventions, almost as a discursive habit, the viewpoint written into the text shifts imperceptibly to the standard sociological standpoint. The young men's view is supplanted.

Much theoretical and methodological work is done to transfer the constructs of discourse to the subjects, producing them as 'figments' of discourse. This has the effect, as so many such devices do, of making invisible the transition from subjects' viewpoint to researchers', by attributing the latter to the former.[17] The researchers want to interpret the behaviour of the young men on the football ground as governed by rules. They also want to be able to treat such rules as the sociological expression of the views and actions of the young men. They hold that they are entitled to use the concept of rule in this way if they can show that in fact their subjects do use rules in guiding their actions. This can be established if respondents talk rules.[18] Thus what the young men do can be interpreted as an expression of a 'rule' if the respondents themselves will tell or talk about a rule or rules. And indeed they do produce 'rule-like' statements. However, in the extracts of interviews that are provided, such statements are made *in response to questions about the reasons why the young men did such and such.* 'Rule-like' statements would thus appear to be the joint product of interviewer and respondent; and hence, the researchers are complicit in producing the 'rules' attributed to respondents.

At the beginning of the book, they describe the young men they studied as the 'dramatis personae.' The metaphor expresses exactly the sociological relation created in the text. Respondents have the appearance of free agents. They have the appearance of speaking with their own voices. But, in fact, the sociologists' script prescribes how they appear and what they say. The sociologists speak through their dramatis personae.[19] Standpoint has in effect been conceptually shifted from that of the young men with whom they talked, and whose viewpoint they had wanted to make central, back to the standpoint of the discourse locating the reading subject in the relations of ruling.

Feminist Resistance

Sociology as a discipline arises in and never manages to leave behind its struggle to extricate the discursive subject from the society in which actual subjects are always necessarily embedded. Unlike the natural sciences, it has never developed technologies of encounter with reality that fully and as a practical matter constitute it as other. Its objectifications are always at odds with the lived actuality in which they are accomplished. This essential fracture continually breaks through as each next attempt to resolve the contradiction re-creates it. Sociological discourse is riven with breaks and discontinuities as we are nudged once again by our own life experience to make it somehow say what it will not say, or will say only partially. There is a constant struggle going on to remake the discourse in order to incorporate the missing, the unclaimed, or the unspoken that disturb it (Stinchcombe 1983).

But the problem we have confronted is more than simply a disjuncture between the world and the discourse that knows it. The feminist critique has questioned the standpoint from which sociology is written. Sociological discourse builds in a standpoint in the ruling relations, which have been occupied almost exclusively by white men, and the phenomenal world it has created has been the view from their site. Here is Patricia Hill Collins's critique of the categories vesting the sociological representation of the family that absent the experience and consciousness of Afro-American women:

Sociological generalizations about families that do not account for Black women's experience will fail to see how the public/private split shaping household composition varies across social and class groupings, how racial/ethnic family members are differentially integrated into wage labour, and how families alter their household structure in response to changing political economies (e.g., adding more people and becoming extended, fragmenting family and becoming female-headed and migrating to locate better opportunities). Black women's family experiences represent a clear case of the workings of race, gender, and class oppression in shaping family life. Bringing undistorted observations of Afro-American women's family experiences into the centre of analysis again raises the question of how other families are affected by these same forces. (Collins 1986: S29)

Indeed, bringing undistorted observations of Afro-American women's family experiences into the centre of analysis does more than raise questions about the effect of these forces on other families.[20] It subverts the sociological relation that has written into sociology the exclusion of Afro-American women,[21] and it continues to write in other exclusions whose representatives have still to be heard. As Sandra Harding (1986) has pointed out, the opening of public discourse to multiple voices and perspectives calls into question the very notion of a single standpoint from which a final overriding version of the world can be written. Indeed the constitution of society as object accomplished by conformity to the founding conventions of sociology also constitutes the singular omnipresent Archimedean subject that feminism calls into question. The specific competence of the founding conventions is the resolution of multiplicity into one.

Of course, sociology has back doors through which the local historical actualities of sociologists' experience leak into the sociological text, as Arthur Stinchcombe (1983) has described; but, as he also describes, the end product is a reworking of the object.[22] At each historical point, the society objectified in sociological discourse crystallizes the invisible presences and concerns of its makers; at each historical point, it sanctifies through such objectification the institutionalized exclusions, as subjects, from the discourses of power, of women as a social category, of people of colour, and of members of non-dominant classes. Sociology's constitutive conventions are organizers of those relations among ourselves and among ourselves in relation to others. They have their political effect. They subdue people's ordinary everyday/everynight knowledge of society; they seal off sociology, as a systematically developed consciousness of society, from modes of knowing beginning where people are, in their lives, who are not among the makers of discourse or participants in ruling.

To seek alternatives is also to revise our relations, to seek a sociology that, as a systematic consciousness of society, learns it from inside, from precisely the multiple standpoints from which the social relations in which we are active and that determine our lives are known, creating accounts of their organization and dynamics that are constantly enriched as they are explored again from a new site.

Susan Sherwin (1988) writes about the differences between how masculinist and feminist philosophers proceed. She proposes a feminist transformation of the relations of knowing, contrasting a feminist ideal of cooperative, collective work with the competition for certainties, the zero/sum approach to truth, characteristic of traditional masculinist philosophy.[23] Feminist ideals call for very different social relations of knowledge:

Scholarship in pursuit of a shared goal is to be undertaken as a collective enterprise where different people do piece-work on different aspects of the problem ... Each contribution is related to the larger system of ideas, the larger project, and is not offered as a private theory then to bear one's name. (Sherwin 1988: 23)

Of course, a sociology for women, for people, seeking a knowledge of how our lives and relations (direct and indirect) are shaped, directs us towards a knowledge community beyond our discipline. Discovering and uncovering how our societies are put together must embrace in its cooperative growing those who have formerly been the objects of our study and must now be, in a new sense, its subjects, its knowers.

We do not despise our knowledge and our skills. It is not these as such that divide sociologists from those to whom we would be responsible and responsive. A revolution must also have a division of labour. And others have skills and knowledge we do not have. But we are hampered by methods of writing into texts that seal in a knowledge divorced from the lively part it might play in coming with others to know, together, our relations and society differently, from within yet not subjectively, knowing them as we actively participate in them and as they are brought into being in the actual practices of actual people in the multiple sites of their experiencing.

Part Two:
Theory

5

The Ruling Relations

Introduction

This chapter explores the complex of objectified social relations that organize and regulate our lives in contemporary society. Its inquiry is driven by experiences in the women's movement of a dual consciousness, with the particularities of being mother and housewife, on the one hand, and, on the other, the abstracted discourses and forms of organization creating the matrix of a consciousness outside the local and particular. Developing a sociology from women's standpoint proposes an inquiry beginning in the local particularities of everyday experience that would explore how these relations are accomplished as local practices. A strategy for sociological inquiry is formulated which does not begin from a discursively structured position within those relations, but from a standpoint traditionally women's, located in the actualities of the everyday of people's embodied living.

The paper goes on to describe an historical trajectory in which these objectified relations have emerged as increasingly independent and increasingly pervasive as organizers of people's everyday/everynight activities. The intersection of everyday local settings and the abstracted, extra-local ruling relations is mediated by the materiality of printed and electronic texts. The texts integral to the social organization of these forms are complemented by technologies or disciplined practices that produce standardized local states of affairs or events corresponding to the standardized texts. Finally the topic returns to the issue of gender, showing how the dual consciousness which brings the objectified extra-local character of these relations into view has itself been defined in the historical trajectory of their emergence. It is in this context that a sociology from the standpoint of women can be seen as proposing an alternative organization of knowledge which does not reproduce the ruling relations, but rather explicates just those relations in which our lives are embedded.

A Sociology from Women's Standpoint

The sociology for women I propose begins in the actualities of women's lived experience. Its aim is to discover the social as it comes into view from an experiencing of life that is not already defined within the ruling relations. It does not speak only of women. Rather, it seeks a sociology, a method of inquiry, that extends and expands what we can discover from the local settings of our everyday/everynight living.

The standpoint of women establishes a place to open inquiry that begins with a consciousness located in a particular local site. Hence it problematizes the move into transcendence, the ego that slots into subject positions defined and determined discursively, bureaucratically, administratively, managerially, etc. The theories, concepts, and methods of the discourses in which we participate as intellectuals constitute the objectified standpoints through which we are related to the world as if we stood outside it. The experience of those whose particularizing work in relation to children, spouse, and household forms their consciousness is obliterated. I used to find, using standard sociological approaches, that we'd begin with the honest intention of doing research that was oriented towards people's interests and from their viewpoint, but that in doing the work inexorably, it seemed, our good and competent knowledge of how to do valid research led us into producing accounts which objectified them from a standpoint in the ruling relations. To reconstruct sociology as inquiry into the social from a standpoint in people's everyday experience means reconstructing its methods of thinking.

A sociology from women's standpoint in the local actualities of our everyday lives must be put together quite differently from the traditional objectifying sociologies. Committed to exploring the society from within people's experience of it, rather than objectifying them or explaining their behaviour, it would investigate how that society organizes and shapes the everyday world of experience. Its project is to explicate the actual social relations in which people's lives are embedded and to make these visible to them/ourselves.

This means a sociology beginning in a world of activity, the doings of actual people, and finding the social as the object of sociology's inquiry into how their activities are concerted and coordinated. It explores the social from within the same everyday/everynight world as we experience in its living. The subject/knower of inquiry is not a transcendent subject but situated in the actualities of her own living, in relations with others as they are. Whatever exists socially is produced/accomplished by people 'at work,' that is, active, thinking, intending, feeling, in the actual local settings of their living and in relationships that are fundamentally among particular others – even though the categories of ruling produce particular others as expressions of its order.

Thus the knowing subject of this sociology is located in a lived world in which both theory and practice go on, in which theory is itself a practice, in time, and in which the divide between the two can itself be brought under examination. The entry into text-mediated discourse and the relations of text-mediated discourse are themselves actual as activities and the ordering of activities. They happen – always in the time they occurred in and during the time they perdured. Concepts, beliefs, ideas, knowledge, and so on (what Marxists know as consciousness) are included in this ontology of the social (see chapter 1) as practices that are integral to the concerting and coordinating of people's activities.

Thus, discourse, and the ruling relations in general, are, ontologically, fields of socially organized activity. People enter and participate in them, reading/watching/operating/writing/drawing texts; they are at work, and their work is regulated textually; whatever form of agency is accessible to them is accessible textually as courses of action in a text-mediated mode. Society is emphatically, from this viewpoint, *not* an ensemble of meaning. The social *happens*; included in the happening/activities are concepts, ideologies, theories, ideas, and so forth. Their deceitful stasis is an effect of how the printed text enables us to return to them again, find them again, as if nothing had changed. But each such iteration is the actual local practice of a particular individual, reading just where she is, for just the what-comes-next that her reading initiates.

In projecting inquiry into social relations coordinating multiple local sites of activity, the investigation of the text-mediation of social relations is foundational. The reason is this: the standpoint of women locates us in bodily sites, local, actual, particular; it problematizes, therefore, the coordination of people's activities as social relations organized outside local historical settings, connecting people in modes that do not depend on particularized relationships between people. The ruling relations are of this kind, coordinating the activities of people in the local sites of their bodily being into relations operating independently of person, place, and time. In putting in question the making of the extra-local and extrapersonal ruling relations, women's standpoint does not proclaim them invalid, but rather recognizes the extra-locality of relations as itself a social organization of actual people's practices. In these relations, the particularity of individuals, their actual situation and site of work, the ephemerality of the lived moment, and so on, disappear; their disappearance is itself an accomplishment of what particular people do, in their actual situations and sites of work, as they live, are active, and experience the evanescence of lived time.

From this standpoint, the ruling relations themselves, including the social organization of knowledge, are problematized for investigation. They too exist in the ongoing concerting of actual people's activities in the particular local sites of our bodily being. How can consciousness operate as if it had no body and were not located in a particular local site, in place and time? What are the specific forms of social relations that provide for the subject's modes of being and action in and through texts? How is it that language and discourse appear as if they were autonomous systems, forgetting the irremediably local historicity of speakers, readers, and writers? How can we take up post-structuralism's discovery of how discourse speaks through us and beyond our intended meaning, while at the same time avoiding its solipsistic confinement to discourse?

The Ruling Relations

In developing an account of consciousness that takes advantage of this method of thinking, I have traced Marx's later thinking on the emergence of the economy as relations that have taken on an independent existence over against those whose work brings them into being and 'drives' them. The notion of ruling relations is analogous to Marx's (1973) specification of the 'object' of his investigations of capital as the specialization and differentiation of relations of dependence. Relations of dependence were originally relations between persons. He tells us that

when we look at social relations which create an undeveloped system of exchange, of exchange values and of money ... then it is clear from the outset that the individuals in such a society, although their relations appear to be more personal, enter into connection with one another only as individuals imprisoned with a certain definition, as feudal lord and vassal, landlord and serf, etc., or as members of a caste etc. or as members of an estate etc. In the ... developed system of exchange ... the ties of personal dependence, of distinctions of blood, education, etc. are in fact exploded, ripped up ... So far from constituting the removal of a 'state of dependence,' these external relationships represent its disintegration into a general form, or better, they are the elaboration of the general basis of personal states of dependence. Here too individuals come into relation with one another only in a determined role. These material states of dependence, as opposed to the personal states, are also characterized by the fact that individuals are now controlled only by abstractions, whereas earlier they depended on one another. (Marx 1973: 163–4)

The abstractions by which individuals are controlled are relations of exchange between people mediated by money and commodities. Differentiated and specialized, these are the relations we know as the economy. In Marx's view, people's existence is produced by their concerted work, and hence they depend on one another. Relations of dependence differ in different modes of production. Before capitalism, relations of dependence were between particular individuals: kinsfolk, feudal lord and serf, and so forth. The market progressively displaces these relations of dependence, substituting for them relations among people mediated by money and commodities (Rubin 1973). The market in its capitalist form is a specialized organization of relations of dependence driven by exchange value. People's dependence on one another's work as members of a society becomes unidimensional and abstract as it is objectified in the exchange of money and commodities.

I envisage the ruling relations and the historical trajectory of their development as an analogous process of differentiation and specialization, but, in this case, of the relations of consciousness (in Marx's sense of 'social consciousness') and agency. The ruling relations 'extract' the coordinative and concerting of people's everyday/everynight activities and subject them to technological and technical specialization, elaboration, differentiation, and objectification. They become independent of particular individuals; individuals participate in them through the forms of agency and subjectivity they provide. Organization is produced as a differentiated function. Coordination and concerting are leached out of localized and particularized relations and transferred to modes in which they are subjected to specialized and technical development.

The ruling relations are text-mediated and text-based systems of 'communication,' 'knowledge,' 'information,' 'regulation,' 'control,' and the like. The functions of 'knowledge, judgment, and will' that Marx saw as wrested from the original 'producer' and transferred to capital become built into a specialized complex of *objectified* forms of organization and relationship. Max Weber's (1978) account of bureaucracy is an early spec-

ification, and indeed it is part of an examination of the historical differentiation of person and organization in the exercise of political power.
But these developments are not confined to the state. Knowledge, judgment, and will are less and less properties of the individual subject and
more and more of objectified organization. They are constituted as actual
forms of concerting and concerted activities and *can be investigated as such.*
'Objectivity,' the focus of postmodernist critique, is only one form of
objectification, though objectified organization relies extensively on text-
mediated virtual realities. Forget crude and reductive notions such as
'superstructure.' Social consciousness exists now as a complex of externalized or objectified social relations through which people's everyday/
everynight activities organize and coordinate contemporary society.

Contrary to some interpretations, Marx (1976) clearly theorized consciousness as an attribute of individuals. Buried in his critical treatment of
German ideology is an analysis of the historical institutions which create
the conditions under which consciousness comes to be conceived as an
independent power over against actual individuals. Men doing mental
work under the peculiar conditions of an intelligentsia or judiciary – philosophers, judges, and the like – experience ideas as having power in and
of themselves. But, in fact, there are only 'the real individuals themselves
and consciousness is considered solely as *their* consciousness' (Marx and
Engels 1976: 42–3; original emphasis).

The concept of the ruling relations identifies an historical development of forms of social consciousness that can no longer be adequately
conceived as arising in the life conditions of actual individuals. It directs
investigation to a complex of objectified relations, coordinating the activities of many, many people whose consciousness as subjects is formed
within those relations. Conceptions such as Louis Althusser's (1971) of
the ideologically constituted subject, or Michel Foucault's (1972) of discourse without authorial intention, or post-structuralism's adaption of de
Saussure's (1959) theory, which construe the subject as a function of a
symbolic order that determines, rather than is determined by, the individual's intentions, or, in the very different tradition of organizational
theory, a theory of institutions and institutionalization as cultural rules
constructing the 'existence' of actors and viewing action as enacting institutional scripts (Meyer et al. 1994): these and other related theoretical
discoveries are of the complex of relations I'm indicating by the term 'the
ruling relations.' They mark a transition from the social conditions of
Marx's theorizing of consciousness as an attribute of individuals to 'consciousness' as the workings of objectifying organization and relations

mediated by texts and computer technologies. Information, knowledge, reasoning, decision-making, 'culture,' scientific theorizing, and the like become properties of organization grounded in and relying on the materiality of the text and its increasingly complex technological expansions.

While the ruling relations are an organization of power, it is misleading to reduce them to relations of domination or hegemony, or to view them as monolithic or manipulated. I emphasize again: the ruling relations form a complex field of coordinated activities, based in technologies of print, and increasingly in computer technologies. They are activities in and in relation to texts, and texts coordinate them as relations. Text-mediated relations are the forms in which power is generated and held in contemporary societies. Printed or electronic texts have the generally neglected property of indefinite replicability. Replicability of identical forms of meaning that can be activated in multiple local settings is fundamental to the ruling relations. The materiality of the text and its replicability create a peculiar ground in which it can seem that language, thought, culture, formal organization, have their own being, outside lived time and the actualities of people's living – other than, as the latter become, objects of action or investigation from within the textual. The material text creates a join between local and particular, and the generalizing and generalized organization of the ruling relations. It is the materiality of the text itself that connects the local setting at the moment of reading into the non-local relations that it bears. Its technology, its system of distribution, and its economy are foundational to the peculiar property of abstraction that provides for forms of social relations that have no particular place or time in which they happen. To use a metaphor introduced earlier (see chapter 1), the text creates something like an escape hatch out of the actual and is foundational to any possibility of social forms of abstraction of whatever kind, including this one written here.

This concept of text diverges from the theorizing of the text that originated in Roland Barthes's essay 'From Work to Text' (1977). In that essay, Barthes distinguishes between 'work' and 'text.' In making his move from the finality of a work's authority to the text as 'produced' in the reader-text relation and as experienced only as the reader is active in production, Barthes also discards the text as a material (physical) presence. The theorizing of the text developed from Barthes's (1977) distinction specifically denies or ignores its materiality,[1] that is, the text as concrete – book, pamphlet, magazine article, TV program, etc. My use of the concept of text reunites the text as material and the text as produced in and by the reader through her participation in an intertextual or interpretive site (discourse, formal organization, etc.). Practices of reading are activities of that site and are not wholly determined in the text's form of words. Yet the text *is* material, a definite physical entity, and its standardized reproduction in multiple sites of reading *as an identical form of words* is presupposed in the theorizing of the text as distinct from the work.

Texts are the mediators and bases of discourses and ruling relations that regulate and coordinate beyond the particular local setting of their reading or writing. But they are always occurrences in time and space: they happen; they are constituents and organizers of actions and courses of action; they are activated at a particular moment of reading in the time it takes to do that reading and in a particular place. The act of reading is very deceitful in this respect; it conceals its particularity, its being in time and place. Reading is experienced as a course of action within the text and in textual time. The reading subject is subordinated in the act of reading to the dimensionality of the text. For this reason, it is difficult to recognize that the text and its reading are always also in an actual time and place and that texts activated in a course of reading are always *in the actual* and being read in 'real time.' Though the course of reading/writing in the interactional mode of the computer is more recognizable as being in 'real time,' it shares with other text-mediated forms modes of being and action 'lifted out' of the local time and place of the bodily being of the reader/writer. The materiality of the text is key to investigating the ruling relations as the local and ongoing concerting of people's activities.

Post-structuralist/postmodernist theorizing of discourse (Foucault 1970, 1972, 1981; Flax 1990, 1993; Lyotard 1984; Butler and Scott 1992) captures the displacement of locally situated subjects precisely in its insistence on the absence of subjects from the determination of meaning and on the self-referentiality of language and discourse in this new mode. Yet it leaves unanalysed the socially organized practices and relations that objectify, even those visible in discourse itself. Its constitutional rules confine subjects to a standpoint in discourse and hence in the ruling relations. They eliminate the matrix of local practices of actual people that brings objectification of discourse into existence. Taking women's standpoint, we remember that we, the actual readers/writers/speakers/hearers, who disappear in the relations of intertextuality, are also those who participate, generate, provide the dynamic of the ruling relations. We are also those whose local activities are organized and shaped by and in these relations, just as, at least in Rubin's (1973) version of Marx, the interrelations of money and commodities relate people to one another and organize the local actualities of our/their lives.

The Textual Mediation of Capital

The development of the ruling relations as an historical trajectory has progressively transferred organization from persons to objectified forms. The complex that has evolved is characterized by a capacity to replicate the same forms, courses of action, relations, etc., in the varieties and multiplicities of the local settings in which they operate and which they regulate. The textual bases that objectify knowledge, organization, and decision processes are essential to this ubiquity. On these bases, forms of replicable organization are built that distinguish what individuals are in themselves from what they do organizationally and professionally, or as participants in a discourse. Properties of formal organization, profession, or discourse are constituted that cannot be reduced to properties of individuals.

People are active in specific local settings as participants in social relations concerted with those of others in multiple local settings. Objectifying social relations constitute subject positions organized at a level transcending particular local settings and organizing sequences of action across multiple local sites. Forms of organization such as the stock market are objectified in the sense that they are not reducible to individuals or the actions of individuals and become, indeed, the everyday/everynight condition, circumstance, means, and terrain of people's financial activities. Subjectivity as well as agency are constituted in these relations; people's capacities to act arise within them. Take Joel Kovel's composite picture, based on a number of men who had been in therapy with him, of the subjectivity of a banker:

An uncommon degree of intellectual perspicacity and personal daring was required for the job, and Curtis had both qualities in great measure. To instantly weigh the complex effects of rates of exchange, tax possibilities and investment risks – such the potential for revolution in a foreign market – and a host of other technical factors demanded a clear understanding of the subtleties involved as the numbers both had a truth of their own and were the ever-shifting abstraction of innumerable human tendencies. Moreover, those tendencies were personified by whoever was across the negotiating table from Curtis: another man or group of men (and only men) – colleague, antagonist, adviser, perhaps all three. One had to weigh him as well, constantly gauging the odds, calculating that hundredth of a percentage point around which millions of dollars turned, establishing trust, and, yes, dominating the other men because that is how successful deals were made ... (Kovel 1982: 42–3)

For the competing bankers, categories such as 'rates of exchange,' 'tax possibilities,' and 'investment risks,' and their shifiting values, give objectified discursive presence to the dynamic of capitalist social relations. Their phenomenal universe is constituted of the different forms in which exchange value appears. These 'surfaces' both organize and conceal the social relations through which the outcomes of their competition are fed into the lives and doing of others, becoming their constraints, contingencies, opportunities, and disasters. To explore the ruling relations is to explore those peculiar forms of power that are diffused through complexes of text-mediated social relations constituting subjectivity and agency. It is the relations that rule, and people rule and are ruled through them.

Exploring the ruling relations, discovering the interrelations and intersections of organization as a product of inquiry, can in principle begin anywhere. Here, however, I want to bring into view an aspect of these relations that is not ordinarily treated as text-based or text-mediated. The social organization of capital itself is an objectification of value. But formulating this purely as theory (as Marx does) evades the historically specific transformations of the relations that constitute it. Capital as a social form is not just wealth, it is wealth perpetuated through time as a capacity to generate wealth. It is constituted beyond individuals at first through the regulation of familial relationships and inheritance.[2] The emergence of the corporation and joint stock companies as an organization of capital independent of particular individual owners superseded familial modes of organizing the perpetuation of capital from one generation to the next. The emergence of corporate forms of capital relies on technological innovations in the reproduction of corporate 'paper' – letters, memoranda, rules, schedules, accounts, and so on.

JoAnne Yates (1989) describes both the late-nineteenth-century technological innovations in the 'hardware' of records and files that underlie organizational objectification, and transitions from organization identified with individual owners and managers to objectified organization relying on these technologies. She presents several case studies drawn from histories of various companies. One of them is the Du Pont company, significant not just in itself but also for its later influence on the establishment of new forms of management in General Motors.

Originally the Du Pont company, manufacturing explosives, was managed in 'word-of-mouth' style and through personal written communications among the male members of the family dominated by the patriarchal Pierre Du Pont. A painting from the first half of the nineteenth century is reproduced in Yates's book. It shows the founder of the company standing on the veranda of his mansion with a bull-horn at his lips. It is thought that Pierre Du Pont is giving orders to his plants in the valley below, the three of them judiciously separated so that if one blew up the others would not be involved (they are not visible in the picture). Here is direct personal management, linked intimately to family ownership of the company. All major managerial responsibilities were undertaken by family members, either sons or sons-in-law. Communication was direct and personal. During the latter part of the nineteenth century, members of the family involved in management conducted much managerial business with each other, including reporting on the state of affairs in different parts of the growing company by writing personal letters to each other, even though they lived in the same house.

By the end of the nineteenth century, the company had secured a monopoly over the manufacture of explosives in the United States. In 1902 the Du Pont company's management was transformed:

A new generation of the Du Pont family took over the business and within two years had consolidated much of the American explosives industry into a single operating company. At the same time, the management of the newly expanded firm was rapidly systematized. A complex and extensive formal internal communication system grew up practically overnight. (Yates 1989: 201)

Lammot Du Pont, a nephew, was the most advanced. He was allowed to take over a chemical manufacturing company which the family owned, and to run it as he wished. He introduced a system of management that involved a committee of department heads under a general manager; department heads wrote papers reporting on their departmental situation for discussion and problem-solving in committee; discussions were recorded; new approaches to collecting operating information and reporting it up the hierarchy were developed; new technologies of copying and filing records were developed. Thus 'systems of upward and downward communication to standardize, control, and evaluate its sales force and to collect operational data' were set up (Yates 1989: 227). These innovations proved later to be influential in the systematization of management that was being generalized at this period.

Among the systematizations of management and record-keeping were new technologies of accounting. The 'rational capitalistic establishment' is one with capital accounting. It is an establishment which 'determines its income yielding power by calculation according to the methods of modern bookkeeping and the striking of a balance' (Weber 1978: 207). Transformed accounting technologies contributed to the transformation of the social organization of capital from the individual to the corporate form associated with the late-nineteenth and early twentieth-century North America (Chandler 1977; Sloan 1964). Albert Sloan (1964) identifies the managerial revolution he introduced into General Motors when he became its chief executive officer early in the twentieth century as a change from 'subjective' to 'objective' organization or management. Systems of accounting, management systems, 'Taylorism' as a corresponding organization of production, and their articulation of financial markets constitute an internally self-referential order of text-mediated and text-based practices and courses of action.

Concurrently, and on parallel lines, the bases of civil society, at least as Gramsci (1971) conceived it, in individuals, particularly in an intelligentsia, were transformed to the objectified social relations of discourse and large-scale organization. These are the developments that provide the historical ground precipitating the structuralist move to dump as a theoretical strategy interpretations in terms of the individual author and his/her intentions. Knowledge is no longer an attribute of individuals but of an immense institutionalized order of discursive networks (Latour 1990), universities, think-tanks, etc., in and through which an intelligentsia comes to participate institutionally as employees, contractors, etc.

The Ruling Relations as Hyper-realities

Baudrillard's (1994) notion of simulation or 'hyper-reality' has relevance here, beyond its interest as an analysis of contemporary cultural technologies. At an accelerating pace in the twentieth century, the ruling relations come to form hyper-realities that can be operated and acted in rather than merely written and read.[3] Of hyper-reality, Baudrillard writes, 'Whereas representation tries to absorb simulation by interpreting it as false representation, simulation envelops the whole edifice of representation as itself a simulacrum' (1994: 6). His paradigmatic instance is Disneyland, an 'imaginary station' (1994: 13) demarcated from an American reality which is itself a simulation. But his account of Disneyland is as a stranger, so that for him the people are included in the spectacle. He doesn't attend to the dialogic connection that people familiar with the media-born Disney images (movies, TV cartoons, comic strips) bring actively to the mini-world, discovering the images life-size and lively, and on speaking terms with them. The creation of local forms that realize for people's local experience and in their local practices, 'on the ground,' images generalized through media technologies *is* the simulacrum as an ordinary daily accomplishment.

I emphasize the 'walk-in' character of what Baudrillard calls hyper-realities. They are made to be operated, reproduced, acted in. Here's a glimpse of one such from an account of the leveraged buy-out of RJR/Nabisco. The protagonist, Ross Johnson, then CEO of RJR/Nabisco, is in the course of trying to decide whether to go ahead with the LBO. His son had just been seriously injured in a car accident and was in a coma. There was nothing for his parents to do but wait. It was suggested to Ross Johnson that work would help to take his mind off his anxieties. So he re-entered the hyper-reality of finance:

Walking into his office, Johnson brought out a sharp pencil, a calculator, and an accounting spreadsheet, the kind he learned to use at General Electric thirty-five years before. All around him, on the floor and the furniture, piled reports from his planning department, blue-book statements, studies from investment bankers, and computer printouts. He wanted to see for himself if an LBO made sense, for he no longer trusted investment bankers or computers to give him the answer ...

For the first time Johnson submerged himself in the possibilities and challenges of an LBO. For five hours he and Benevento waded through the numbers, dissecting cash flows, market shares, profit, and sales projections for every RJR Nabisco business. From time to time, Johnson stood and called Atlanta or Winston-Salem to get up-to-date figures.

Johnson wanted to value each business, determine what it might sell for. That, plus tobacco's future cash flows, would go a long way toward determining what price, if any, he could offer in an LBO. (Burrough and Helyar 1991: 125)

Look carefully and you see a mode of action entirely in texts. Taxes, rates of exchange, investment risks, and so forth are texts of various kinds based on complex textual technologies that both express and organize the forms of domination that translate action in texts into effects at ground zero. The postmodernist critique of representation has its application beyond the zones where the aesthetic of postmodernism cares to venture, into the very organization of capital in a textual medium. The post-structuralist theorizing of the subject as an effect of discourse theorizes a shift that has already taken place in the social relations of and the division of functions within capital[4] and is now integral to the social organization of its relations.

These are not neutral systems of representation external to the organization they produce and regulate. The production of forms to correspond to and realize locally the forms and norms borne by text-mediated discourse is not confined to Disneyland. The creation of standardized forms giving local and material expression and local possibilities of action to the ubiquitous, alocal, images/versions/theories vested in printed texts is more general. Shapin and Shaffer's (1985) account of Robert Boyle's contribution to the early development of science makes it clear that the technology of the air pump that he invented was intended to enable the replication of standardized events at different times and in different places. In fact, it was not entirely successful in doing so. Nonetheless, Boyle provided careful, detailed instructions and drawings, and made detailed descriptions of experiments to standardize both the experimental 'machine' and experimental procedures. Experimenters at work in settings far apart could recognize, in going from text to machine, the same events as those the text describes. The correspondence of textual and mechanical processes created the conditions under which experiments done at different sites could be considered as pertaining to the same phenomena and as being comparable to one another.

A standardized and standardizing technology and work organization in the laboratory (or its simulacra) *produce* the conditions of correspondence between events and texts. Such standardization of events-to-texts has been technologically elaborated to constitute a universe of locally occurring events iterable trans-situationally to coordinate with the ubiquity of the printed text. It is essential to the development of science as we know it today. Boyle's innovations established new procedures for operating in a print medium that shifted from the individual narrator as source of information to the scientific text authorized or guaranteed by specialized procedures for going from actualities to objectified, text-based representations. The very possibility of dwelling in a domain of scientific theorizing, as Alfred Schutz's (1962) inhabitant of the theoretical domain is described as doing, relies on the creation of a world of exact (created) correspondence between events observed and their in-text theoretical expressions.

Reproducibility constitutes a 'reality' corresponding to the circulation of the (printed) text. For example, the notion, and practice, of the replicability of scientific experiments relies on the interrelations between the theories, categories, quantities, etc., of scientific discourse and the standardization of laboratory technologies that reproduce as 'the same for all practical purposes' (though, of course, they are not the same) the local actualities that the theories, categories, and measurements account for.

Unlike Disneyland, of course, it is a hyper-reality whose business is the ongoing production of change in both the theories and the technologies standardizing the local actualities in correspondence with them.

It is not only in science that methods of standardizing the potentially inexhaustible configurations of local settings produce local events as readable in the texts of ruling. The technologies, regulations, and arts of creating a standardized 'environment' of events are fundamental to the organization of societies governable within the ruling relations. As Charles Perrow (1986) points out, 'any machine is a complex bundle of rules that are built into the machine itself. Machines ensure standardized products, thus eliminating rules regarding dimensional characteristics. They ensure even output time; they also indicate precisely what kind of material can be fed into them' (Perrow 1986: 23). However, machinery does more than displace rules. The replication of local 'events' as identical (though identity is always more or less a fiction) makes possible, for example, systems of measurement, the accumulation of statistical data, the formulation of rules and instructions applicable from one setting and time to others, and other textual practices of science, management, and the market.[5]

The numbers that Johnson and Benevento were 'wading through' connect the financial regulation of the various businesses with the regulation of production, ultimately an exercise of control at the level of the shop-floor. Control of production process at the level of the shop-floor is tied into accounting systems and other computerized technologies of management that render the company operable within the field of capitalist social relations.

The situation in which Ross Johnson is acting is organized by text-mediated relations intersecting institutions and interpenetrating corporations. For example, the historical development of accounting and accountancy comes to organize the relations between particular capitals and the generalized relations of capital at the level of the market for stocks and shares. The objectified system of corporate management described above represents only one side of a development the obverse of which is the separation of ownership from control and the emergence of a market in stocks and shares. In public companies, the financial statement of an enterprise is a public document subject to state regulation; it mediates the internal state of company transactions and the stock market. It is no accident that in Canada the development of accounting associations is closely connected with the late-nineteenth- and early twentieth-century problems with unregulated stock markets (Naylor 1975; Murphy

1980, 1984). Whereas in the nineteenth century, 'audits' were often done by members of the board, or by shareholders (Brockholdt 1983), new statutes required that companies' financial statements be 'witnessed' independently and objectively (Murphy 1980). A new level of organization, and hence new levels of coordinated activity and agency, were constituted, organizing the internal regulation of value of particular capitals in relation to the state, financial markets, and so on.[6]

Accounting is more than a source of information travelling between work organization at the level of the shop-floor to the decision-making level of corporate executives and financial managers. It is an actual *organizer* of the relations articulating people's work, particularly the processes of production and sales but also of management, to the capitalist project. Accounting and related textual technologies of management coordinate local work processes at the shop-floor level, or of consumers in malls, supermarkets, and in other companies, or in the office, with the conditions of capitalist accumulation, tying them in to the relations of capital investment in banking, the stock market, and so on. The story of Ross Johnson in his office presents his data as mere paper, containing information for him and his associate to use in their calculations. But burrowing (metaphorically) beneath that to the actual practices of actual individuals who are there somewhere buried in the accounts, we can see or at least envisage how the hyper-realities of the ruling relations are actively accomplished by many people, most of whom are not themselves constituted as agents within those relations.

The data Johnson was appraising were a product, in part, of the kind of discursive processes and procedures described in the previous section; they were records produced by systematic and technical management practices; they were financial accounts; etc. Such data are the product of the technologies of text-mediated management and accounting. Technologies of production and sales have been created to coordinate with such practices of management. They produce (for management) and enforce (for workers) a local order of accountability fully compatible with and interpretable in terms of the corporate system of accounting. At the managerial level, these technologies produce the texts of the virtual, or hyper-, reality of large-scale capitalist organization; at the level of the shop-floor, there are correlative technologies, regulations, and supervision that discipline workers to produce 'events' that are standardized in form and time so that the value created is accountable within the text-based ordering that produces it as a component of the hyper-reality within which 'Johnsons' act.

There is a relational order here that is both present *in* its paper or computer representation and concealed by it. The local work organization of the shop-floor is present, effective, and invisible. Below the surface of the text as read is the text-mediated organization tying action at the managerial level, or the financial entrepreneurial level at which Ross Johnson was operating, to the ordering of people's work and the wages they receive at all levels of large-scale organization. The regulation of the shop-floor by managerial/accounting technologies is illustrated in Sallie Westwood's (1984) description of women at work in a British textile factory. She is quoting from an interview with one of the workers:

'The minutes, you know what that means? It just means that they break everything down more to speed it up so that we work more. We know that is what they are doing.' 'The minutes' was common parlance for the measured day-work (MDW) system in operation in the factory ... an MDW system is one which is fixed against a *specified* level of performance. The system depends on some form of work measurement to set the performance level required and to monitor the actual level achieved. [Workers were graded on the basis of production performance.] Each grade had a specific production level which guaranteed a certain wage packet; bonuses could be earned by producing more in less time. Workers were subject to monthly assessments at a meeting of management, supervisors and trade union representatives. (Westwood 1984: 39–40)[7]

'Taylorism' is an ideology of management that focuses on the design of work disciplines that will produce in local settings of production a standardization of work practices corresponding to the systematics of the accounting text. The system of measuring and remunerating performance that Westwood describes does not prescribe movements or sequences of movements in a design for the most 'efficient' sequence as did Taylor. It is a system based on production in discrete units that can (a) be counted; and (b) be identified as the production of individual workers. The standardization of local practices in the shop-floor is produced by the workers themselves as their own production orients to the grade of performance and pay set for them by the establishment of a standard time frame as the basis for the rate. This is the 'work measurement [that] set the performance level required' in Westwood's description. Coordination is at the point where the amount each worker produces in a given time translates into a *rate* as the basis of her pay. Thus workers themselves produce the standardization of the relationship between the textual order and the local settings of production. In other contexts, however, such as some of the 'lean production' regimes recently introduced into North American manufacture, workers' movements, how they carry tools, the time taken by each sequence, are precisely designed and prescribed to standardize work processes to the standardizing machinery.

Accounting is not an exact science; it is the technical articulation of capital as a regime. Firms of accountants, participants in the professional/technical discourses of accounting and management, act as consultants to the corporations they audit. Through them the companies they audit are connected up with new designs for wages, productivity incentives, and so on, combining more effective motivations for workers to increase productivity with making the process and its products more effectively accountable within the system articulating the internal financial processes of a corporation to the financial markets. Thus changing accountancy and managerial practices disorganizes and disrupts the accommodations workers have established to give them some control over work processes and relationships. Accounting is more than a tool of management; it is an integral part of the organization and reproduction of class relations in the workplace. That this is so is the ordinary working knowledge of financial analysts. For example, an editorial in the *Financial Times* in 1993 described initiatives by German corporations to participate in U.S.-designed capital markets. To do so, they would be required to adopt the accounting practices of the New York Stock Exchange. The editorial speculates that such a change in accounting practices would likely endanger the 'harmonious relations between management and workers within the compan[ies]' that contribute to the 'success of German industry.' U.S. accounting practices give labour costs greater weight in measuring profitability than do German companies, hence encouraging managers to give primacy to the reduction of labour costs in improving the visible profitability of their company and hence its standing in capital markets.

The process of capital accumulation is driven through the text-based systems that hook production and marketing into financial management and financial markets. The expansion of capital is also an expansion of forms of ruling increasingly abstracted from local ties. The reorganization of work and wage reaches beyond particular corporations into institutional systems reproducing knowledge and technical skills. Education transforms the multiplicity of regional and ethnic cultures into a standardized labour force that is foundational to the possibility of generalizing organization from one local site to the corporate order at large. Trans-regional forms of economic organization create pressure for a professionalization of skills and practices of 'mind' out of body that standardize the latter across regions and nations. A complex of text-mediated relations evolves constituting a division of the labour of consciousness that objectifies in its hyper-realities the formerly individual attributes of knowledge, judgment, and will as a field of *action* and domination.

Returning to Gender and Women's Standpoint

In delineating the ruling relations, I have focused on the texts as integral to an ontology of capital in contemporary society. Traditional social science ontologies, conforming to disciplinary divisions, write a sharp separation between the social and economic. The version of the social that I have put forward above follows Rubin (1973) in breaking with this practice. The ruling relations as a text-mediated organization of relations extend into the economic sphere and can be investigated as accomplished by and organizing the activities of actual people. It is important, however, to keep in mind that the ruling relations are a more general dimension of the organization of society, extending into its systems of discourse, science, mass media, large-scale organization of all kinds, professional organization, and so on.[8]

The historical trajectory of the ruling relations, from their fragmentary beginnings in the seventeenth and eighteenth centuries to their increasing comprehensiveness and complexity in our own time, has been profoundly gendered. In the middle classes, in particular, gender relations were radically reorganized. The dual consciousness that I experienced, one located in the objectified ruling relations and the other in the particularizing work of childcare and home, is located in this trajectory. The experiencing of these two kinds of consciousness cuts across historical time. Experience is always now and hence embedded in an historical trajectory, coming into being dialogically in the discourse of its time. Historically the division between these two worlds of work and consciousness has been gender-organized. The emerging capitalism of seventeenth-century Europe reorganized women's and men's relation to the economy; indeed, it brought into being the economy as a discrete and specialized system of relations mediated by money. Among the middle classes, the domestic setting became sharply differentiated from the relations of capital and of the public sphere (Davidoff and Hall 1987, Habermas 1989), so that forms of consciousness became differentiated by gender. While women remained at work in the particularities of domesticity, men, particularly of the middle classes, were active in businesses that connected them to the impersonal, extra-local dynamic of the market, and in the clubs and coffee-houses of Europe and the saloons and places of public assembly in North America (Ryan 1993), and, as readers, in the journals, newspapers and books that constituted the discourse of the public sphere. 'The new world of political economy necessitated a new sphere of domestic economy' (Davidoff and Hall 1987: 74).

This, of course, was only a beginning. The gender divide that emerged among the middle classes widened and deepened as the powers, technologies, and scope of the extra-local organization of the relations of the economy, the state, and public discourse increased, while the domestic sphere became increasingly ancillary. This is the historical trajectory of which my experience of these two consciousnesses was a moment.

These foundations to the ruling relations, grounded in capitalist social relations, created a radical division between the spheres of action and of consciousness of men and women. The peculiar out-of-body modes of consciousness of the nascent ruling relations required a specialization of subject and agency. The formation of the middle-class male subject in education and ideology aimed at creating that extraordinary form of modern consciousness that is capable of agency in modes that displace or subdue a local bodily existence. Rousseau's *Emile* designs an educational regime aimed at creating the autonomous male subject of civil society. His complement is a woman equally highly trained, but not for autonomy. It's her role to sop up the bodily needs that are residual to the masculine project; she is never to appear for herself or as herself in the zone of civil society that is his preserve.

During the nineteenth century, in particular, the barriers excluding women from participating as subjects and agents in civil society were policed by parents, educators, and the spokesmen of the public sphere. Middle-class women might be actively deprived of education, particularly of education that would give them the skills needed to participate in the discourse of reason – opportunities to learn philosophy, mathematics, and science. Books were taken away; women who read were told they would go mad if they didn't desist; women of knowledge were ridiculed publicly. Later in the century, as education for women became institutionalized, it was as a gender-differentiating system. In Germany, for example, the rise of an administrative class of civil servants was complemented by an educational system for women emphasizing preparation for the domestic sphere in which the rearing of men was central (Kittler 1990). As universal public educational systems were established in the late nineteenth century in both Europe and North America, they were also created as gender-differentiating systems, developing for the sons of the middle class the moral and intellectual capacities they would need in order to act as agents in the field I'm calling the ruling relations, and among women the skills and ideologies of subordination, passivity, and modes of agency restricted to family, home, and neighbourhood.

The women's movement of the late 1960s and early 1970s was a radical break with this formation of the social consciousness. It created, at least momentarily, a breach between the objectified text-based modes of consciousness of the ruling relations, and what had been formed and institutionalized for middle-class women as their place. Here, then, was a contradictory site of consciousness for women, bridging the intellectual functions of the ruling relations and the local particularizations of women's domestic sphere – woman as mother, as housewife, as neighbour, as sexual partner or object, at work, at play, in sex. It may be indeed that the increasing scope of the ruling relations progressively supersedes differentiations of persons on the basis of bodily being that locates them in particular local sites and in particularized relations, and that the women's movement in North America and Europe seized upon the possibilities, ironies, and frustrations emerging in this situation to seek a remaking of the relations of public discourse. Certainly the standpoint of women systematizes an historical bridging across the historical gap. This sociology traverses it from this, women's side, beginning in the local particularities of people's lives. It seeks to redesign knowledge of the social, recognizing that it is in and of the same world as the one we live in.

Standard sociological conventions of writing society into the text represent the ruling relations as system or structure. They can be found, for example, in recent attempts in organizational theory to deal with the new realities of the ruling relations[9] which recapitulate in the theory exactly those relations that should be the focus of inquiry. By contrast, a sociology developed from the standpoint of women, as I've formulated it here, returns us to the actualities of people's lives and activities. It is only there that organization can be found as text-mediated relations that coordinate local sites of work across time and space. Texts and text-mediated organization and relations must be explored as they are 'in action' and constitute media of action. Their conceptual dimensions must be held, not as meaning, but as 'organizers' packaged in texts that transmit 'organization' invented in one site of ruling to multiple sites (see chapters 8 and 9 below), regulating the local activities of particular people.

The standardization of the local, whether through machine or computer technologies, government regulation, work discipline, or a socialization of consciousness, is the essential local complement to the ubiquity of the organizing text. Forms, sites, and media of agency are created; worlds are created within which there is agency, at least for some, and beneath which and sustaining them is an organization of people's activities that transforms the localization of the everyday/everynight of people's living into the Disneylands of the ruling relations, real in their simulacrity and real also in their consequences and their power to subjugate. I imagine, therefore, examining the ruling relations, not only with respect to their content, but also with respect to the relations among people they organize. I honour the great democratic impulse of the movements of the 1960s and 1970s. I have seen taking up inquiry from women's standpoint as setting up very different relationships between the actualities of people's everyday/everynight lives and the forms of knowledge of the social that might be developed for them. This theorizing would insist on recognizing in those forms something like the DNA of social organization. Knowledge is socially organized; its characteristic textual forms bear and replicate social relations. Hence knowledge must be differently written and differently designed if it is to bear other social relations than those of ruling. The forms of knowledge we take for granted in social science have been created externally from our local actualities, standing over against us in a relation of dominance and authority. This is the world of discourse that Foucault (1980) characterizes in terms of power/knowledge. But despite his commitment to subjugated knowledges, theorizing the subject as a creature of discourse provides no ground on which different perspectives could arise. There is in his theory (though not, of course, in fact) no place other than discursively determined subject positions to speak from and no language other than that which intersects with 'the law of the father' (Lacan 1977) in which to mean. I do not accept Foucault's view, or at least its popularization, that knowledge is necessarily a relation of power. The intersection of knowledge and power is an effect of the integration of the ruling relations, establishing subject positions within discourse from which experience can be known only externally and from within an order of domination.

What I'm putting forward proposes a reworking of that social organization. By returning us to a standpoint in the actualities of people's living, I'm not proposing just an alternative method of inquiry; rather, I am also looking for a revision of the relations of knowing. The method of inquiry into the social I'm proposing would extend people's own good knowledge of the local practices and terrains of their everyday/everynight living, enlarging the scope of what becomes visible from that site, mapping the relations that connect one local site to others. Like a map, it would be through and through indexical to the local sites of people's experience, making visible how we are connected into the extended social ruling relations and the economy. And though some of the work of inquiry must be technical, as making a map is, its product could be ordinarily accessible and usable, just as a map is.

6

Telling the Truth after Postmodernism[1]

Introduction

The consciousness-raising practices of the early days of the women's movement in the 1960s and 1970s relied on a telling of women's experiences. The project of a sociology developed from women's standpoint and for, rather than of or about, people is modelled on this method. It is not, however, exclusively about or for women. Women's standpoint means beginning in the actualities of people's lives as they experience them, and a sociology for people developed from this *point d'appui* orients to the social as it organizes people's everyday/everynight living. It proposes to create a knowledge of the social grounded in people's experience of their own lives. It does not treat experience as knowledge, but as a place to begin inquiry. The aim of inquiry is not, as in established sociologies, to explain people's behaviour, but to explain to people the social – or society – as it enters into and shapes their lives and activities.

Speaking from experience speaks from the only site of consciousness – in an individual's own living, and hence as it is, and must be, embedded and active in social relations and organization that are not contained in what people can speak of directly. Experience, as spoken, is always social and always bears its social organization. A sociology for people proposes to explore from experience but beyond it, beginning in the living as people can speak of it rather than in the pre-givens of theoretically designed discourse. Discourse itself, and other dimensions of the objectified organization of corporations, government, professions, etc., are themselves also understood as being 'in the living' and hence investigatable as people's actual practices.[2] The object of sociological inquiry is, not order nor action as such, but the ongoing coordinating or concerting of actual people's activities.[3] Consciousness, subjectivity, and the subject are hence always embedded, active, and constituted in the concerting of people's activities with each other; concepts, theories, ideas, and other terms identifying operations of thought are themselves activities or practices and enter into the coordination of action. This is a social ontology not of meaning but of a concerting of activities that actually happens. Hence the social must be conceived as an ongoing process (cf. Garfinkel 1967, 1972), in time and in actual local sites of people's bodily existence, even when the coordination may be of large-scale organization or of social relations implicating multiplicities such as those theorized by Marx.

A sociology beginning in people's everyday/everynight experience takes for granted that experience is as various as people are. It does not seek to supersede this variety by constructing a version that overrides all others. Differences in experience arise in a matrix of everyday/everynight activities and through how they are entered into and coordinated with others' activities. The project is to explore concerting and co-ordering and hence also the relations that generate the varieties of lived experience.

As a project of inquiry rather than of theory, it must rely on the possibility that truth can be told in the following very ordinary sense: that when people disagree about statements made about the world, accuracy or truth is not decided on the basis of 'authority' or on the shared beliefs of a community but by referring back, in principle at least, to an original state of affairs, extraneous to the accounts they have given. In a sense, it wants an account of knowledge which takes for granted that people's experiences are various and can be coordinated, and that a social theory of knowledge grasps it as a definite mode of coordinating people's activities.

This sociology is of the same lived world of which it writes; it aims at producing a knowledge of that world which is itself in and of the social. It is committed to inquiry and investigation, to *finding out* 'how things are put together,' and hence to producing knowledge that represents the social as it happens. Clearly, then, it must find some alternative to post-structuralism/postmodernism's[4] rejection of the possibility of referring to what exists beyond discourse and independently of discourse's positing. That critique has addressed, and been addressed primarily in, the social sciences. In anthropology, it has led to a deep questioning of the very project of ethnography; in sociology, the very possibility of a knowledge of society or the social is put in question.[5]

The project of a sociology from women's standpoint, as it is taken up here, joins with post-structuralism/postmodernism in rejecting sociologies requiring an Archimedean point, objectifying as authoritative a unitary consciousness grounded in and reproducing existing relations of power. It also rejects the totalizing of a theory that subdues all forms of consciousness to its own dominating system of interpretation. However, post-structuralism/postmodernism is challenged on two fronts: I argue here that the post-structuralist/postmodernist critique of theories of language, meaning, reference, and representation has 'slipped into the form' of the theories it criticizes[6] by importing the very universalized subject of knowledge it has repudiated. The unitary subject of modernity is rejected only to be multiplied as subjects constituted in diverse and fragmented discourses. Secondly, post-structuralism/postmodernism transfers the function of the subject to language or discourse, reinforcing the traditional separation of the bases of consciousness from the local historical activities of people's everyday lives. Once this step has been taken, the inquirer cannot find her way back to a world in which people are active and in which we are constantly bringing what we do into relation to others. She is confined to a phenomenal world in which nothing ever happens.

Using theoretical resources drawn from George Herbert Mead (1938, 1947), Valentin I. Vološinov (1973), and Mikhail M. Bakhtin (1981, 1986), this paper puts forward an alternative and social theory of knowledge which begins in a world of activity, the doings of actual people. The subject/knower of inquiry is not a transcendent subject but situated in the actualities of her own living, in relations with others as they too are active. Hence, theory must formulate referring, representing, inquiry, and discovery as the locally organized social practices of actual people. Mead's, Vološinov's, and Bakhtin's theories locate self and language in the social processes of people's everyday activities. Mead theorizes a fully social self arising in and organizing the social act; he conceives of the meaning of symbolic communication – indeed, its very symbolic character – as a property of ongoing social interaction. Vološinov and Bakhtin complement Mead. They are equally decisive in rejecting conceptions of language and ideology as systems independent of the local production of language and meaning. Bakhtin presents an essentially dialogic conception of meaning and of language, not as an autonomous system, but as continually remade in settings of its use. Their theory and analysis contribute what is so strikingly absent in Mead, namely, an account of language as meaning given determination prior to any particular local interaction and hence as playing a powerful role in the local organization of the social. I draw on both these lines of thinking and analysis to develop an account of 'referring' or 'representing,' indeed knowledge, as *essentially* social and as an organization of social action *among participating subjects* rather than as a function, such as perception or cognition or experience, extrapolated from the consciousness of an individuated subject.

The Post-structuralist/Postmodernist Alternative

Established sociology has come to take for granted that the categories of its discourse represent dimensions of the social world. It has taken for granted the possibility of producing objective accounts of society and of the social determinants of people's behaviour. The technical sophistication of its methodologies, particularly quantitative methodologies, has been dedicated to producing accounts and explanations that are both 'unbiased' and veridical. The methodologies of sociology constitute a position from which the object of knowledge can be displayed uncontaminated by the positions and interests of sociology's practitioners. The developing intellectual debates loosely described as post-structuralism/postmodernism are united in denying the validity of such a transcendental standpoint. Post-structuralism and postmodernism remove the foundations of this project in removing the primacy of the subject-object relationship, insisting that both are effects of discourse. They posit language and discourse as having properties and dynamics independent of people's intentions to mean and deny that categories and concepts can refer to and represent a reality beyond them, indeed, that it is meaningful to speak of a reality which is not in language. They reject the notion that there can be an overriding truth to which alternative views, theories, and versions of the world must be subordinated. Charles Lemert (1994) formulates the challenge for sociology thus:

In a world where reality is constituted in and by means of texts, everything is theoretical in some sense, because everything is discursive and, in situations where this is the case, what other reality is there? (Lemert 1994: 279)

Lemert follows Roland Barthes's (1979) distinction between 'work' and 'text.' A work is the book or paper held in the hand, which originated in the intentions of an author; 'text' is 'held in language' (Barthes 1979: 75) and in an intertextual field[7] in which no one person can be considered its originator. Subject and object and the subject-object relation disappear. To be a subject is conditional on entry to discourse; to enter discourse is to forgo the very possibility of knowing the object:

... with entry into the symbolic order, our immersion in the immediacy of the real is forever lost; we are forced to assume an irreducible loss; the word entails the (symbolic) murder of the thing, etc. (Žižek 1993: 92)

Writing and interpreting texts are practices of and in the intertextual field. Language or discourse, not the objects or events, determine representation. There can be, therefore, no reality posited beyond the text with reference to which meaning can be stabilized among different subjects. The notion of referring to or representing in the text a reality beyond discourse which authorizes theory or explanation is rejected – '[Truth] cannot be the representation or mirror of an external or universal substance ("presence") or subject because none exists' ... (Flax 1990: 200):

All criteria for distinguishing between truth and falsehood, for evaluating theory, require that one choose between categories, or they expect one to establish a hierarchy of values that designates some as good and others as bad. Post-modernists reject such distinctions and rather emphasize multiple realities and the view that no single interpretation of any phenomenon can be claimed superior to any other. (Rosenau 1992: 80)

The intersection of knowledge and power arises as the claim to truth overpowers alternative and subjugated knowledges (Foucault 1980). Postmodernism displaces totalizing claims to truth with notions such as Jean-François Lyotard's (1984) conception of multiple language games, each with its rules and practices, no one of which can declare its primacy over others. In Jane Flax's terms:

Truth for postmodernists is an effect of discourse. Each discourse has its own distinctive set of rules or procedures that govern the production of what is to count as a meaningful or truthful statement. Each discourse or 'discursive formation' is simultaneously enabling and limiting. The rules of a discourse enable us to make certain sorts of statements and to make truth claims, but the same rules force us to remain within the system and to make only those statements that conform to these rules. A discourse as a whole cannot be true or false because truth is always contextual and rule dependent. Discourses are local, heterogeneous, and often incommensurable. No discourse-independent or transcendental rules exist that could govern all discourses or a choice between them. Truth claims are in principle 'undecidable' outside of or between discourses. This does not mean that there is no truth but rather that truth is discourse dependent. Truth claims can be made by those who accept the rules of a discourse or who are willing to bridge across several. However, there is no trump available which we can rely on to solve all disputes. Prior agreement on rules, not the compelling power of objective truth, makes conflict resolution possible. (Flax 1992: 452)[8]

It follows that as social scientists we cannot create a unified disciplinary subject of a unified system of knowledge, but must reconcile ourselves to multiple narratives revealing varied and many-sided versions of the world from multiple and fragmented discursively constituted positions. Nancy Fraser and Linda Nicholson (1994), writing for feminism, propose a 'postmodern-feminist theory' which

would be pragmatic and falliblistic. It would tailor its methods and categories to the specific task at hand, using multiple categories when appropriate and fore-swearing the metaphysical comfort of a single 'feminist method' or 'feminist epis-temology.' In short, this theory would look more like a tapestry composed of threads of many different hues than one woven in a single color. (Fraser and Nicholson 1994: 258)[9]

Thus post-structuralism/postmodernism challenges the very project on which sociological theory had been based, namely, its 'claim to speak the Truth, to be an epistemically privileged discourse' (Seidman 1994: 119). In this view, the project of knowledge for sociology has to be abandoned in favour of regional social, rather than sociological, theorizing 'with a moral intent' (Seidman 1994: 126–7).[10]

Feminism's recognition of the imbrication of knowledge, authority, and masculine hegemony has rejoiced theoretically in the critical possi-bilities offered by postmodernism. It has been argued that the concep-tion of a unitary and universalized subject is corrupted by a desire for dominance (Flax 1992) and that claims to universality cannot be sus-tained against their demonstrable ethnocentricity or class and gender positioning. Even the authority claimed for experience by many in the women's movement is denied. 'Experience,' interpreted as a function of the modernist unitary subject, cannot provide a direct and uncontami-nated access to reality since it is already discursively determined. For fem-inism and for the sciences of the social, the project of 'representing' the object in discourse is no longer viable for there is no object that is not already posited discursively:

To posit a materiality outside of language is still to posit that materiality, and the materiality so posited will retain that positing in its constitutive condition. (Butler 1993: 67–8; see also Laclau and Mouffe 1985)

The circularity of Butler's formulation repudiates the very possibility of *discovering what is not already posited*. The validity of inquiry as a project is removed.

The individuated subject's perception giving unmediated access to reality has been foundational to traditional philosophical epistemologies. Francis Bacon (1900) formulated this as a knowledge wholly transparent to its object. Such epistemologies assume that language enters only at the point of naming what has been perceived. Philosophical theorists of language – Frege, for example (Dummett 1981) – have indeed sought to construct rules for language so that it could perform fully scientific representation. They have believed in the possibility of a language in which meaning is determined by, or indeed *is*, reference.

Post-structuralists extrapolated from de Saussure's structuralist theory of signs and signification to put such theories of meaning in question. De Saussure (1959) starts from the discipline of linguistics as it had developed in the late nineteenth century. Though his theory is profoundly original, it also takes for granted the incisive move that had already been made, namely, the treatment of language as an object of systematic study independent of its local occurrences in talk and text and hence of local historical contexts of utterance. In his view, it is not thought that seeks expression in language, but the system of signs that gives body and organization to ideas. Nor does the meaning of signs rely on an object world; hence, reference is excluded as determination of meaning. On the contrary, individual signs depend for their meaning on the system of signs of which they are constituents. Meaning is treated as a determinate property that signs carry around with them, independent of actual contexts of speaking-hearing and reading-writing. People's actual practices of talk or writing/reading lack discursive presence in this theory; hence, the social character of systems of signs is also cut away.

Building on this theoretical basis, post-structuralist/postmodernist critique insists on a dynamic internal to discourse or language determining meaning beyond intentions seeking expression in a particular utterance. Hence language or discourse cannot represent the object purely and directly because both are systems of meaning determined internally in processes of differentiation[11] independent of the object represented. When we speak and write, a discourse speaks through us. We speak/write/image only within its play of signification. The sign's capacity to signify is an effect of the play of difference within language or discourse. Since experience and perception are always mediated discursively and are never pure themselves, claims to knowledge grounded in them must be discounted. If meaning is determined internally to the system of signs itself, how can it be wholly transparent to the object?

In an analogous fashion, discourse is understood as determined inter-textually and beyond the intention of individual speakers or writers. There can be no one-on-one correspondence between a category and the object it designates; every such category is determined by the opposing and determining complement from which it is differentiated and carries with it traces of what it is not. Any category, any term, draws into the text or talk as a tacit subtext the other that defines it in difference. There is no discrete category that does not contain internally the other from which it is differentiated. So there is no way in which concept or category can function purely representationally, no exact and reproduceable corre-spondence between term and object. We must always mean more and other than we mean to say/write. Precision of reference, indeed the very possibility of consistent, reproduceable reference, is precluded. Where there is no possibility of inquiry or reference to the beyond-the-text, even a denotational language-game can only circle around itself. The object of inquiry cannot be pushy, cannot surprise those who think they are explor-ing it, cannot be a common point of reference in deciding who is right in arguments about what is.

There is nothing, then, against which the text can be evaluated except that text again or another text. Theorizing is substituted for, even dis-places, inquiry. There is no outside to go to, no beyond-the-text to check the text against. Theory retreats into interpretation (Alexander 1995;[12] Seidman 1992, 1994); once rules of evidence and argument constraining inquiry are obviated, theory's discursive field can expand indefinitely. Ann Game's deconstructive sociology insists that her analyses of the 'social texts' of Australia's Bondi Beach 'make no claims to being the best or correct reading; on the contrary, one of the central concerns here is to develop a form of analysis that invites further rewritings' (Game 1991: 8). Discourse as a field of study is an endless resource without destination or conclusion. Within this frame, sociology has no ground for inquiry that could claim to discover a world inclusive and exceeding textuality and discourse in which actual people are active and in which the social that we create among us actually happens. A sociological inquiry positing as its object the ways in which people coordinate their activities – the sociol-ogy recommended by women's standpoint – is pre-empted. The object of

knowledge is already there; it has already been posited, already discursively constituted. There can be no discovery. Sociological discourse, feminist discourse too, become open-ended intertextual territories which
theory builds as it goes along.

The Unitary Subject

Post-structuralism/postmodernism rejects the unitary subject of the
Enlightenment's project of rational objectivity. The latter presupposes a
subject who experiences the world independently of the language or discourse in which statements about that world are made and can therefore
evaluate their truth. The Enlightenment's conception of the individuated
subject of reason and self-reflection as it was formulated at its foundational moment by Descartes has been elegantly stated by Rodolphe
Gasché:[13]

> By lifting the ego out of its immediate entanglement in the world and by thema-
> tizing the subject of thought itself, Descartes establishes the apodictic certainty of
> self as a result of the clarity and distinctness with which it perceives itself. Through
> self-reflection, the self – the ego, the subject – is put on its own feet, set free from
> all unmediate [sic] relation to being. In giving priority to the human being's
> determination as a thinking being, self-reflection marks the human being's rise to
> the rank of a subject. (Gasché 1986: 14)

The unitary subject transcends its bodily sites of being and hence also its
historical situation. It is the foundation of the Enlightenment's project of
knowledge. Knowledge of logical and mathematical truths is complemented by knowledge that relies on perception. The endemic and perhaps unsolvable problems of the relation between Descartes's subject, the
ego cogitans, and the object known or sought have been the generating
dynamic of Western philosophy since Immanuel Kant published his *Critique of Pure Reason*. It is projected even, as Gasché (1986) demonstrates,
into the deconstructive work of Jacques Derrida.

   The subject of philosophy is not only unitary, he is also alone in his
encounter with an external world. He is that mind the functions of whose
consciousness are universalized by Kant in his *Critique of Pure Reason* as
'cognition,' 'intuition,' 'understanding,' 'sense,' and so on. The problematic of reason and knowledge is set out in a way that conceals a shift from
activities of the individual subject to universalized functions. Through
such devices and through stylistic conventions, the individuated (male)

subject is raised to the level of the universal: '[M]an,' says Heidegger, 'becomes the measure and the centre of beings. Man is what lies at the bottom of all beings; that is, in modern terms, at the bottom of all objecti-fication and representability' (quoted in Kolb 1986: 137). In such univer-salizations of the unitary and individuated subject, we can locate the class, gender, and imperial subtexts of Western epistemologies, expanding the masculine subject of the West to correspond with the global project of imperialism. Ironically, the individuated subject of the Enlightenment, which was foundational to concepts of freedom from traditional authori-ties whether of monarch or Church, becomes foundational to new forms of authority and power (Foucault 1980).

Post-structuralist and postmodernist theorists have raised a fundamen-tal challenge to this conception of the unitary subject and its associated claims to authority. Michel Foucault (1970, 1972, 1981) insisted that the history of discourse cannot be read off from the intentions of participat-ing subjects. Rather, discourse is an order of concepts, schemata, consti-tuted objects, systems of representation, rules of evidence, and so forth, with its own internal structure and relations which impose themselves on subjects as the medium of their thought. Discourse constitutes subjects, subduing them to the diffuse, decentred processes of power that it articu-lates (Foucault 1979, 1980). Lyotard (1984) argues that the postmodern condition undermines the unitary subject, replacing it with a multiplicity of subject positions fragmented among multiple language games which lack an overriding philosophical principle that could assign primacy to any one. Sandra Harding (1986), offering a feminist critique of scientific epistemologies, argues for a multiplication of knowledges corresponding to subjects situated variously in relation to gender, race, and class. Judith Butler (1990) criticizes the unitary concept of woman as subject which replicates in the women's movement 'the very structures of power through which emancipation is sought' (2). Gender identities, she argues, are not 'always constituted coherently ... because gender inter-sects with racial, class, ethnic, sexual, and regional modalities of discur-sively constituted identities' (Butler 1990: 3).

While this critique dispenses with the unitary subject of 'the modern,' the idea of an individuated subject is *carried forward as a foundational struc-ture.* In challenging Husserl's conceptions of 'solitary mental life' and of 'interior monologue' as an unmediated self-presence of meaning, Derr-ida (1973) deploys de Saussure's (1959) theory of language in arguing that self, presence, and meaning are secondary to language and its struc-turing of signification. His critique, and his subsequent theoretical work, do not displace, however, the individuated subject and the problematic of knowledge that it generates.[14] Lacan's subject is an individuated consciousness permanently in exile from 'reality.' Though there are mother and father, these are ideal rather than actual people. Neither is a subject for her- or himself; neither speaks back. There is no social *process*; no interrelating; no context; no history.[15] The subject travels his solitary path among parents who are no more than mythologized functions in the Oedipal story (Lacan 1977; Mitchell and Rose 1982; Grosz 1990: 50–81), the father a Name and the mother voiceless. There is no interplay.[16] 'The subject is born insofar as the signifier emerges in the field of the Other' (Lacan 1977: 199). The individuated subject of his formulation echoes Descartes's *cogito* reconstructed for Lacan's own theory as, in Renata Salecl's (1994) vivid phrase, a 'substanceless point of self-reflection' (115).[17] The intervention of the symbolic order constitutes the (individuated) subject at the same time as it bars him forever from unmediated access to reality.

The individuated subject appears as the normal state of the knower in postmodernist discourse. For Steven Seidman (1994), for example, it is an individuated knower, ineluctably situated historically and in specific positions in society, who puts in question the very possibility of universally valid social theory:

Postmodernists have evoked the suspicion tht the products of the human studies – concepts, explanations, theories – bear the imprint of the particular prejudices and interests of their creators. This suspicion may be posed as follows: How can a knowing subject, who has particular interests and prejudices by virtue of living in a specific society at a particular historical juncture and occupying a specific social position defined by his or her class, gender, race, sexual orientation, and ethnic and religious status, produce concepts, explanations, and standards of validity that are universally valid? (Seidman 1994: 123)

Notice in this formulation how the social is also individuated by attaching it to an individuated knower as a position defined by various classes of membership categories, a device that has been methodologically standardized in sociology's survey methods.

The feminist critique also remains committed to the individuated subject. True, she is now 'an effect of discourse' (Flax 1990); or is distributed among different social categories of oppression such as gender, race, and class (Harding 1986); or is multiplied in correspondence with the multiplicities of discourses; or, as identity, is fragmented across these multiple intersecting discourses; or, as Lacan's subject, is divided like a layer cake between the subject who enunciates and the subject who is the speaker. Though postmodernism rejects the unitary subject, knowing and knowledge remain functions of an individuated consciousness. Throughout, the individuation of the subject is preserved, whether as fragmented, multiplied, layered, or various.

Yet the social returns in odd ways. Presumably finding that language and discourse are somehow insufficient, the practitioners of post-structuralism/postmodernism reintroduce the social, using *ad hoc* notions of social context, history, institutions, and so on. Foucault falls back on 'institutions'; Richard Rorty (1994), on 'community.' It is worth considering in more detail how Judith Butler (1994) deploys J.L. Austin's (1962) concept of 'performative' to supply the missing 'social' and to return us within discourse to a world of activity that the post-structuralist/postmodernist theorizing of discourse does not encompass.

'Performative' is a conception introduced by Austin in discovering for philosophy utterances that are not constative, that is, factual, statements. He uses as examples formulaic statements such as the 'I do' that is part of the Anglican wedding ceremony or the formula used at the ceremonial launching of a ship. These are utterances that 'perform' an act rather than make a statement. But for Austin, and also for Butler, performatives proceed from the individuated subject. Careful to avoid attributing anything to the individual actor, Butler adopts a device much like those sociology has used for similar reasons – the verb is nominalized to create an abstraction. 'Perform' via Austin's gerund becomes 'performativity.'

Performatives, Butler (1994: 134) argues, are the 'effects' of language conventions. Language conventions are sedimented historically. They cannot be attributed to individual intentions.[18] The individuated consciousness is structurally displaced by language to reappear as a subject who is an effect of language or discourse; 'performativity' substitutes for intention as the originator of action. Any notion of the social is preempted – a striking effect when we consider that Austin and Butler use examples such as marriage. In effect, the notion of performative reduces to the speech act of an individual what can only be accomplished by people together in concerted action. For Austin, 'I promise' promises and 'I do' marries. In order to overcome the difficulties this creates, Austin introduces two more concepts: the notion of the illocutionary force of a speech act – what makes a particular form of words a promise or an invitation; and its perlocutionary force or what is getting done by the illocutionary force of the speech act – a marriage, the organization of a social event, etc. Through such devices, Austin and Butler seek to overcome the inhibitions created by the traditional commitment of philosophy to the individuated consciousness. 'Effects,' 'effectivity,' 'force,' 'power,' or 'linguistic conventions' are added to 'performativity' or to language, displacing, even repressing, the social:

For a performative to work, it must draw upon and recite a set of linguistic conventions which have traditionally worked to bind or engage certain kinds of effects. The force or effectivity of a performative will be derived from its capacity to draw on and reencode the historicity of those conventions in a present act. This power of recitation is not a function of an individual's *intention*, but is an effect of historically sedimented linguistic conventions. (Butler 1994: 137)

The same drifts of metaphor can be seen in Flax's formulation of the subject as an 'effect of discourse' (1990) and in Foucault's association of knowledge and power. In displacing the subject, agency or causal efficacy is reassigned to discourse, language, or culture. Power is ascribed to knowledge, the subject is an 'effect' of discourse, the force of the performative is derived from historically deposited linguistic conventions, and so on. Discourse *is* the social (Laclau 1980); the dynamic of discourse drives those it interpellates as subjects. Throughout, the original individuation of the subject remains, though now as site in which discourse or the force of the performative has its effect. The social, conceived as the ongoing concerting of activities among people, is reduced to a solo performance, such that promising, marrying, or launching a ship (Austin 1962) is an act of an individual, a problem replicated in John Searle's (1969) theory of speech acts: 'in speech act theory, a speech act is conceived as a closed totality where the intention corresponds to the act itself' (Salecl 1994: 30). The social remains unexplicated, even unnoticed.[19]

Positing the individuated subject means that problems of knowledge must be solved with reference to states of individual consciousness – perception, cognition, experience – and the objects they perceive, know, experience, or otherwise apprehend. Post-structuralism/postmodernism blocks this route to knowledge by depriving the traditional unitary subject of authority, shifting determinations of consciousness, and hence of the object of knowledge, to discourse and language. As an epiphenomenon of language and discourse, the subject is incapable of giving access to a something extraneous to language or discourse that the latter can be forced to express, to which they refer, or which is represented in them. A new solipsism is created. It is no longer one which confounds reality with the perception of reality, a problem created by the Cartesian individuation of the subject. Now it is a solipsism of discourse, admirably expressed in the quotation earlier from Judith Butler (1994) which reinvents Plato's *Meno* in a new form, trapping us in the paradox that nothing can be known which is not already known.

Post-structuralism/postmodernism substitutes discourse for the knower: what is posited as beyond discourse is already discursively constituted. The multiplication of discourses multiplies subject positions. Different standpoints produce different knowledges (Stanley and Wise 1983, 1993). There is no social process in which subjects thinking differently might seek to evaluate discourses relative to one another; and there is nothing extraneous to the discourses constituting them as subjects about which they might argue and to which they can refer in seeking to persuade others of the veracity, accuracy, and adequacy of a representation.

Theorizing Self and Language as Social

Post-structuralism/postmodernism boxes us into a theorizing of knowledge that precludes the significance of inquiry and denies even the possibility of discovery. An alternative is a theory which does not view 'knowledge' as a solipsism of discourse, but preserves people's active presence and views knowledge as a definite form of social act in which an object world is constituted by participants as a world in common. Such a theory does not suspend the divergent perspectives and experience of actual individuals in the theoretical construction of a unitary subject. Rather, it focuses in a dual fashion on how divergence is coordinated and how the forms of coordination (social relations) generate divergence.

Although Mead's[20] conceptions of mind and self remain within the general framework of the individuated subject, they are exceptional in being fully social. For Mead, self is differentiated from objects and others in the development of the social act. But self is more than difference; it is an incorporation of the organization of the act and others' attitudes into the individual's psychic organization. It is the mechanism through which individuals are able to bring their consciousness and actions into a coordinated relation to ongoing processes of social action with others. Quite unlike the post-structuralist/postmodernist conception of the subject constituted in discourse, self is *active* in the ongoing concerting of activities with others. It is also dependent on symbolic communication since it is only in language that the individual is able to respond to his or her own actions as others might.

Of course, the self cannot be simply laid over the post-structuralist/post-modernist conception of the subject. Unlike the latter, Mead's conception of self is essentially dialogic. Far from treating the subject as an effect of discourse (or social act), the self is active dialogically in coordinating the individual's unfolding line of action within the social processes in which s/he is engaged.[21] The social as an ongoing social act is the matrix in which the self is individuated. The self is also the form of consciousness which brings a person's conduct into a coordinated relationship to those with whom s/he acts. Mead's theory embraces both notions of the social as arising from the mindful activity of subjects creatively engaged with others in the social process, and an explication of the mechanisms of the self as at once differentiating and coordinating individual conduct.

Mead's theory of the self and of mind is also a theory of language and meaning. Self arises and operates only in the context of symbolic communication. His theory of language or symbolic communication is fully social. The symbol itself is generated in a social act in act-response sequences. The meaning of any given gesture or symbol is never already given, but is always accomplished by people active in the social act. Hence, for Mead, meaning isn't bound to signs that are transferred from one speaker to another, but is interactionally determined in the temporal sequence of an act (gesture) that calls out a response.[22] Language for Mead is an inter-individual organization of consciousness; it is both within and 'between' people; when one speaks and the other hears and responds, the one who speaks also hears and responds. Language picks out meanings, Mead said, and not just for the individual but for speakers and hearers participating together in a social act. Such a formulation of what Mead calls 'symbolic communication' directs us towards an understanding of knowledge as grounded socially in an inter-individual territory constituted by the language-mediated organization of the social act, rather than in a typal individual consciousness.

Mead, however, insists on the fluid, open-ended character of the ongoing concerting of social activity, and the distinctively human forms of that coordination. For him the social act is always an emergent; it is an ongoing coordination of activity among people in which what it has been emerges only as a moment in a social act. Meaning is generated in the social process and is not a property of language as an independent system of signs that 'carry' their meanings around with them. Rather, Mead sees language as *controlling* meaning in the local settings of its use; and, at the same time, how it means is determined by the responses of both speaker and hearer within the social act.

Mead's theory of what he calls 'symbolic communication' (stressing, in this phrase, the inter-individuality of language) also departs radically from conceptions of sense as determined by the intention of the speaker. The significant symbol *aligns* the consciousnesses/responses of speaker and hearer(s). The verbal symbol is heard as the same for both speaker and hearer; within the social act, it elicits a coordinate organization of meanings for both. The significance of an utterance is not a discrete effect of the words that it assembles; rather, it is determined retrospectively by what has gone before and gives determination to the emerging organization of the social act. Symbolic communication gives control over meanings arising in the social act and brings into the social process objects the constitution of which is rooted in the organism's responses or attitudes in its environment. Throughout, Mead's theory is striking in his insistence – sometimes his struggle – to conceive of self, object, symbol, and meaning as coming into being in the ongoing continuities of individual and social action.

There remains, however, a deep problem in Mead's conception of symbolic communication. Mead's notion of meaning as arising in the social act insists that meaning must be in life and cannot 'occur' other than in activities among people. This, however, does not account for how language already has a determinate capacity to mean before it is activated in actual situations of action; or, indeed, how it is that symbolic communication can have that property so essential to Mead's theory, namely, that speaker and hearer can hear and respond to the speaker's words in the same way. He lacks a theorizing of language and discourse (as does this ontological tradition, in general), or a means of making forays into social organization and relations beyond the matrix of the social act in which the self arises.[23] Despite Mead's treatment of symbolic communication and of the social grounding of the self-reflective self or mind, he lacks *a fully social conception of knowledge and language* which could integrate the discoveries and analytic innovations of post-structuralism/postmodernism.[24]

Mead's conception of language and how language means is interestingly concordant with an apparently entirely independent tradition, identified with the names of Valentin I. Vološinov (1973) and Mikhail Bakhtin (1981, 1986) and originating in the Soviet Union at approximately the same period as Mead was writing in the United States. Like Mead, Vološinov, a member of Bakhtin's circle, rejected theories of meaning in which signification is a property of determinations independent of local contexts of utterance. He is specifically critical of de Saussure's structuralist theory of language. He views meaning as something like a field interpenetrating the psyche and the social. Language operates in this field neither fully in individuals' consciousnesses nor as a property of a system or structure distinct from them. Like Mead, Vološinov theorizes language as creating an inter-individual territory. The sign is 'inter-individual' (Vološinov 1973: 12):

[A] *word is a two-sided act.* It is determined equally by *whose* word it is and *for whom* it is meant. As word, it is precisely *the product of the reciprocal relationship between speaker and listener, addresser and addressee.* Each and every word expresses the 'one' in relation to the 'other.' I give myself verbal shape from another's point of view ... (Vološinov 1973: 86; original emphasis)

His formulation of how words mean as inter-individual, within and beyond the psyche, is strikingly concordant with Mead's insistence that language – *symbolic* communication – calls out the same response in the speaker as it does in the hearer. Mead's theorizing of the self as arising in a reciprocity of perspectives in the ongoing social act could be viewed as supplementing Vološinov's unfinalized conception of the psyche as continuous with the social.

Mead's notion of meaning as arising in ongoing social acts presupposes (in his notion of language as a controller of meaning) that words carry a capacity to mean independently of particular local settings of action. But he lacks a theory of how words can bring an already determined meaning into a setting, for this must be presupposed if language is to be effective in controlling the field of meaning generated in the social act. Structuralist theories, by contrast, provide for how words already mean before particular local settings of their uttering; they enter anyone's communicative use as already determined and trailing a debris of meaning beyond the intention to mean of the speaker/writer. Though critical of Saussurean structuralism, Vološinov and Bakhtin, unlike Mead, share conceptions similar to contemporary post-structuralist conceptions of language and discourse as formative of how people can mean. In particular, Bakhtin envisages the ongoing multiple historical production of meaning as sedimenting 'speech genres' which transmit their 'taste' into each new moment of speaking or writing, while at the same time, like Mead, he preserves the moment of utterance as the ontological site of meaning:

For any individual consciousness living in it, language is not an abstract system of normative forms but rather a concrete heteroglot conception of the world. All words have the 'taste' of a profession, a genre, a tendency, a party, a particular work, a particular person, a generation, an age group, the day and hour. Each word tastes of the context and contexts in which it has lived its socially charged life; all words and forms are populated by intentions. Contextual overtones (generic, tendentious, individualistic) are inevitable in the word. (Bakhtin 1981: 293)

In contrast to post-structuralism/postmodernism's motiveless subject at the mercy of the winds of intertextuality, Bakhtin views every utterance as 'containing' the speaker/writer's creative struggle to make a language that is pregiven and determines how she can mean, mean what she wants in the actual local settings in which she speaks or writes. For Bakhtin, the pre-givenness of language is always in movement as each new moment of people's creative struggle to get meaning done in actual settings of utterance is entered into the pre-given of language for those who come later:

As a living, socio-ideological concrete thing, as heteroglot opinion, language, for the individual consciousness, lies on the borderline between oneself and the other. The word in language is half someone else's. It becomes 'one's own' only when the speaker populates it with his own intention, his own accent, when he appropriates the word, adapting it to his own semantic and expressive intention. Prior to this moment of appropriation, the word does not exist in a neutral and impersonal language (it is not, after all, out of a dictionary that the speaker gets his words!), but rather it exists in other people's mouths, in other people's contexts, serving other people's intentions: it is from there that one must take the word, and make it one's own. (Bakhtin 1981: 293–4)

Bakhtin's theory preserves a conception of the meaning of words as already sedimented historically by past activities and hence as determined prior to a given moment of speech or writing, but he also insists on meaning as produced and shaped in the local historical contexts of utterances. Concrete utterances are essentially dialogic, an active interplay between past determinations of meaning and their creative shaping to the speaker's or writer's current intentions (Bakhtin 1981: 272).

Thus, both Mead and Bakhtin in different ways locate language in and of the settings and among the people who are speaking and hearing, reading and writing. *And nowhere else.* For Mead, the significant symbol is always an organization of responses in the social act; Bakhtin contributes the determination of a sign as product of the speech genres in which it plays a part and the speaker/writer's struggle to make it express her intention in an actual utterance which is formative of the meaning the sign comes to bear forward. In returning on this basis to the problem of how signs may be taken as referring to 'out there,' I follow on from these theorists' location of meaning as an active moment in an ongoing social act involving more than one participant.

Observing Referring

In Mead's view, the object constituted in the social act is not external to its naming. Mead's conception of objects is always as they arise in action. Objects come into being for the organism as it engages actively in and with its environment and are social as they are constituted in a social course of action as objects for participants:

... the social process, as involving communication, is in a sense responsible for the appearance of new objects in the field of experience of the individual organisms implicated in that process ... objects are constituted in terms of meanings within the social process of experience and behavior through the mutual adjustment to one another of the responses or actions of the various individual organisms involved in that process. (Mead 1947: 77)

For Mead, the term for an object is an aspect of how its social character is produced:

Symbolization constitutes objects not constituted before, objects which would not exist except for the context of social relationships wherein symbolization occurs. Language does not simply symbolize a situation or object which is already there in advance; it makes possible the existence or the appearance of that situation or object, for it is part of the mechanism whereby that situation or object is constituted. The social process relates the responses of one individual to the gestures of another, as the meanings of the latter, and is thus responsible for the rise and existence of new objects in the social situation, objects dependent upon or constituted by these meanings. (Mead 1947: 78)

In Mead's view, language, rather than simply expressing meaning, controls it. It is a mechanism capable of creating new objects because it selects meanings developing in a social process and brings them into the shared and social space that symbolic communication creates.

Here I draw on observations, my own or others, as 'specimens'[25] in which we can find practices of referring to objects as moments in a social act. Rather than an individuated subject, *subjects are plural*. Practices of referring to an object are not an effect of discourse in the individuated subject and hence moot; rather, they are practices that organize among participants in a social act a shared universe of objects. 'Referring' is a concerting of consciousnesses through symbolic communication that gives presence to an object for participants in the emerging course of a social act.

The archaeology of the first of my observations reveals a relatively primitive layer of my understanding of Mead's thought and certainly of language. At one time, I used to teach the 'social significance of language' in courses on social psychology. To illustrate the structuring or organizing effect of language, as I then thought of it, I used to tell the story of one of my children's first word. When Dave was about eighteen months old, we lived in a second-floor apartment in Berkeley, California. One morning, a bird flying by the window, I pointed to it and said, 'Bird.' He repeated the word, also pointing to the window where the bird had flown by. Shortly thereafter, we were at a doctor's office where there was a fish tank with tropical fish. Dave pointed to the fish and said, 'Bird.' And I said, 'No, not bird. Fish!' In class I used this anecdote to illustrate how language structures the way we can see/talk about the world. I suggested that there was a possible organization in Dave's analysis of a world in which 'bird' collected not only those beings that flew through air but any living object that moved through space and was seen through glass.

I think differently about that incident/instance now. Earlier I had been interested in how the name or concept organized or collected objects. I was teaching my son how to name objects properly. I was teaching him a word-meaning relation. The meaning would attach to the word. The word would pick out the object. What I now see is something rather different, namely, that the word-meaning relation, the act of referring and teaching a child how to refer, was itself a social act. My naming the bird as I pointed it out to my son was more than teaching him the 'correct' way to use a word. I was inducting him into the social act which constitutes an object as *being there for participants.* Dave and I were there together, looking together, looking at the same 'thing.' 'Looking at the same thing' was more than a subjective orientation of consciousness; it was also the pointing that coordinated the direction of our looking.[26] Pointing brings the other's gaze into alignment with her/his own. There becomes an object. It is not yet an object for them before this alignment. We could 'know' we were looking at the same thing as I named it and he repeated what was becoming for him – *in this social act* – a word. In learning to refer, he was learning how to constitute an object in a social act and for its participants, for us. And in the social act in which 'bird' is differentiated from 'fish,' a socially organized order of *objects constituted in a system of relations* is being established for him.

Referring to objects, as Dave was learning then, is a socially organizing practice that 'implies' the presence of another and 'implies' what Mead would call the shared 'attitude' of looking that objectifies. Naming objects is more than naming what is already constituted. It sets up a social organization of relations among subjects and 'what is there' that naming coordinates as the perception or recognition of an object in an ongoing social act. There is an alignment of the individual consciousnesses via the utterance. A virtual, if not an actual, other is always already implicated in utterances referring to objects; *a place is already prepared for the or an/other whether she is present or not.* Reference from language to objects always, in this view, carries the implication of a plurality of subjects.

Mead's conception of the social act is of an ongoing development of activity coordinated in its course among and by more than one; symbolic communication is an organization *between* consciousnesses, constitutive of subjects within the social act. Helen Keller's story of her 'miracle' exhibits just this structure. Made blind and deaf by an illness early in her child-hood, Keller was unable to communicate other than in gestures (signs) that expressed her needs; her teacher, Anne Mansfield Sullivan, taught her to extend the range of this form of communication by spelling out the letters of words on her hand. 'I did not know that I was spelling a word or even that words existed' (Keller 1909: 22). Sullivan describes her difficul-ties with getting Keller past using these spellings merely as expressions of her needs (Sullivan in Keller 1909: 312). She had difficulty getting her to move to the fully social organization of 'symbolic' communication.

Keller was, in a sense, alone with her desires; 'nouns' signed on the palms of her teacher's or others' hands were merely expressions of a consciousness lonely in its own desire, lacking other subjects. Keller did not discover 'that everything has a name' and an entry to fully symbolic discourse until one day when her teacher ran water from the pump over her hand while at the same time spelling out the letters *W A T E R* on her palm. Here was the moment when she entered, with Anne Sullivan, the social act in which objects are constituted as present to more than one, and hence into a world in which there are other subjects. The symbolically constituted world is also a social world, an open-ended territory; Helen Keller's world was enlarged and transformed as it was given an existence in the consciousnesses of others as it existed in hers.[27] For the first time, as Sullivan's letters inform us, Keller's world became one in which the presence of objects was given to her as a presence for other subjects: she wanted to know the names of everything she encountered; she wanted to encounter so as to name; and, for the first time, she wanted to know who her teacher was (Sullivan in Keller 1909: 315–16). 'What happened at the well-house was that the nothingness vanished' (Keller 1956: 42).[28]

The presence of the other is *in and not separable from* the act of referring to the object by naming it. To repeat Vološinov: 'Signs can arise only on *interindividual territory*' (1973: 12). In a sense, signs (in Vološinov's sense) *organize* an inter-individual territory – the named and known-in-common object world. In practices of referring, others are always implicitly present; they carry and reproduce an attitude that objectifies 'things' as 'between' consciousnesses. Naming objects is a three-way relation; not just subject-object, but subject-object-subject. It is this three-way relationship that constitutes objects as social or that constitutes objects as such.

Referring has, I suggest, social grammar, a definite socially organized sequence of practices which is learned as a whole bundle. Not too long ago walking home, I saw a small child with her mother, who was standing talking to another adult. The child was tugging her mother's skirt and saying, in a crescendo, 'A cat, a cat, momma, look, a cat.' She was pointing across the street to a black cat engaged in a leisurely toilet on the sunny sidewalk. Her mother eventually responded by looking briefly in the direction in which the child was pointing and said, 'Yes, Karen, a cat!' The child stopped pulling, as well as her excited yelling. Here (it seemed to me) was a child's practice of the social organization constituting an object *among* participants. The other's look and recognition of the object 'seen' and named by a speaker is made accountable by the mother's 'yes.' 'Cat' is thereby constituted or completed *as object* as the other accountably recognizes what the speaker sees. The *social* 'grammar' of naming and identifying or referring to objects called for a missing complement, the other's 'recognition' in her assent, her glance towards the object, and her repetition of 'its' name. Once the mother 'completed' the sequence by registering that she had seen the cat Karen indicated, the sequence was completed to Karen's apparent satisfaction.

Karen could be seen re-enacting the discovery of the other as subject in the moment of naming an object. Perhaps the sequence brings some of the same pleasures as Helen Keller experienced so sharply. Referring is a social act involving more than one in which 'the appearance of the situation or object' (Mead 1947: 78) is accomplished in a sequence concluding in the other's recognizing what becomes, *for both of them*, the object referred to.

The social organization of referring constitutes the object as independent of the experience or perception of any one individual. The independence is not theoretical; *it is produced in the socially organized practices that coordinate different subjectivities with different perspectives and experience* in relation to what becomes for them, in common, an object. This does not mean that there is no world that the organism, as Mead would say, encounters and finds 'ordered' in a bodily mode prior to its social and human organization. Indeed, the objects that thus come into presence for participants in a social act must somehow be built into this substratum, including the neuro-muscular organization of the world as separate from self[29] (the social organization of referring relies on physiological organization shared by the human species). The name-look-recognition sequence among people produces the object world *among us* and for each other. Practices of referring that fail, as Karen's importuning of her mother to see the cat failed at first, are incomplete.

The symbolic order articulates socially an object world that is built as an everyday/everynight practice on how the human organism engages with the physical world it is born into. Maurice Merleau-Ponty's *The Phenomenology of Perception* (1962) explores from the standpoint of the individuated consciousness the subject's active perceptual organization of its world; Jean Piaget (1958) explored ethnographically how the 'play' of infants with objects appearing and disappearing organizes for consciousness the world existing independently of consciousness that Piaget calls 'reality' (the Freud/Lacan '*Fort-Da*' anecdote is a fragmentary observation of an extended process).[30] Practices installed at a neuro-muscular level of organization and articulated *socially* through the symbolic order establish the physiological grounding among members of this species necessary for the very possibility of social objects, known in common. It is striking in Helen Keller's (1955) story how her teacher relies, in the absence of sight and hearing, on Helen's ability to *feel* the water splashing from the pump onto her hand to create the foundation of symbolic communication.

In Mead's account of the *social* object, that is, the object that arises or is accomplished as such in a social act, name and object are interdependent, though neither is a function of the other. In the above accounts, we can see the object *as in the course of arising in a social act*. An object is *coming into* presence for participants. There is a sequence here. A name picks out for participants in the act the object to be recognized in common; its status as real, that is, as object for others as well as for the speaker, is completed in responsive acts of recognition: the mother's 'Yes, Karen, a cat!'

in the specimen above; or the mother's 'No, Dave, not bird. Fish!' in my own story. Even when the response corrects, the object has already been brought into the social act. Naming accomplishes it as presence in common, as an object *for* participants. Responses according agreement to the naming produces the object as known by participants as known. Karen sees the cat; Karen names 'cat' to her mother; her mother sees the cat that Karen *sees and makes herself accountable to Karen for her seeing*. The object produced ostensively as 'inter-individual' is produced in a *sequence* of interactions among people. It is completed in the inter-individual mode in the other's 'recognition' of what the speaker names and points to. The inter-individual object is a dialogic production. It presupposes that the subjects constituted in the social act can perceive things differently. One may see what another does not, or see it differently; as one names and indicates, the other/others know how to find it. Here there is no 'reciprocity of perspectives,' positing an interchangeability of standpoints (Schutz 1962a) as a way of overcoming for sociology its assumption of an individuated consciousness. Subjects active and defined as subjects in this social act may see something from different angles, be in motion differently towards it, see it at different times, yet at the moment of finding and recognizing, the object enters, indeed organizes, a kind of community of attention *in the course of a social act.* An inter-individual territory (Vološinov 1973) comes into being at the intersection of the different consciousnesses constituted as subjects in relation to what all can also see.[31] Naming gathers and concerts different consciousnesses in 'motion'; it does not resolve their differences.

Discourse and Reference

In the previous section, we looked at 'referring' as everyday sequences of talking and looking among people. But not all such dialogues share co-presence. Where speaker and hearer are together and the object being identified is present, recognition can be made accountable, misrecognition correctable, in the course of the social act. The speaker can point to the object she names just as I did in introducing the word 'bird' to my son or as Karen did, pointing out the cat to her mother. Corrections can be introduced, as I introduced a correction of name when Dave identified a fish as 'bird.' Recognition of the object that completes the social act of referring is made on the spot, as it is in Karen's mother's 'Yes, Karen, a cat.' But the writer of a text does not share the situation of the text's readers and, however many precise instructions the text includes, the writer may not be able to anticipate comprehensively the contigencies of finding and recognition in particular local settings.[32]

Bakhtin inserts another kind of dialogue, one between local settings of speech and action and the meanings sedimented in speech genres or discourses which are carried forward from past into present. In contrast to post-structuralism/postmodernism's theorized capture of subject and meaning by discourse, Bakhtin theorizes local utterances as in dialogue with the speech genres. A speaker draws on a symbolic inventory determined prior to the setting and moment of her speaking. Meanings that words carry with them have already been shaped in previous settings of their use. Speech genres are configurations of meaning which have developed in the context and bear the imprint of the characteristic usages associated with the activities of a group – a work organization, a professional practice, the experience of a generation, and the like. The relation between any given occasion of speaking or writing and the terms and characteristic syntactic and stylistic practices of a speech genre on which a speaker draws to speak and her hearer to understand, is dialogic. As words are drawn into an actual interchange, an utterance (speech or text) comes to meaning in an interplay between the speech genres which have given the words meaning before and the new life given them in the utterance. Thus, rather than treating meaning or signification as simply attached to words and transferred in an unproblematic way to the hearer or reader, Bakhtin conceives meaning as a dialogic accomplishment specific to the utterance's setting or context (Bakhtin 1981).

Bakhtin (1986) makes a distinction between primary and secondary speech genres, the latter corresponding pretty closely to the notion of a discourse as the term has been used here. 'Secondary speech genres' are

novels, dramas, all kinds of scientific research, major genres of commentary and so forth [and] arise in more complex and comparatively highly developed and organized cultural communication ... artistic, scientific, sociopolitical ... (Bakhtin 1986: 61–2)

Unlike the conceptions of discourse which stem from Foucault (see, particularly, Foucault 1981), Bakhtin's conception is one that emphasizes the socially active character of secondary speech genres. They are communication rather than rules, categories, statements, texts, and so on (Foucault 1981). This active and relational character of Bakhtin's conception is congenial to the sociology from the standpoint of women deployed in this paper. Discourse here is viewed as a socially organized activity among people. That the relations it creates among people are mediated by texts means that it is easy to forget that people are present and provide its dynamic. But Bakhtin reminds us that discourse's local accomplishment is an active dialogue between what people are trying to get said and get done at any given moment of speech or writing, and what has been given prior discursive shape.

In the context of discourse or secondary speech genres, the sequencing of the social act of referring originates elsewhere, entering dialogically into any local phase of the overall sequence. Hooking a local sequence of action into a discourse-driven dialogue means that readers/hearers must know how to 'find' objects beyond-the-text that can be recognized as the object or objects to which the text refers. The ostensive act that joins name and 'experience' – the woman seeing a bird, pointing to focus her son's gaze as hers is, and saying 'bird'; Helen Keller's teacher pumping water over Helen's hand and tracing the letters $W A\ T E R$ on her palm – isn't available. The reader in her practice of referring must bring to her reading of the text a procedure for indexing a universe of socially constituted objects.[33]

Frederick Grinnell's (1987) account of teaching biology has direct parallels to the woman teaching her child to find the 'bird.' Here, however, what is being taught draws the discourse of biology into the local accomplishment of referring. The 'cell concept' is of central importance in learning biology, but it is incomplete without its complement: being able to see a cell and recognize it as such. Grinnell writes that he has

shown ... pictures [of cells and cell debris] to 1st-grade elementary school students, and they were unable to identify the cells. If, however, I showed them which of the objects were cells and which were debris, the students subsequently were able to recognize other similar cells. More dramatically, the average medical student often is unable to distinguish between cells and cell nuclei when first shown light micrographs of tissue sections ... After studying histology the same students are able not only to make such distinctions but also to discriminate among the different tissues and recognize the specific cell types of which they are composed. (Grinnell 1987: 10)

Far from the mere positing of the object within discourse that Butler theorizes, here is an active social process in which students learn to bring the concepts of discourse into the local work of finding and recognizing cells or differentiating cells and cell nuclei under the microscope.

Mead holds that a 'symbol of communication' abstracts the 'universal character' of an object (Mead 1938: 370) and that this 'function' of language is systematically developed in science. Science confronts as a problem that of 'successful reference to identical objects and characters through identical symbols mutually employed by different selves' (Mead 1938: 53):

> The world that is there has taken up into itself all the order, definition, and necessity of earlier scientific advance. It is not there as hypothesis, in so far as the hypotheses have justified themselves in experience, nor is it there as analyzed relations, events, and particles. These characters have passed into things, and for the time being at any rate, they are there unanalyzed, with the same authority as that of the so-called sensible experience. (Mead 1938: 50)

Mead's formulation of the social always situates it in the experience[34] of the individual 'organism' in action. The individual's experience within the social act is always more than the symbolic ordering of the act brings into focus; meanings arising in the social process are always more than those controlled by participants' utterances. From an attentional field evolving in an ongoing activity, symbols pick out and focus attention on the 'universal character' of some aspect or feature present in that field, which becomes *in this process* what we call generically an object.[35]

The technologies of the laboratory standardize the production of discriminable events that scientists can recognize as the same object in the multiple settings of their work. This account is, of course, in direct disagreement with those who take up science as wholly within language or discourse, as, it seems, does Richard Rorty (1994), who argues that the difference between Galileo and Aristotle was not Galileo's telescope or his fascination with the *observed* movement of objects, but his 'terminology' (Rorty 1994: 48). Among other things, Galileo observed spots on the sun through his telescope. Others used telescopes to see if they could find again what Galileo had reported. Recognizing the sequential grammar of identifying objects enables us to see how the social act of naming and referring brings into being the basis of community, as well as the potential for its destruction: an established 'terminology' could not survive a confrontation with what it could not properly name; observing spots on the sun *discredited a discourse* of the sun's unsullied surface; in the dissolution of a socially constituted object, the subjects who have been its sustaining community are put in jeopardy.

The microscope created a new encounter between human perception and an original, unnamed world of living beings. Naming them and learning the continuities of their differences has been the patient work of biological scientists. Maps and mapping recognize and formulate a terrain that is known as it cannot be from ground level but can only be found and recognized there. The trained discriminations that the scientist learns to make are indeed posited by the technical categories of the science, but making them is always a local practice of finding again the technically standardized category-object connection. Grinnell's students are being instructed to find *what others have found before them*. The categorization, criteria, methods of measurement and of identifying the continuities and differences of an object, etc., are the technical practices which produce for a scientific discourse, not just what differentiates itself within an individuated consciousness, but an object *for the discourse* (Carr 1964). Such objects are produced and reproduced *as* social in the social acts of science, whether in the work of inquiry or of teaching, as we saw in the case of Grinnell's biology instructor at work. They become present to *and coordinate* individual consciousnesses as discursive subjects in locally accomplished sequences of referring, finding, and recognizing the objects as the same.

The specialized objects constituted in the technical practices of science are not external to the terms that name and locate them, nor are its objects simply expressions of its discourse as in Butler's (1993: 67–8) mechanical account of the dependence of the posited materiality on that positing as its constitutive condition. Producing an object for science is a technical work bound dialogically to others in relations mediated by the intertextuality of that science's discourse. Actuality becomes a resource for scientific technologies that distill effects recognizable to a scientific discourse. The technology of science systematically produces objects and events which can be found and recognized as the same in the multiple settings of scientific discourse, including its research practices. *The technical standardization of objects across local sites of research is essential.* Stabilizing reference from one site of research to another relies on reproducing objects that are recognizably the 'same.' Böhme (1977) analyses a controversy dating from the early days of experimental psychology concerning the radically different findings of experimental studies of reaction times by the Leipzig School and an American psychologist. Differences in the findings of the two schools are attributable to differences in how each constituted the experimental object. His conclusions emphasize the importance for science of 'guarantee[ing] to members of a scientific community that the object of their research is identical' (Böhme 1977: 139).

Garfinkel, Lynch, and Livingston's (1981) paper analysing the discovery of an 'optically discovered pulsar' provides an account of a conversation between two astronomers leading up to and at the moment of discovery of a pulsar. Their talk and the note-taking recording their observational procedures are dialogically coordinated with the discourse of astronomy,[36] to which they are accountable. Their local practices attend to what Foucault (1981) calls the rules of inclusion and exclusion of the discourse of astronomy. Their excitement as they begin to think that they have found something incorporates the significance their discovery will have for other participants.

Scientific techniques and technologies of observation, and systematic note-taking, supplant the immediacy of Karen's cries and pointing to the cat, but they are organized by the same sequential 'grammar.' They are intended to enable other astronomers to track and find the object they have introduced into this particular sequence of the social act of science. It is that sequence as a whole, including the confirmation of their observations by other astronomers, that produces for science, and accountably, the optically discovered pulsar. Indeed, the optically discovered pulsar of Garfinkel, Lynch, and Livingston's (1981) paper was not yet a discovery for the science of astronomy on that evening when the astronomers were recorded in the process of 'discovering' it. The sequence of finding, 'pointing' (however technical), and making the object accountably present to others had not yet been completed. If it is to come to have 'the same authority' as 'sensible experience,' others, deploying these same techniques and technologies, must come to 'recognize' the object and affirm it. Like Karen, the pulsar's discoverers had to get others to 'see' just what they 'saw,' before anything had been discovered. The scientific paper reporting the 'discovery' appended to Garfinkel, Lynch, and Livingston's analysis invites others to recognize the object and affirm its existence as an object the scientific properties of which have passed into its existence for astronomy. Indeed, Garfinkel, Lynch, and Livingston's paper leaves the achievement of the object at the 'Mommy, there's a cat' stage. A scientific discovery is not a one-time-through event. It is a sequential coordinated of interchange among participants in a scientific discourse, in which the already dialogic ordering of the work of discovery gets hooked into the work of other scientists through the publication of 'findings.' There is an implicit or explicit argument in which others, following the directions supplied in publications, try to find again what the discoverers claim is there. And then there may – or may not – be the final moment in which the discovery is recognized and affirmed in further publications, journal reviews, or the like.[37]

In imagining the forms of knowledge and their indexical operation in a dialogic relationship with the knowing subjects, I have used in the previous chapter the metaphor of a map. Reading a map in an actual situation of finding one's way is a distinctive kind of dialogue. I think of Ann, my son's partner, and I driving to dinner with friends. It was dark. We had never been to their house before, and it is in an area of Vancouver with which we aren't familiar. I am driving; Ann is navigating. She goes back and forth between the map and the not always well-lit streets and street names. From the map and its conventions for describing the layout and its naming of the streets, she goes to the street names she can see and the configuration of the intersecting streets in the area we are driving through. She is able to give me advance notice of how a street intersects with another diagonally and then curves to connect with the street (overlooking Burrard Inlet) we want. And she's good at this, so that I'm looking confidently for streets that 'behave' as she tells me they will from her reading of the map. And they do. Under her guidance, we are successful in finding our friend's house. Finding our way involves going back and forth between the text of the map and the actual streets, and 'connecting' its conventionalized signs with the actual configuration of the streets that we're travelling, the street signs, and so on. This dialogue relies on the cartography's systematic and technical development of symbols and of procedures for going from the actualities of the local terrain to the technically systematized features and relations of the map. In local situations of reading, the reader goes back and forth between their actualities and what she can find and recognize as the features iconically represented on the map she is reading. This is an actual and social process. The map is inert. It doesn't happen until it is read. Its dialogic capacity is potentiated by the reader. The competent reader knows how to locate her subjectivity in the universe of extension, a Cartesian universe, activating it as a 'player' in the sequence of referring. Even if she is alone, in reading the text of the map, she initiates a dialogue in which she plays both parts; she activates the instructions it carries and looks for what it tells her she can find. The map 'tells' her what features of the world to find and recognize as expressions of the relations it draws, *but she has to look outside the map to find them.*

The map-reader dialogue has two movements: the reader takes up the iconic markings of the map as instructions to look for features and relations of the landscape about her, and finds (or does not find) the features and relations that she can recognize as in correspondence with those instructions. This completes the circle of indexicality (Garfinkel

1967). Referring is not achieved wholly within language; beyond any given utterance, it relies on a differentiation in the world that is humanly discoverable and discriminable somehow or other. Referring is a social act in which the category used by the speaker provides something like a set of instructions for the hearer to look for and recognize an object that can be treated as fitted to the category. The hearer may not be successful; she may get it wrong; or the instructions may be inaccurate and misdirect her. But a good map will tell the truth if we know how to read from it to the features it indexes (they *become* features in the reader's local practices of indexing) – the complex of differences between pavement and side-walk, the lined-up houses, the street lights, the signs at the intersections – and how to carry on the dialogue it potentiates. Thus, as a sequential social act, Ann and I severally 'find' the streets we are driving through as the streets identified on the map, and can find our way.

In Ann's reading of the map, she brings into play the product of a complex technical development of mapping and representational conventions. As she 'reads' the map, we both orient to an object world that both see; features of the local environment become objects of attention to both; our relevancies are the same. The local environment and its features are indexed by the map. What is there becomes a feature for us as it is 'named' by the map's icons: 'There should be a cross street pretty soon,' Ann might have said, and I'd be looking out for it. But even if she were on her own, the dialogic of map and reader would be just as active, as she went from map to looking out of the window to find street intersections, names, and the park shown in green that would tell her that she'd overshot the turn she needed to take.

Maps are built from locally recognizable differentiations to produce a standardized iconic representation. The relation between the objects symbolized on the map and the streets and parks are not in any sense *in* the map. The map reader must know how to find the local particularities of the terrain as the objects indexed by the map; they are not contained in cartographic discourse. The relation of referring is brought into being in an actual course of action in which a reader takes up the map as pointing beyond it to what she might be able to recognize as the object it names. A local practice of referring picks out the objects indexed by the map from a field of experience which is always more and other than can be recognized by a reader under the map's instructions. She may be alone, but in reading the map and finding her way she brings discourse into active dialogue with the present in which she's looking for direction; she is participating in a social act. Knowledge is not the product of the solitary Cartesian consciousness, nor is it contained within a discursive field. Sense, meaning, truth – and falsehood – are always the local achievements of people whose coordinated and coordinating activities bring about the connectedness of statements about the world and the world they index during that time, in that place, and among those who participate in the social act, whether present to one another or not.

Conclusion

Postmodernism focuses its critique on theories of and claims to knowledge founded in the experience or perception of the individuated subject. Holding that the subject-object relation is constituted wholly within discourse undoes the very possibility of telling the truth in the sense of making reference to what is beyond discourse. Here, however, I have argued that referring is a social act in which more than one subject is active and is always a local practice of finding and recognizing what is named and indicated. A scientific discourse sets up procedures standardizing the production and replication of local practices of knowing which are drawn dialogically into actual situations, just as we could see in the account of reading a map. Referring is always a local achievement of some actual occasion or sequence of occasions. As such it is always problematic. In a sense, the development of science can be seen as accumulating successes in the local achievement of reference. Knowledge, and hence the possibility of telling the truth and of getting it wrong, is always among people in concerted sequences of action who know how to take up the instructions discourse provides and to find, recognize, and affirm, or sometimes fail to find, what discourse tells is there, as well as relying on just such dialogic sequences to settle disputes about what is. Knowledge, thus conceived, is always in time, always in action among people, and always potentiates a world in common as, once again, known in common. This account of knowledge and telling the truth represents them not as functions of the individuated consciousness of post-Cartesian philosophy, but as dialogic sequences of action in which the coordinating of divergent consciousnesses is mediated by a world they can find in common.

The problem of telling the truth that is postmodernism's challenge to sociology cannot be resolved by remaining within the assumptions of the individuated consciousness that postmodernism preserves while rejecting the unitary subject of modernity. Here I have argued that a fully social, dialogic account of knowledge and truth holds out for systematic inquiry the possibility of telling the truth about what it finds. I have centred attention on the problem of referring and representing since these are central problems presented by post-structuralism/postmodernism to sociology. I have put forward as an alternative an account which presupposes more than one subject. Drawing on the work of Mead (1938, 1947) and Bakhtin (1981, 1986) (and, to a lesser extent, of Vološinov [1973]), I have presented an account of reference as an interactional sequence relating word and object in a practical process of telling, finding, and recognizing. This is a social act implicating more than one consciousness; *each participant could perceive things differently; their perceptions are coordinated in it.* Knowledge joins consciousnesses whose perspectives are necessarily divergent, giving us what can be *known as known* in common. Perspectives are subdued to the virtual of what we can treat as there for you as it is for me – the water flowing over Helen Keller's hand becomes the water which she can 'know' as what is known both to her and her teacher.

Experience is fragmented and diverse, arising out of different biographies and different sites and projects in a given setting; the dialogic of knowing creates the virtual space of a world recognized as known in common. Divergent perspectives are coordinated in the social act of referring and, more generally, of knowledge. Rather than undermining the very possibility of truth being told, it is precisely the multiplicity of experience and perspective among people that is a necessary condition of truth. Telling the truth is an active coordination of people's subjectivities in a social act and presupposes difference. In this view, telling the truth is itself a social act in more than the obvious sense that 'telling' gives us. Here it is truth itself, knowledge itself, which is resolved from its conceptual stasis into sequences of concerted action which methodically accomplish for participants what they can know as known in common. Truth and knowledge are grounded in the foundational moments in which the social comes into being through language and through the sensory ground which human organisms share. Through these *together,* individual experience becomes hooked up to a world known in common and is radically and forever transmuted. Referring to an object is a social act, performed in actual settings of people's activities, and producing for those present what is first named, or pointed to, or referred to in some other way, as what is to be dialogically achieved in its 'recognition' by another, whether the actual other of the local setting or the virtual others of text-mediated discourse. Referring is a sequential and active dialogue among speakers and hearers, or text and readers, implicating and relying on the humanly shared senses of participants, their bodily being and activities of looking, touching, smelling, hearing, etc., to discover, to actively pick out, what becomes for them the object referred to in the course of dialogue. We have seen 'referring' as essentially dialogic, both in the local sequences of the social act in which Karen's mother finds and recognizes the cat that Karen is telling her to see, and in relation to the dialogue between discourse and local actualities in which the map reader finds her way.

The text of a map never stands alone; it is always waiting for its connection with the local actualities it intends; the sense that it can make is incomplete without that local practice of referring, yet that reference is not contained within it. It is indeed always indexical, to use Garfinkel's phrase, but in a stronger sense than he intended. A map does not stand alone; it relies on the actual terrain it can reference in the hands of the map-reader. The grammar of the dialogue is the same. Fictional maps mime the operation of a map that enables the complete sequence of reading and taking the map's instructions to look beyond it and recognize in that beyond-the-map the features it instructs the reader to find. They instigate the motion of referring to a somewhere sometime, but it does not exist; the map has no indexical complement. Fictional maps initiate a local dialogic of referring. They tell the reader to look beyond the map to find the map's complement in a world: Rivendell, the Misty Mountains, Smaug's lair under the Lonely Mountain. The very movement of this dialogue posits a beyond-the-text; its grammar projects the map's complement into the imaginary.

As much as does postmodernism, the method of writing the social as a knowledge for people put forward in this book rejects the grand imaginary maps of the Marxisms of the 1960s and 1970s (distinguish them from Marx himself!), which were held in suspension outside local practices of finding and recognizing. It rejects equally sociologies which give primacy to theory, whose phenomenal universe is constituted by abstractions and in which sequences of referring are completed entirely within discourse in returning to its own discursively constituted objects. Instead it aims at knowing the social as people actually bring it into being. Its objects would not be meaning but the actual ongoing ways in which people's activities are coordinated, particularly those forms of social organization and relations that connect up multiple and various sites of experience since these are what are ordinarily inaccessible to people. It aims at taking up just such a dialogic relation to the actualities of people's lives as we have seen in my description of Ann reading the map of Vancouver and our finding our way. And unlike maps of lands, seas, and sea coasts, these have to be maps of relations in motion, the dynamic of which generates changes in how we are related, what we experience, and what we do and can do.

Just as in the development of cartography, there is technical work to be done in discovering just how to find, represent, and name the features and dynamic of the social. Technical development relies on actualities to correct and refine its representational practices. It relies on the possibility of discriminating what it indexes. In a sense, it enters into a dialogue with actuality in order to create representations of the social that are capable of initiating sequences of referring that people can reliably complete in local settings. The ability of such a sociology to tell the truth would be in just how it could be entered dialogically, just as a map can be, into every-day activities of finding and recognizing where we are in relation to others, and how what we are doing and what is happening are hooked into such relations.

Here there is no massive pre-empting of multiple and divergent perspectives by a single overarching view which claims an hegemony of consciousness. This sociology is just as resistant to the pre-empting of many divergent perspectives by a single objectified stance as is postmodernism, but does not come to rest there. The metaphor of a map directs us to a form of knowledge of the social that shows relations between various and differentiated local sites of experience without subsuming or displacing them. Such a sociology develops from inquiry and not from theorizing; it aims at discoveries enabling us to locate ourselves in the complex relations with others arising from and determining our lives; its capacity to tell the truth is never contained in the text but arises in the map-reader's dialogic of finding and recognizing in the world what the text, itself a product of such inquiry, tells her she might look for.

Part Three:
Investigations

7

Exploring the Social Relations of Discourse: Sociological Theory and the Dialogic of Sociology[1]

Introduction

If we begin as ourselves, active in the local settings of our living, we know sociology as we live it, as its readers, writers, speakers, and hearers. We are in the middle of it, in our reading in a library, in an office, at home. Our reading is active, responsive, attentive to possible uses, and reactive to what we identify as error – sometimes it makes us angry, sometimes it gives us pleasure. Though we rarely if ever attend to it this way, it is always being discovered again as an actual course of action projecting into what comes next – whether teaching, writing, or speaking at a conference. Writing sociology, too, engages actively with the discourse; it references and is in dialogue with our reading. Explicit references are only a small part of it; it is deeply embedded in and draws on language-uses as they come to hand already determined historically by their uses in multiple disciplinary sites, as well as beyond the discipline. For, of course, sociological language isn't clean. It is contaminated in multiple ways by sociology's dialogue with the heteroglossia of the society. Sociology pulls other forms of language in to do its discursive work, language that trails with it a debris of meaning from its original site. Reciprocally, the language of sociological discourse goes out into the world and is taken over to do work outside that discourse.

This paper draws on Mikhail M. Bakhtin's theory of the novel, of language, and of speech genres to investigate discourse as social organization. It takes up this project as an investigation into sociology as a discourse because I know this discourse as an 'insider'; I am a participant; I know it as a local practice in my own life (and it is this that provides the main resource for this investigation). In this I move away from Foucault's

(1981) conception of discourse. Brilliant as it is, it accredits the stasis of the text. That we can return again, and at different points, to the utterance embodied in the printed text permits, perhaps even creates, the appearance of discourse as statements or meaning.

Foucault displaces the traditional 'unities' of the history of thought, such as a book or a body of work, as the unit of analysis, replacing them with a conception of a field 'made up of the totality of all effective statements (whether spoken or written), in their dispersion as events and in the occurrence that is proper to them' (Foucault 1981: 27). In so doing, he discards actual subjects, whether as 'author' or as reader, and the materiality of the text as in print, on screen, or in some other mode in which it enters local settings of reading, watching, etc. I have no thought of returning to the older history of ideas that Foucault sets aside. But here the materiality of the text, its replicability, and hence iterability, is key to addressing discourse as actual social relations between reading, writing, speaking, hearing subjects – actual people, you and me. Just as in Marx's *Capital* the commodity mediates the concrete and particularized labour of the producers and the abstract and universalized relations of exchange, the printed, and hence many-times replicable, text mediates between the actual people engaged in their particular local activities as participants in a discourse and the intertextual organization of the discourse. The latter is the level Foucault comes in at. In contrast, I'm shifting ground, rather as Marx does, to attend to how the latter mediates relations among those who are – as readers, writers, viewers, and so on – discursively active.

And so this chapter explores discourse as what we are part of and active in, including, of course, what we use to think, write, and interpret others' texts with, since these are *the local practices of the discourse*. In a sense, I want to lift the discourse off the page and pull it into life; I want to step outside the artifice of the text's stasis and rediscover discourse as an actually happening, actually performed, local organization of consciousness.

In this I am helped by Bakhtin's differentiation between utterances in and of direct encounters between people and those mediated by texts. The latter he calls 'secondary speech genres' (Bakhtin 1986), a term that corresponds closely to Foucault's concept of 'discourse' and to my usage of the latter term here. For Bakhtin, speech genres 'originate' in 'spheres of activity':

All the diverse areas of human activity involve the use of language. Quite understandably, the nature and forms of this use are just as diverse as are the areas of human activity. This, of course, in no way disaffirms the national unity of language. Language is realized in this form of individual concrete utterances (oral and written) by participants in the various areas of human activity. These utterances reflect the specific conditions and goals of each such area not only through their content (thematic) and linguistic style, that is, the selection of the lexical, phraseological, and grammatical resources of the language, but above all through their compositional structure. All three of these aspects – thematic content, style, and compositional structure – are inseparably linked to the *whole* of the utterance and are equally determined by the specific nature of the particular sphere of communication. Each separate utterance is individual, of course, but each sphere in which language is used develops its own *relatively stable types* of these utterances. These we may call *speech genres*. (Bakhtin 1986: 60; original emphases)

The concept of 'speech genres' reflects a textual separation of utterances from locally situated speakers and writers, hearers and readers. It is from the standpoint of the already 'in-text' that speech genres appear as distinct from 'spheres of activity.' Secondary speech genres/discourses are also just as much spheres of activity as the speech genre of pickpockets (Maurer 1981).

Precipitated out of its textual security, sociology is a sphere of activity. Sociologists are reading, writing, teaching, learning sociology; going to conferences and listening to sociologists; worrying about their sociological competitors; getting together in departments to defend the sociological enterprise against administrative marauders and upstart theoretical factions; participating in networks, orienting to leaders, deciding who's in and who's out. All this is not apart from its texts, for its texts are 'activated' in these activities as local events coordinating the local practices of this sociologist here with those of others, most of whom appear to her only as virtual participants of discourse.

Sociology's Dialogic

I have written of texts as 'active' (Smith 1990b). I mean to see them as being like speakers in a conversation; that is, though deprived of the possibility of hearing and responding to us, as nonetheless present and active in 'speaking' to us as our reading activates them. Our reading operates the text; in our reading, it becomes active. The artifice of the text detaches it from the local historicity of living and activity, or seems to do so. But its making was work done in actual settings by one or more people and as part of a course of action, whether of an individual, a group, an organization of some kind, or of an extended social relation concerting the activities of many. And its reading also is in time and in an actual place, and enters again into someone's course of action and has, in that course of action, a speaking part; it becomes active in that course of action. Just so, sociological texts are active in sociological discourse.

Bakhtin, in theorizing language and the novel, insists that the meanings of words have already been given determination as they have been used in multiple local settings; they enter local utterances trailing meaning from the past, 'tasting,' to use Bakhtin's term, of the settings and intentions of their use elsewhere and elsewhen:

As a living, socio-ideological concrete thing, as heteroglot opinion, language, for the individual consciousness, lies on the borderline between oneself and the other. The word in language is half someone else's. It becomes 'one's own' only when the speaker populates it with his own intention, his own accent, when he appropriates the word, adapting it to his own semantic and expressive intention. Prior to this moment of appropriation, the word does not exist in a neutral and impersonal language (it is not, after all, out of a dictionary that the speaker gets his words!), but rather it exists in other people's mouths, in other people's contexts, serving other people's intentions: it is from there that one must take the word, and make it one's own. (Bakhtin 1981: 294)

To speak or write is thus always essentially dialogic. A given utterance (Bakhtin's general term comprises both speech and writing) is intrinsically dialogic in its reworking of terms that have already been given determinate, if essentially transitory, meaning elsewhere and elsewhen in the utterances of others. And it contributes prospectively to what others may be able to say elsewhere and elsewhen down the line.

Bakhtin's theory of the novel builds on this notion of dialogue. Our everyday use of language appropriates, for what we want to get done, meanings determined by a multiplicity of contexted utterances. Of course, these aren't unique to individuals. Bakhtin stresses language as a property of groups and relations. Styles of usage are established among groups or forms of organization, professions, bureaucracy, trades, social circles, social movements, generations, regions, and so on. The novel's distinctive project draws such speech genres into a dialogue within the text. Its themes orchestrate diverse speech genres, bringing them into dialogic relations with one another. Dialogue is present not only in the overall thematic organization of the novel. The dialogic thematic organization is worked out, in and worked into, specific passages and even sentences. The diversity of voices in dialogue is not only in the representation of different voices as speakers in the text, and in reported speech, but in hybrid sentences in which the author's voice draws in and subdues another's speech, in irony where the author's voice reflects on others, and in movements between one voice and another in narrative sequences so that one reflects on (is in dialogue with) another.

In Bakhtin's thinking, the novel as a literary form is of and embedded in a society of diverse forms of speaking and writing. The many voices of the society are the resources on which the novel-writer draws. She relies on them and determines how they will be presented in the order of the text. Their dialogic forms and relations (tensions, conflicts, hierarchies) are at her disposal, to be given determinate thematic value in the text she creates. Her text creates a new dialogic ordering among the speech genres of the society.

Sociology, too, is embedded in the heteroglossia of a diverse society. Sociology, too, relies on and writes into its texts and hence draws into its discourse (as the text-mediated conversation among sociologists) a diversity of voices. It relies on the same resources as the novel does; indeed, sociologists have recognized this kinship, though not knowing quite what to do with it. Perhaps we should be writing novels rather than sociology; some sociologists have written novels (Harvey Swados, for example); some have thought novels are a better form of sociology than sociology itself. Sociology draws into the discourse, covertly or explicitly, the social organization carried by the 'speech genres' of the people who have been its object or resource. It brings into the text, though not necessarily explicitly, not just a language but a linkage back into the 'sphere of activity' in which the language originated.

Imagine sociologists reading newspapers, magazines, novels, poetry, biographies, history, and watching television, and going to see films, as well as doing our proper sociological reading. We participate in the multi-discoursed relations of ruling and are competent practitioners of the speech genre bearing the social organization of our place of work. There is constant leakage from the multi-voiced society in which we do our work into our sociological work. More than that, however, is the discourse's necessary dialogue with its subject matter. It is full of voices, though often they are unrecognizable as such because, before they even arrive at the threshold of sociology, they have already been transformed into textual products, for example, in the demographic data produced by the state census procedures or the legally mandated procedures for registering births, deaths, and marriages, and so forth. The dialogic of the interchange between state and the people who are the originals of the data enters sidling into the sociological text. Sociologists listen to conversations and, after converting them into texts as tape- or video-recorded voices and then as written transcripts, analyse them; we talk to people out there in what we call the 'real world' in contradistinction to the world we generate in our texts, which is not real; we ask them questions and bring their answers home with us to build representations of those with whom we spoke. Some script the dialogue between sociology and respondent so that the latter's voice is heard only as a refraction of the sociological discourse; other methods, such as oral history or ethnography, expose the sociologist to the native speaking of society, leaving it for her later work, after she's brought her notes, recordings, and recollections back to home or office, to subdue the original genres abstracted from their sphere of activity to the magisterial language of the discipline. Within sociological texts themselves, we find traces and presences of diverse voices: passages quoted from interviews, passages from field notes giving accounts of what was said and done on a particular occasion, texts of a variety of kinds used for what the sociologist thinks they might be able to tell her about what was on the other side of the text in the 'real world.'[2] Recommendations and prescriptions for how to regulate these dialogues appear in the endless publications on methods of 'qualitative' research.

Sociology's dialogic has the potential for eroding from within the discursive coherence on which sociology's existence *as a discipline* depends. The speech genres drawn into its texts carry their own intentions, perspectives, experience, and social organization:

... there are no 'neutral' words and forms – words and forms that can belong to 'no one'; language has been completely taken over, shot through with intentions and accents. For any individual consciousness living in it, language is not an abstract system of normative forms but rather a concrete heteroglot conception of the world. All words have the 'taste' of a profession, a genre, a tendency, a party, a particular work, a particular person, a generation, an age group, the day and hour. Each word tastes of the context and contexts in which it has lived its socially charged life; all words and forms are populated by intentions. Contextual overtones (generic, tendentious, individualistic) are inevitable in the word. (Bakhtin 1981: 293)

In a sense, sociology is exposed to capture by ways of seeing and representing the world that are those of speech genres other than its own. It does not have a material technology to produce its differentiation from the world which is its object. Its tenuous separation is an achievement of its discursive order. In contrast with the novel, as Bakhtin theorizes it, its stylistics, rather than preserving the 'inserted genres' and the 'speech of characters,' have been regulated theoretically so that the diverse speech genres or voices that appear directly in the text are provided with standardized discursive frames. Dialogue is subdued to the monologic or unitary language, a situation which Bakhtin contrasted with the dialogized interplay of voices in the novel:

Monologism, for Bakhtin, describes a condition wherein the matrix of ideological values, signifying practices, and creative impulses which constitute the living reality of language are subordinated to the hegemony of a single, unified consciousness or perspective. Whatever cannot be subsumed under this transcendent consciousness is regarded as extraneous or superfluous. (Gardiner 1992: 26)

As we have seen in chapter 4, Durkheim's constitutional rules for sociology specifically suppress the presence of actual people, whose activities *are* 'the types of conduct or thought [that] are not only external to the individual but are, moreover, endowed with coercive power, by virtue of which they impose themselves upon him, independent of his individual will' (Durkheim 1964: 2). Constitutional rules of one kind or another objectify sociology's phenomena, producing a discursive universe in which the people's utterances and other actions can appear as if there were no actors. So far as sociology is concerned there is an ambiguity in Bakhtin's notion that monologism can displace dialogue,[3] since sociology's monologisms subdue or bury but do not do away with its necessary dialogue with other voices. Nonetheless, the notion of an *imposed* monologism suggests a regulatory device. It cannot be a particular author's since it is a monologism standardized for a discourse rather than an individual and adopted by individual participants of the discourse as a 'single, unified consciousness or perspective' (Gardiner op. cit.) that all know how to practise as their sociological competence. This device, I suggest, is sociological theory.[4]

As a regulatory device, sociological theory subordinates the intentions and perspectives of the original speakers to the 'order of discourse' (Foucault 1981) managing sociology's intra-textual dialogues and supplanting the original intentions of the 'subjects' with an authorized system of discursive intentions. It standardizes the local interpretive practices of its participants and sets up a unitary organization of subject positions determining how the reading sociologist (or other reader) can enter into the dialogic relations of the text. The regulatory work of sociology's theoretical vocabulary can be seen in the following two examples. The first is from a paper by Hilary Graham and Ann Oakley (1981) called 'Competing Ideologies of Reproduction: Medical and Maternal Perspectives on Pregnancy' (discussed previously in chapter 4). Two different and conflicting 'perspectives' on childbirth are described, that of obstetricians and that of women in childbirth:

Specifically, our data suggest that mothers and doctors disagree on whether pregnancy is a natural or a medical process and whether as a consequence, pregnancy should be abstracted from the woman's life-experiences and treated as an isolated medical event. (Graham and Oakley 1981: 56)

Obstetricians and patients are not observed arguing with one another. The conflicts are 'between medical and maternal frames of reference' (ibid.). The 'perspectives' or 'frames of reference' are constructed *in the text* from rather different kinds of materials: the obstetricians' are inferred from observations obtained during consultations with patients;[5] the mothers,' on the other hand, from extensive open-ended interviews – the respondents speaking directly to the researchers. The theory of ideology that defines the paper's topic frames a lower-level set of categories – 'perspective,' 'frame of reference,' and so on. These, in turn, transform the original stuff of observations and interviews into expressions of ideology. Utterances recorded from the original setting are cited as 'manifestations' (ibid.) of an underlying reality.

The second example is Eric Rothenbuhler's (1990) interpretation of the 1912 strike in Lawrence, Massachusetts (organized by the International Workers of the World), as ritual. Here theory manages the conflicting voices by differentially privileging one and suppressing the other. Rothenbuhler quotes from a newspaper editorial written during the strike. Here is part of it:

Are we to expect that instead of playing the game respectfully, or else breaking out into lawless riot which we know well enough how to deal with, the laborers are to listen to a subtle anarchistic philosophy which challenges the fundamental idea of law and order, inculcating such strange doctrines as those of 'direct action,' 'sabotage,' 'syndicalism,' 'the general strike,' and 'violence'? (Rothenbuhler 1990: 68)

Rothenbuhler combines Victor Turner's (1969) analysis of rites of passage and Emile Durkheim's *The Elementary Forms of Religious Life* to produce an objectified and generalized version of this as follows:

when ... some members of a society reside in a liminal zone that is not part of that society's legitimate ritual code, their behavior cannot be meaningfully explained by the governing myths. (ibid.: 67)

Theory transposes the standpoint of the newspaper editorial into the monologic of the sociological text, elaborating theoretical categories that deprive the 'laborers,' and their organization and theory, of sense and intentionality. The subject-other relation projected in the newspaper editorial is transposed into a monologic form; its 'transcendent consciousness' (Gardiner 1992) has prior commitments to one side of a struggle between striking workers and employers.

In these examples, sociological theory is brought to bear in subduing what people have said in different actual settings to intentions projected at the level of sociological discourse. Theory is deployed to pick out and tailor extracts from the original events to appear conceptually reconstructed or as fragments of speech or writing sustaining the discursive project. The hybrid text is riddled with the dialogics in which it originates, but theory represents their fragmentary appearance at the surface of the text as its instances or expressions, assimilated to the order of discourse (Foucault 1981) and appropriated by the latter's 'transcendent consciousness' (Gardiner 1992) as its own.

Language, 'Speech Genres,' and Social Organization

Language comes to be thought as distinct from local practices of speaking, writing, hearing, and reading when technologies of print have created the conditions under which it can appear as replicable independently of particular contexts of reading or writing (see chapter 5). The abstraction of language and meaning from settings that is foundational to semiotics or semantics is, I suggest, an artifice of its textualization which separates and preserves utterances as independent of local settings and makes possible its regulation through the development of technologies of meaning, as in dictionaries and thesauruses. It is the investigation of language as possessing meaning independently of the local settings of its use that produces as a problem the ongoing historical and contextual reworking of meaning that Bakhtin emphasizes.

In general, models of meaning are grounded in this experience of language as being meaningful independently of its local practice. The artifice of the text is presupposed in lexical models that locate meaning in the coupling of word and meaning or reference, signifier and signified, even when meaning is held to arise as a function of differentiations within a system. Words/signs carry meanings around, can be carried from mouth to ear and transmitted unblemished from one mind to another. To such models, the theories of Bakhtin, V.I. Vološinov, and George Herbert Mead offer a radical contrast. Vološinov's conception is of language as essentially social, and signs as both within and external to the individual. Rather than 'communication' from one consciousness to another, language is 'inter-individual' (Vološinov 1973: 12):

> *A word is a two-sided act.* It is determined equally by *whose* word it is and *for whom* it is meant. As word, it is precisely *the product of the reciprocal relationship between speaker and listener, addresser and addressee.* Each and every word expresses the 'one' in relation to the 'other.' I give myself verbal shape from another's point of view ...
> (Vološinov 1973: 86; original emphases)

For Bakhtin also, the meaning of an utterance always arises 'two-sidedly' in particular local settings; while for George Herbert Mead, the spoken word appears between people, is heard by both, and generates the same responses in speaker and hearer – its meaning organizing the consciousness of both in the ongoing social act. For these thinkers, meaning is always relational, processual, and *two-sided.* Such a formulation is readily expanded in terms of my interests in the social as the concerting of people's activities, enabling language or, rather, speech and writing, to be explored for how they coordinate or align individual consciousnesses, hence as *organization.*

In moving away from lexical models of meaning, speech/writing (or 'utterances,' to use Bakhtin's general term for both) is conceived as projecting organization into ongoing sequences of people's activities and bringing them into an active coordination with the activities of others. To preserve this sense of utterances, language, and meaning, I have tried to use terms such as 'regulating,' 'controlling,' giving 'instructions,' and so on, that project their forward-looking, organizing capacity into local settings of people's activities.

The organizing work language will do, its selecting, ordering, assembling operations, is transferred from setting to setting. A word exists already 'in other people's mouths, in other people's contexts, serving other people's intentions' (Bakhtin 1981: 294):

Each separate utterance is individual, of course, but each sphere in which language is used develops its own *relatively stable type* of these utterances. These we may call *speech genres* ... each sphere of activity contains an entire repertoire of speech genres that differentiate and grow as the particular sphere develops and becomes more complex ... (Bakhtin 1986: 60)

The speech genres that are the dialogic ground of the novel are themselves grounded in 'spheres of activity,' scientific, literary, political, bureaucratic, occupational, regional, and so on.[6] The 'social organization' of what Bakhtin calls 'spheres of activity' is carried by the ordinary and taken-for-granted terminologies and syntactic conventions generating the utterances of the participants in those ongoing activities. Here is the source of the familiar feeling you have when you are new to a socially organized setting of not knowing quite how to speak. It is not a problem strictly of knowing the language, but rather of how to insert properly made sentences into local sequences of action (including, of course, talk and writing).

Since Bakhtin is primarily concerned with the novel, a literary form, his focus is on language. Though he sees speech genres as arising in the spheres of activity of groups of people, he is interested in the forms of language and not in its relation to the people who use it or the activity it arises in and organizes. Because he is working exclusively with textual materials (and almost exclusively with novels), he can lift out the speech genre and forget about spheres of activity. The operation is entirely within language, though, in a sense, language uses extracted from one setting are imported into another But the fictional form does not claim to represent a reality beyond itself, as sociology does. Sociology is concerned with 'forms of life' (Wittgenstein 1953) in which people are active. Whether or not these are actually its topic in any particular case, its ground is always and necessarily in the 'spheres of activity' that bring its phenomenal universe, however defined, into being. The distinctive language uses that Bakhtin calls speech genres – terminology, syntactic conventions, stylistics, and so on – carry and regenerate the social organization of groups, large-scale organizations, discourse, indeed, all forms of social life in which people together are concerting their activities in some specialized way. David Maurer's (1981) account of pickpockets' 'talk' shows us a speech genre viewed in relation to a sphere of activity:

When a professional criminal learns his occupation, as, for instance, thievery, with specialization as a pickpocket, he starts with the very specialized techniques of pocket picking in terms of a specific language. More than that, he constantly thinks of his occupation in terms of that language and discusses his work with other pickpockets in terms of their common language. In other words, his entire occupational frame of reference is both technical and linguistic, and the language is fundamental not only to the perpetuation of the craft of thievery but to its practice. (Maurer 1981: 261)

Maurer's account shows the intimate connection between learning an occupation and learning a language. He emphasizes here, and in his study of the practices and social organization of pickpockets, *Whiz Mob* (Maurer 1964), how the 'language' of thievery (surely what Bakhtin would call a speech genre) organizes a thief's activities and his (or her) working relations with others. In the study from which the above quotation is taken, Maurer has worked up his material as a lexicon of pickpockets' language. Scanning the lexicon, we can see how the terms locate categories of person in the organization of a division of the 'labour' of thievery: there is the 'mark' – focus of the pickpocket attempt; the respectably appearing 'front,' who unbuttons the mark's coat so that the 'tool' can get into the mark's inside pockets; a 'cannon broad' is a skilled and experience woman pickpocket; the 'local' will not work outside the area with which he or she is familiar. Hazards are named, including, of course, police and detectives, settings and areas are constituted in relation to the relevancies of thievery – a locality that is 'burned up' is one that has been hit so often that it is 'hot' (Maurer 1981: 234–56).

These are not just items in a lexicon; they are terms that operate as the carriers of an inter-individual organization of consciousnesses among pickpockets, constituting a shared universe of actors, practices, environment, objects, and their relations on which practitioners can draw in coordinating their work. The terms transport the sedimented experiences of previous usages into the current situations of utterance among the thieves. Language doesn't appear as if it were detached from the settings, objects, persons, and activities that it names. It coordinates the focus of the speakers' and listeners' consciousnesses in ongoing courses of action: marshalling news, passing on tips, sharing achievements and failures, telling jokes, locating known-in-common points of reference, and filling out the future projects with local detail.

We could say that the talk here 'expresses' a social organization. That would direct us to an analysis of such texts for what underlies them. We would be instructed to look for structure or organization underlying the form of words the texts contains. We could also confine our interest, as ethnomethodology's conversational analysis does, to the ordering of the talk itself. But carrying Bakhtin's line of thinking into the analysis of spheres of activity attends to how utterances generated by the relevant speech genre organize consciousnesses in courses of action. They regenerate or activate forms of coordination that have been laid down in the past and are carried in the terminology, the characteristic syntactic forms, the styles, and so on. Social organization is continually reanalysed, explicated, and elaborated in talk and writing/reading that concerts particular activities ongoingly across particular local encounters, occasions, and so on. In coordinating particular local sequences of activity among participants, utterances reaffirm, regenerate, and modify social organization as it is projected towards the next occasion of action together.

No less, then, the social organization of those spheres of activity we call a discourse. The peculiarity of a discourse is the standardization of methods of producing utterances across the multiple texts claiming membership in it; indeed, membership is claimed in part by the recognizable standardization of the methods by which such texts have been produced. Sociological theories, however various, provide for sociological discourse standardized strategies for reducing the multiple voices and speech genres of the society to monologism. A variety of theoretical enclaves have formed in sociology around competing monologisms. Sustaining the dominance of a particular standpoint as universal means excluding alternative practices of sociology's dialogue with the world full of other voices that it is its business to bring to discursive order. No one procedure for producing monologism will suffice; every one is exposed to the possibility of being unseated by what it cannot subdue.

The 'work' of sociological theory in regulating the potentially destabilizing dialogues of sociological discourse with people is a local practice of sociologists. It is at work as sociologists plan and carry out research, devising interview schedules and coding systems, and interpreting the product as they write it up for presentation or publication. It is at work also as sociologists read sociology, and hence in sociology's dialogic relationship to the unregulated intertextuality and heteroglossia of contemporary society. Reading sociology is no less a local practice than doing research. Reading is not entirely in the text, for at the point of reading, the reader both activates the text and is responding to it. Here is another dimension of the regulatory work of theory. While practices that rework, reduce, or mush the heteroglossia of our time are organized or instructed by the text, it is the reader who performs them. The following section explores observations of my own local practices of reading a passage of sociological theory and discovering theory's regulatory capacity as it organized the dialogic of my encounters with voices from other sources.

How Theory Regulates the Local Organization of Reading: Analysis of a Specimen

In this section, I report analysis and observation of my experience of reading a passage from an essay on sociology by Anthony Giddens. A footnote to the essay tells us that it was originally written for presentation to the assembled members of Cambridge University. It can be read therefore as a dialogue between sociology and the dons and fellows of Cambridge University, in which Anthony Giddens plays in a kind of ambassadorial role, acting as sociology's representative and champion. At the same time, it is written to be 'overheard,'[7] appearing in a collection entitled *Social Theory and Modern Sociology*, which admits readers as official eavesdroppers.

The ethnomethodological device of writing 'of and in settings' pre- serves ethnomethodology's insistence that activities occur in settings and canot be treated independently of them *and* that settings themselves are constituted *as* settings through members' activities. Here, the setting is sociological discourse; the activity in and of the setting, constituting it as a setting of the discourse, is reading theory. The discursive setting is sig- nalled by the title and related cues, such as the name of a well-known sociological theorist as its author. If we think of an actual local setting of reading, we can see how it becomes a setting of sociological discourse as the reader picks up the book (she bought it recently at the university bookstore or got it out of the library) and begins her conversation with it. The discourse comes into play as the reader 'activates' or 'operates' the text, deploying the methods of reading of the discursive genre in which Giddens writes. But reading, like conversation, is also two-sided; the reader's consciousness is not wholly subdued to the text; she brings her own sociological projects and concerns to the reading, as well as resources of memory and attention. As is typical of sociology, the inter- change between reader and text is not insulated from other and non- sociological speech genres / spheres of activity. Activated by a particular reader, the text provides a set of instructions organizing the reader's selections from other texts and even from the local relevancies of her life.

For the reader, so long as she is reading, the text pursues its remorse- less way, unresponsive to the impassioned marginal notes, the exclama- tion points, the question marks, the underlinings, through which the reader tries to force dialogue on it. It is untouched by the reader's part in her conversation with it. It scripts her part in the conversation, and in the order of reading, she has no choice. Yet text and reader are in dialogue, and not only at the time of actual engagement in reading the text. Dialogue may also appear as afterthoughts, supplements, additions, a return to particularly troubling passages, or connections between the dialogic of the text and other texts or talk that the reader is engaged in. This is the dialogue in which I am interested here, for when I was reading Giddens's book some while back in an apartment in Eugene, Oregon, I noticed how a particular passage occasioned a kind of argument with other things I was reading or had been reading, and how it regulated, through me, their admissibility to or implications for sociological discourse. I found the latter observation troubling and decided to investigate it.

Here is the passage:

It is intrinsic to human action that, in any given situation, the agent, as philosophers sometimes say, could have acted otherwise. However oppressively the burden of particular circumstances may weigh upon us, we feel ourselves to be free in the sense that we decide upon an action in the light of what we know about ourselves, the context of our activities and their likely outcomes. This feeling is not spurious for it is arguable that it is analytical to the concept of agency that the actor in some sense 'could have done otherwise' – or could have refrained from whatever course of action was followed. (Giddens 1987: 3)

The author has a dual role or, perhaps better, is present at different levels of the text. He is scripted, as any of us is, as participant in the 'we' to whom all these scripted determinations of subjectivity apply; he is also Anthony Giddens, major sociological theorist, whose authority has already passed from the title page to the text we read. He speaks in the magisterial voice of one who can claim to speak for sociology, even legislate for it. The magisterial voice is more than just the voice of the sociologist. He is not alone; one sentence bears an internal dialogue – a hybrid utterance to use Bakhtin's term. A proposition is started – 'It is intrinsic to human action ...' – and then interrupted to make explicit its appropriation of phraseology from philosophy for its concluding clause, the agent 'could have acted otherwise.' An intersection of discourses is signalled; a kind of collaboration in which the phraseology of another discourse is deployed to buttress the discourse *in situ*. The appeal is to a discourse that is in the business of formulating rules, principles, and procedures for thinking and inquiry for other discourses. A supplementary authority is invoked.

Our participation in the text is directly scripted. 'We' are accorded properties of consciousness: 'we feel ourselves to be free'; 'we' 'decide upon an action in the light of what we know.' As reading subject, I am entered into the text as a local course of action; I come to stand as proxy for the text; in a sense, I speak its sentences. As reader activating the text, I participate in the 'we' who 'feel ourselves to be free' and 'decide upon an action in the light of what we know.' The power of this device is such that in reading we wouldn't ordinarily stop to check out whether we do indeed feel free, and so on, or whether indeed we can be sure we know what 'feeling free' feels like. The autonomy of the subject's consciousness is surrendered to the text. [W]e feel ourselves to be free ...' establishes the application of what philosophers sometimes say to she who reads. She is /I am among those who feel free.

The subject thus positioned in the text participates in a scripted dialogue with the magisterial and positionless voice: 'We feel ourselves to be free ...' we intone, and antiphonally the magisterial voice assures us, 'This feeling is not spurious.' Our feeling is authenticated theoretically: '... it is analytical to the concept of agency that the actor ... "could have done otherwise" ...' Our textually scripted subjective states of consciousness are properly authorized.

At the time of my reading, I was on leave and had time to read eclectically and for other than strictly sociological purposes. Under the text's mapping of my consciousness, I began a dialogue between Smith as its local proxy and other texts. In the account that follows, intertextuality is transposed from its primarily literary force to explore a particular reader's local practice of dialogue among texts, escaping in this way from the stasis of the text into the lived actuality where discourse, like any other speech genre, belongs to a sphere of activity.

Here, for me, the concepts of 'agent' and 'agency,' and of 'freedom' to choose a course of action, select and collect beyond the terms of the text, hooking into other and subversive discourses. The disk head skitters over time, pulling out examples from later reading and setting up arguments against the constant and impervious text. It picks out passages from newspapers and books, and from what people say. I recall Jessie Bernard's (1973) early feminist critique of the agentic assumptions of sociology, and my use of that in reflecting on my own experience as a woman *who did not choose* (Smith 1987) or, I suppose, had chosen, a form of marriage that relinquished choice.

'We feel' locates us, readers/audience, as members of the class of human agents, summoning us to join the text's course. Yet, in retrospect,

I think the pronoun creates a rent in the text which a more impersonal form might have avoided. The formulation claims universality that the pronoun subverts. The 'we' is for anyone, but not everyone feels free. My intertextual dialogue, thinking about Giddens and reading eclectically over several days, engaged with more than one passage in which people wrote or were recorded as saying they do not feel free. In a study of women and depression, I encounter women who lacked a sense of themselves as agents: one of the women says that 'the traditional sort of role that I played in my marriage was almost like an automatic pilot' (Jack 1991: 73); another: 'Most of my feelings about what a woman is are tied directly into a man. A woman isn't anything by herself' (ibid.: 116). I remember a woman speaking in a group of 'psychiatrized' women (the self-naming of women who have been hospitalized for mental illness). She described herself as having been taught as a girl that she was *not* an agent, that she did not have the power to decide anything for herself, that she existed purely as an extension of, means to, men's doings, men's actions, men's projects. How can these women's experience be 'claimed' by this theory of human action and agency?

I had just read Marcia Dimen's experiential and analytic account of sexual domination. Giddens's text as regulator of Smith's consciousness singled out a passage that also registered as an exception. Dimen writes of 'the loss of one's sense of and wish for autonomy, as a result of processes that play on one's doubts about the reality and validity of one's self, one's perceptions, and one's values' (Dimen 1989: 37). Her experiential account is more powerful still. It begins with an incident in which she is followed by a man on the street telling her he wants to fuck her; it recounts the responses of her mother, who criticizes her manner of dress, of her father, who wants to beat the man up, of her conscience echoing many voices. An uncle, not himself blameless in such matters, tells her to ignore the man. To the last of these, she replies in the text:

My mind doesn't work as rationally as yours. How can it? My brain hears, my desire is stirred, I lose control of my body. On the street my body is theirs. I am a body on the street. Two tits and no head and a big ass. I am a walking rohrschach. My body becomes a cunt and I am sore from this semiotic rape. (Dimen 1989: 37; italics in original)

The same guide directed me to the memory of a passage in Zora Neale Hurston's *Their Eyes Were Watching God*. Nanny tells her granddaughters, 'Ah was born back due in slavery, so it wasn't for me to fulfill my dreams of whut a woman oughta be and to do' (Hurston 1986: 31–2). Slavery deprived slaves of freedom. They did not cease to be human or indeed to act. What sense of agency or freedom to choose applies here? Reading the Iranian labour newsletter that I then subscribed to, I located another instance. An article in it tells me that, under Iranian labour law, 'the worker is considered a minor and the employers as the owner of the society.' '[A]ny worker who reads this law carefully will say to himself or herself: This law considers me part of the means of production, without a tongue or will of its own' (Saber and Hekmat 1992). The law is enforced by the police and courts. The employer's will is sustained with beatings, jail, and sometimes by death. Iranian workers do not have – rather, they want – the freedom to decide.

In sum, as the text's proxy, my practices of remembering, noticing, and looking out for passages that bear upon it, that it bears upon, are organized by the theory. Though the input is argumentative, it is the text's theory as organizer of my attention and reflection that structures the intertextual dialogue.

The text provides me / the reader with instructions on how to handle instances that 'come to mind' of people who have not felt free. It is not the feeling that validates the generalization. Not any old feeling can be admitted as relevant. The parameters of admissible feelings are laid out. The theory validates feelings selectively. Some would be authorized and others discounted. As proxies acting for the text, we know how to discard the relevance to the argument of the voices of those who declare that they are not, and do not feel, free. What is validation here? It is not simply the text's work, but an implicitly dialogic aspect of the reader's work as proxy of the text. The text lays out theory's command of relevance, but the reader must assent and activate to regulate what feelings of freedom may be entered into the feeling of freedom of those who can enter the 'we' of the text. As the text's proxy, the reader is accountable to the text; she is its enforcer.

The text's trap is that its dialogue with the reader is reader-activated. In becoming the text's proxy, she takes on the text's organizing powers as her own. Just knowing how to read it enables the text to creep into her consciousness and take over (Smith 1990c) – not necessarily forcing the reader to agree with it, of course, but to adopt its organizing framework in selecting and interpreting other texts. This is the special competence of theory. Giddens's text in my consciousness singles out passages read or recalled; it also instructs me how to subdue them to it. Can it not be said of any of the instances I adduced that the 'actor in some sense "could have done otherwise" – or could have refrained from whatever course of action was followed'? An Iranian worker could choose to do otherwise and risk death. 'However oppressively the burden of particular circumstances may weight upon us, we feel ourselves to be free in the sense that we decide upon an action in the light of what we know about ourselves, the context of our activities and their likely outcomes.' Hurston's grandmother could choose within 'the context of [her] activities'; she was, after all, a slave. I have to contort the others, discounting the women with depression (they are 'ill') and treating Dimen's text as metaphor. So long as I undertake to act is its proxy, the text remains impregnable.

The cunning of the theoretical formulation provides for the problem that in none of these examples do the individuals concerned feel free. Here are people who state clearly that they do not feel free, indeed, that they are not free. How to exclude their testimony so that the text is not impugned? We have instructions for how to handle such difficulties right there in the passage I quoted. Feeling free in the text's sense cannot be equated with people's self-reporting of their feelings of freedom or unfreedom. A special sense of feeling free is put in place. It is this: 'we decide upon an action in the light of what we know about ourselves, the context of our activities and their likely outcomes.' If the likely outcome of what we choose to do is torture and death and deciding to avoid them is to accept slavery or forced labour, we have been free to make that choice. The order of the discourse imposes its interpretive authority against the authority of the voice I bring forward in contention.

Giddens has ben careful to define what feeling free might mean. While we, who feel free, are validated – *our* feeling is not 'spurious' – those who do not feel free drop outside the circle of shared subjectivity constituted in the text-reader dialogue. For within that circle, it seems that 'however oppressively the burden of particular circumstances may weigh upon [them], ... [they] could have refrained from whatever course of action was followed.'

Here is demonstrated theory's capacity to control the bolt-holes through which the meaning of other texts or voices might escape its regime. And note that the printed published text has this powerful organizing effect of making the same 'instructions' available, not just to me, but to any other reader who can activate it. Any such reader becomes its proxy. Just as I became proxy of Giddens's text in my reading, others, reading his text in his chapter may find themselves saying, as a colleague of mine did when she read a draft, 'But doesn't she see that they [my collection of other voices] don't apply?' Another might move to a larger scope of the hermeneutics of discourse to point out that I have misinterpreted the issue: Giddens surely is addressing the traditional problematic of the regional moral discourse of Western European philosophy since the Enlightenment, namely, that of free will versus determinism: 'Smith has missed the point altogether.' Here is theory at work in the social organization of discourse.

There is repression here. Whatever way I turned, my collection of stories from people who do not feel free could not engage with the text or enter the circle of authorized subjectivity it constitutes. Trained readers of such texts know how to suspend their own or others' experience when it challenges the theoretically regulated order of the text. They know how to take up instructions provided by the text to subdue the intrusive and potentially disruptive other voices. The dialogue inferior to the text offers no purchase to the challenge offered by counter-examples. They will not fit and cannot be spoken without a discursive shift, such as I'm making in this chapter, that repositions the subject outside the scope established by the theory that regulates from the original text.

Within the theory-regulated dialogic order of the text, the possibility of feeling otherwise, perhaps not free, perhaps not really feeling either one or the other, is not open. The reader who feels a disjuncture here, has also been given instructions to bracket the sources of disjuncture emerging for her from the actualities of her own life, or from her participation in other discourses. No feeling other than that prescibed is admissible to the dialogue within the text, and the reader as the text's proxy is enforcer of that rule.

It is here we find theory's part in organizing the discursive exclusions that are the local practices of monologism. I don't think Giddens would have felt comfortable telling an audience of Iranian workers that 'we feel ourselves to be free' when 'we' is intended to include them. They would be indifferent, perhaps enraged. I imagine Zora Neale Hurston's grandmother turning away in contempt and disgust too profound for rage. The cogency of Giddens's passage is at least in part sustained by the lack of disjuncture between the reader's/audience's feelings of freedom and the subjective state it assigns them. They/we do feel free, or at least don't feel strikingly unfree. 'We' (men and women of European origin and of the middle class) have no sharp history of recent slavery; we have not experienced being confined to a ghetto; 'we' who are men do not experience masculine sexualization of women's public life as a young woman might; we are not Iranian workers, and so on. Here's where an organization of class, race, and gender subtends and is written out of the text. Is agency itself as much a construction of social relations as subject is of discourse?

The override clause that specifies the sense in which we feel free relies for its operation on our being able to centre ourselves where the text centres us, setting up instructions for its exclusionary work in our consciousness. It relies on the lack of specification of who this 'we' is, and on our knowing how to participate in it and adopt the enclosures it calls on us to inscribe. There is no space, operating under the text's instruction, for an alternative 'we' offering a contentious identity. The stylistics of theory universalize, and she or he can find no ground within the text enabling her/his speech. The participant as text's proxy adopts its instructions for her local practices of inclusion and exclusion. And she is not alone. Others, also readers of the theoretical texts, are observing the same boundaries. Our local practices of interpretation are, in this fashion, coordinated across the multiple local settings in which sociological discourse is realized as such.

I notice retrospectively that this passage of sociological theory could subdue these divergent voices only because I treated its unitary standpoint as mine. It, rather than any one of them, was the effective authority in my local practice of reading. Sociological theory is one of a family of discursive practices which shares with other 'institutional processes' characteristic terminologies that have the capacity 'to operate on an account of experience in such a way that it can be seen as an expression of, or as documenting, that institutional process' (Smith 1990c: 154) or, in this case, that theory. Theory coordinates the local practices of sociological discourse, aligning the practical exercise of consciousnesses of participants. Perspectives and voices presenting alternative standpoints are subdued to expressions or examples of the theoretical reading. The stylistics of universality are preserved against the threat of fragmentation and disorder, a threat sociology cannot evade in its dialogue with society. All this, of course, is the work of participants in the discourse who take up the theory as regulator, making its monologic organization of dialogue their own.

I did not know when I started on this analysis that I was going to discover how a passage such as this may inscribe as its hidden subject a white, male-dominant European intelligentsia. I discovered it in finding out how I operated it to exclude its defining others. There is no strident assertion of whiteness of masculinity. Rather, being white and male emerges as complementary to the others whose voices it excludes: it is the not-female, not-African-American, not-Iranian worker. The subtextual subject is constituted in the reader's theory-governed dialogue with the various voices threatening its claim to universality. Here theory can be seen in action as regulator of sociology's dialogue with other voices, inhibiting their capacity to intrude and disrupt the consolidation of a unitary 'we' among members of a discourse.

Discussion

In my introduction to this collection of papers (chapter 1), I wrote of the ontology of the social I have come to work with and of how this breaks with the ontologies in which activities or practices appear on one side and beliefs, concepts, ideologies, knowledge, theory, and so on, on the other. Recognizing the latter also as activities or practices pulls them into the same space of investigation as, say, conversations or local work organization. My interest in this chapter has been to explore further the ways in which sociological theory organizes and defines the sociological project, and in particular its political force in regulating the discourse, a force very clearly declared in Jeffrey Alexander's argument in support of the teaching of the 'founding fathers' of sociology: a classic, he tells us, 'establishes the fundamental criteria in the particular field' (Alexander 1995: 22), and he cites the Bible and the works of Shakespeare as instances. But I have also been interested in developing further the project of bringing discourse into the space of readers' and writers' (and researchers') everyday living, since it's here that discourse happens. Of course, any research project could be investigated as Bruno Latour and Steve Woolgar (1986) investigated laboratory life, but though they 'observed' reading, reading itself as a local activity coordinate with the laboratory's work escaped.

I do not mean to produce an ethnography of reading as such since I am interested in reading as it brings a pre-given form of words, standardized from reader to reader, into the social organization of people's activities. I am interested in making it part of an exploration of what in chapter 5 I described as the 'ruling relations,' among them the relations of discourse. I follow Bakhtin (1986a) in recognizing discourse or what he calls secondary speech genres as 'spheres of activity.' Perhaps rather grandiosely, I have proposed, elaborating on George Herbert Mead's examination of symbolic communication, a rather different way of writing about how words, language, speech, writing mean that attends to how they are active in coordinating consciousness and projecting organization into what comes next. This gives me ways of conceiving texts as entering actively into the organization of a reader's attention, memory, direction, and so on, both as specifically instructed by the text and beyond it.

In exploring my own experience of deploying a piece of theoretical text in argument with other texts, I have been exploring a discourse as what Bakhtin call a sphere of activity. It is explored, not as statements, but as actual practices that are organized as and into a discourse across local settings. Sociology has as deep a dialogic ground as Bakhtin has argued for the novel. This is *in* its texts (as we have seen), in the making of its texts, and in their reading. My interest has been in exploring theory as it regulates the order of discourse. What I discovered had not been previsaged. Analysis of the kind I have done here discovers beyond what the researcher knows before she starts. I learned in the process just how the particular text I had chosen blocked any avenue I could discover of making it responsive to those whose voices I used to interrogate it.

I did not intend an irony in drawing on pickpocketing to provide an example of a sphere of activity and the speech genre that organizes it. I know it was, in part, because I had admired David Maurer's study of pickpockets through their language. At the same time, as is so often the case, there is a kind of inner logic in the choice of metaphor. I see, in the retrospect of writing this concluding section, that I have displayed a sociology that has found ways of appropriating others' voices for 'its' own uses without being accountable to them. Of course, I don't mean here the ordinary professional practice of ethical research. I mean what goes on at the level of the text and how the text is written. Here is theory's role in the appropriation of others' voices and in reducing the essential dialogic character of the society to the monologic of the order of its discourse (Foucault 1981).

In exploring my local practices of reading and reflecting on a piece of Giddens's text, I learned something of the power of a theoretical text to insulate the discourse against subversive voices. Though I could set up an argument with it, I could not make a place for them in it. At every turn, their experience had to be denied. You could choose the theoretical text or choose those voices, but there was no way in. Oddly enough, the very conception of agency that rescues the scholars of Cambridge from feeling that they are somehow pushed around by society and claims for anyone some kind of autonomy as a subject vis-à-vis the determinations of structure, fails at a critical juncture, namely, in its capacity to recognize people as subjects speaking for themselves.

Earlier in this chapter, I described how Rothenbuhler's (1990) theoretical moves replicate monologically a standpoint in the ruling class of the Eastern United States in 1912, constituting the striking workers as an other beyond understanding. I originally read this paper during the same period of residence in Eugene during which I was reading Giddens. I had time then to go to the University of Oregon library and read up on the extensive IWW literature from that period. The voices of people active in the struggle are strong and immediate. People are named and known. They argued and fought with one another as well as fighting against a ruling class. They sang; they spoke on street corners; they went to jail; they lived in camps and travelled on the rails. Here was another dialogue I could have written, bringing their voices to bear on Rothenbuhler's theoretical gloss. But again, the order of discourse would have gone unmarred and unmarked by my argument on their behalf. The use of theory to circumscribe a standpoint and export it to the discourse as its order is obvious here, but no less present in the extract from Giddens with which I worked.

I do not imagine you can have a sociology without standpoint or interests. Rather, the sociology making inquiry into the social as people bring it into being its central project is necessarily in explicit dialogue with them and is necessarily exposed to being changed by that dialogue. Theory, rather than insulating such a discovering discourse from the voices of others, must be seen rather as providing what is good to think with, at least until we find something that does better.

8

The Standard North American Family: SNAF as an Ideological Code[1]

Introduction

Traditional social science has viewed the ruling relations (see chapter 5) as discrete forms or units of organization – state, bureaucracy, formal organization, mass communications, science, popular culture, etc. But their evolution has produced an increasingly coordinated complex, forming a system or field of relations occupying no particular place, but organizing local sites articulated to it. Since the relations of this complex are based in and mediated by texts, important functions of coordination are performed by ideologies, concepts, theories, and the like, that insert their ordering capacities into specialized sites operating otherwise independently. Ideologies, concepts, and theories generate texts (Smith 1990b) and constitute their internal organization; they regulate intertextuality (as we saw in the previous chapter) and interpret texts at sites of reading. Texts generated in different settings – for example, government systems of collecting statistics, social scientific research in universities and think-tanks, policy making in government, and mass media – are coordinated conceptually, producing an internally consistent picture of the world and providing the terms of policy-talk and decisions.

This chapter explores how what I am going to call an 'ideological code' coordinates multiple sites within the intersecting relations of public text-mediated discourses and large-scale organization. Its problematic originates in a reflexive treatment of the experience of doing research on women's work as mothers in relation to their children's schooling. The course of that research, including problems that arose, alerted Alison Griffith and myself (Griffith 1995; Griffith and Smith 1987, 1990a, 1990b) to discursive schemata operating in our own experience of being single parents, in our research problematic drawn from that, our interview design, and the sense-making practices of interviewers and respondents. Opening up this topic as an exploration of the local practices of research links with my concern to explore text-mediated discourse as social relations coordinating multiple local historical sites and the locally bound activities of actual people.

Conceive of discourses that are mediated by texts (I shall call these T-discourses), not as culture, meanings, significations or chains of significations, or texts without located readers, but as skeins of social relations, mediated and organized textually, connecting and coordinating the activities of actual individuals whose local historical sites of reading/hearing/viewing may be geographically and temporally dispersed and institutionally various. My notion of T-discourse goes beyond Foucault's (1972) conception of discourse as a conversation mediated by texts, to include how actual people take them up, the practices and courses of actions ordered by them, and how they coordinate the activities of one with those of another or others. People enter into practices ordered by the texts of the T-discourse and are active participants in its relations.[2] We enter into and participate in such relations in ordinary and unthinking ways. For example, describing someone as mentally ill catches a local moment into the discursive relations organized by psychiatry.[3]

Prevailing cultural theory disconnects culture from its actual practitioners other than as the latter are conceived as expressions of subject positions generated discursively. By contrast, here a T-discourse is conceived as a system of virtual relations coordinating, ordering, hooking up, the activities of individuals in multiple local historical sites.

T-discourses organize; they are also socially organized. There are, for example, complex relations knitting the T-discourse of sociology to multiple professional, policy, and political discourses. The concepts and schemata of such discourses are subdued to a sociological discourse that evolves lumpily and unevenly as its capacity is strained by shifts at the level of ruling practice and of the institutional order. The eclectic character of the program of the annual meetings of the American Sociological Association displays some of these multiple connections of sociology.

This paper proposes that there are 'ideological codes' that order and organize texts across discursive sites, concerting discourse focused on divergent topics and sites, often having divergent audiences, and variously hooked into policy or political practice. This ordering and organizing of texts is integral to the coordination and concerting of the complex of evolving T-discourses.

I am using the term 'ideological code' as an analogy to 'genetic code.' Genetic codes are orderings of the chemical constituents of DNA molecules that transmit genetic information to cells, reproducing in the cells the original ordering. By analogy, an 'ideological code' is a schema that replicates its organization in multiple and various sites. I want to make clear that an 'ideological code' in this sense is not a determinate concept or idea, though it can be expressed as such. Nor is it a formula or a definite form of words. Rather it is a constant generator of *procedures for selecting syntax, categories, and vocabulary in the writing of texts and the production of talk and for interpreting sentences*, written or spoken, ordered by it. An ideological code can generate the same order in widely different settings of talk or writing – in legislative, social scientific, and administrative settings, in popular writing, television advertising, or wherever.

The Standard North American Family (hereafter SNAF) is an ideological code in this sense. It is a conception of The Family as a legally married couple sharing a household. The adult male is in paid employment; his earnings provide the economic basis of the family-household. The adult female may also earn an income, but her primary responsibility is to the care of husband, household, and children. The adult male and female may be parents (in whatever legal sense) of children also resident in the household.[4] Note the language of typification – 'man,' 'woman' – and the use of the atemporal present. This universalizing of the schema locates its function as ideological code. It is not identifiable with any particular family; it applies to any. A classic enunciation of the code can be found in George Murdock's use of files containing summaries of ethnographic data accumulated by anthropologists from different parts of the world to establish the universality of the nuclear family (Murdock 1949). The nuclear family is a theorized version of SNAF. Characteristically, Murdock was able to generate its distinctive form even when ethnographic descriptions contradicted it. Even when the nuclear family is not the 'prevailing form,' it is 'the basic unit from which more complex familial forms are compounded.' It is 'always recognizable' (Murdock 1949: 2).

Sociobiology deploys SNAF in a similar way:

The building block of nearly all human societies is the nuclear family. The populace of an American industrial city, no less than a band of hunter-gatherers in the Australian desert, is organized around this unit. In both cases the family moves between regional communities, maintaining complex ties with primary kin by means of visits (or telephone calls and letters) and the exchange of gifts. During the day the women and children remain in the residential area while the men forage for game or its symbolic equivalent in the form of money. (Wilson 1978: 553)

In this passage, SNAF-ordered terms, sentences, and sequences of sentences synthesize accounts of hunting-and-gathering forms of society and of the contemporary United States. The ideological code generates a common ordering into which descriptive elements from very different societies can be inserted.

SNAF is also foundational to contemporary economic theories of the family. These include the theories of neo-classical economists such as Gary Becker, whose model of the family has a 'head' who 'transfers general purchasing power to all other members because he cares about their welfare' (he is the altruist and they are beneficiaries) as well as Marxist theories of the family, which have been equally committed to SNAF.

We can contrast SNAF-ordered discourse with other representations of family. Rayna Rapp (1978) wrote a sharp critique of it from a feminist standpoint. Carol Stack's (1974) ethnography of the kin relations in an African-American neighbourhood describes kin relations that cross household boundaries and connect people in ways that can't be described in SNAF-generated descriptions. For example, women may have children with more than one father, all of whom maintain their relationship to their children; kin terms are extended to those connected in networks of reciprocal support and exchange; and 'daddies' and 'mommas' may be identified by the care they have provided a child and not by legal status. Jaber Gubrium and James Holstein (1990) have sought a total dissolution of SNAF, exploring the many and various uses of the notion of family in varying contexts and for diverse purposes, individual and collective – talk among people about themselves and their relationships with others (not exclusively 'blood' kin), among people in health-care or judicial settings, and more. Their book defies the reader to find a determinate unit corresponding to the concept of The Family. Though such initiatives may in the long run prevail,[5] they are at present marginal to the ubiquity of SNAF. Indeed, the latter is often preserved in the identification of deviant instances, such as 'female-headed families.' SNAF-defined non-intact families appear to be female-headed families only. The single male-headed family does not appear to be defined as deviant by SNAF. It seems likely that this is because the SNAF code will not generate a male-headed family. It simply falls outside what SNAF 'knows' how to 'order.'

I have stressed above the potential ubiquity of ideological codes. They operate to coordinate multiple sites of representation. Two examples of the operation of SNAF as an ideological code are examined here. Many could be found. They exhibit different ways in which the ideological code operates. The first examines the structuring effect of SNAF in organizing research done by Alison Griffith and myself on the work mothers do in relation to their children's schooling; the second, its effect in William Julius Wilson's *The Truly Disadvantaged: The Inner City, the Underclass, and Public Policy* (1987).

Researching Women's Work as Mothers

When Alison Griffith and I started research concerned with the work mothers do in relation to their children's schooling, we began by talking about our experiences as single parents in relation to our children's schools. Indeed, over a period of two or three years before we decided to undertake the research, we had shared confidences, complaints, miseries, and guilt arising from this relation. Our more systematic discussion resulted in our formulating our problem as that of being, vis-à-vis the school, 'defective families,' families that somehow didn't match up to the parental roles defined as proper by the professional ideology of the school system. We decided that in order to understand how our kind of family was defective, we needed to know more about how the 'normative' or 'intact' family, to use Wilson's (1987) term, worked in relation to the school. We wanted to learn more about the relation between the 'normative family' and the school, and to focus on the work that women in such families were doing in relation to their children's schooling, and perhaps also for the school.

We began, as feminism recommends, from our own experience and worked with some of the notions I've put forward about the everyday world as problematic (Smith 1987). Hence the relevancies of our study were not structured by sociological or educational theory. At the same time, as our work progressed, we became increasingly aware of the ordinary ways in which our thinking and our telling of experience were structured by text-mediated discourse. Telling experience 'naturally' makes use of the speech genres (Bakhtin 1986) of the setting in which experience is being told. Our interest in schools, our own experience, and our feminist concerns with women's unwaged work were embedded in T-discourses. These T-discourses are SNAF-infected through and through. So, therefore, was our research, as gradually became visible to us at a number of points; one being, of course, that our selection of families to interview was SNAF-governed. We confounded the ideological code with the working realities of families in seeking a sample of intact families, as if we could find the logic of the code in the socially organized relations of intact families to the school[6] or treat them as manifestations of the normative form. This was to operate with the same ordering procedure as George Murdock used in his SNAF-governed extraction of nuclear families from the Yale Human Relations Area Files.

We learned painfully, and sometimes too late to rectify in our 'data collection,' that our thinking and research plans were deeply structured by what we have come to call the mothering discourse (Griffith and Smith 1987). Mothering discourse in North America developed historically during the first two decades of the twentieth century. It was and is actively fed by research and thinking produced by psychologists and specialists in child development and is popularly disseminated in women's magazines, television programs, and other popular media. An important aspect of it is directed towards 'managing' women's relation to their children's schooling, enlisting their work and thought in support of the public educational system. Women, particularly middle-class women, were much involved in the early development of this discourse. As housewives and mothers, they continued to participate in the school-mother T-discourse, reading women's magazines and books on child development and child rearing, and deriving guidance, ideas, standards, and schemata for interpreting themselves, their children, and the relationship between what they might be doing and their children's success in school (Griffith and Smith 1987). Though what Alison and I call mothering discourse is not reduceable to SNAF, it is through and through SNAF-ordered, and indeed may have been, historically, among the carriers that generalized SNAF throughout English-speaking North America.

The extent of SNAF invasion of our study is disturbing, given that Alison's thesis had studied the ideology of the single-parent family in the educational context (Griffith 1984, 1995). She had explored the creation in child development and social psychological discourse of effects of the single-parent (female-headed) families on children, showing how they provide for teachers procedures for reading back from what can be observed in the classroom to the defective family.[7] She had also shown how the concept operates in educational administration, in the professional formulations of teachers, and in the news media. Yet when we embarked on our study, we failed to register the extent to which our thinking and research design were organized by the mothering discourse and by conceptions of the Standard North American Family. This is one of the reasons for introducing the notion of an ideological code. What I am calling 'ideological codes' are not necessarily committed to a determinate set of categories or conceptual system, or a determinate content. The code reproduces its *organization* in the discursive texts (including, of course, our interviews) without necessarily being manifested in the use of specific terms. For example, we never thought of, may even have consciously avoided, concepts such as the 'nuclear family.' The discourse on mothering that has flourished in North America since the 1920s is SNAF-ordered; so also is the complementary discourse on family of professional educators; sociological research in education such as James Coleman's (Coleman et al. 1966) is also through and through SNAF-structured; and so was our research.

The school-mother T-discourse lays the primary responsibility for the individual child's school achievement and even his/her success as an adult on the family. SNAF enables interpretation in practical settings to translate 'family' into the mother. The 'intact' family means that the child's mother is available to do the work for the school that is done invisibly in the home. As Griffith (1984) showed for the ideology of the single-parent family, school-mother T-discourse provides for schools and teachers a 'documentary' method of reading back from a child's behaviour in school to its cause in the family; and from a knowledge of family problems to an interpretation of the child's behaviour in school. The documentary method of interpretation (Mannheim 1971) is a circular process. What we see and hear is interpreted in relation to an underlying pattern or schema; the underlying pattern or schema selects and orders the way we attend to things and hence what we see and hear.[8] The school-mother T-discourse worked both ways. Both Alison and I (and presumably other mothers) and the teachers, counsellors, and principals of our children's schools knew how to operate this interpretive circle. We (Alison and I) were viewed at school as defective families; defective families produce defective children; any problem our children might have at school indexed the defective family as its underlying interpreter; we were always guilty. SNAF coordinated our relation to school, the school's relation to us, the school's relation to our children. And children learn SNAF from children's readers. As my small son said one day, arriving home from school: 'There's something awfully wrong with our family.'

In retrospect, the SNAF-structuring of our own experience in being single parents for our children's schools was a powerful effect in our research. Our interest in how SNAF-conforming families worked with the school originated in our experience of being, vis-à-vis the school our children attended, defective families. This is a classic SNAF procedure of reading. Here, of course, we return to where Alison and I started our research, now recognizing what we did not recognize in designing our interview topics: namely, the operation of the school-mother T-discourse in the interview design. Topics such as the typicality of the school day, how mothers kept track of their children's homework, what part they played in school activities, and so forth – these were generated by our ordinary competence in the school-mother T-discourse. Our own participation in this T-discourse and how it had organized our inventory of interview topics only became visible to us rather late in the game and accidentally (Griffith and Smith 1987).

SNAF was perhaps most obviously at work when our interviews addressed women's employment. We and most of the women to whom we talked took for granted, at least for the purposes of the interview, that employment outside the home was not 'standard' for women with small children. Respondents who did work outside the home were careful to describe how they provided for childcare or the exceptional economic situation that required them to do this. The interviewers (there were three, Alison, myself, and a graduate student) were sometimes very tentative in asking the woman about her employment, taking care, as in the following instance, to 'normalize' working outside the home:

I: O.K. so the first thing that we want to start talking about is ... because what we are finding is that some mothers work outside the home part-time, some full-time and some don't work outside the home, and so we can just sort of start with a background and then move on. So have you ever worked outside the home?

SNAF is very much at work here. An account of women working outside the home that normalizes it in terms of what other women do, recognizes that paid employment for women with small children *is a deviation* from the normative intact family. The introduction to the question, redefining employment outside the home as normal, responds implicitly to the SNAF ordering that defines it as deviant.

The SNAF effect was not confined to the design of our study. Many, if not most, of the women we interviewed also operated with the interpretive schema of the mother-school discourse. They oriented to the very interpretive schemata that we used in writing our questionnaire and interpreting their answers. Our questions and our responses to their answers would demonstrate to them our interpretive competence in the (documentary) method they themselves used, and we would find in their answers the sense that could be made as we found them as indices of it. They were practitioners in the discourse of mothering;[9] they were competent. They knew how to address and interpret their lives using the schemata of the school-mother T-discourse. Our use of open-ended interviews that focused on their work practices means that we have accounts of their work that are not wholly constrained or reduced by SNAF. And, of course, we have been committed to explicating the actual ways in which mothers' work vis-à-vis the school is organized, so that our presuppositions are subject to challenge from the actuality. Nonetheless, it has meant that our analysis of our interview data (both questions and responses) has had to take up how it is ordered by the school-mother discourse and the SNAF code operating within it.

SNAF as a Reading of the African-American Family

In his study of the poverty and problems of African-Americans in the inner cities of the United States, William Julius Wilson (1987) distinguishes between 'intact' families and those that are not intact. SNAF-governed descriptions of families represent families lacking an adult male head as deviant from the normative intact family with a male head. Wilson's non-intact families are 'female-headed.'

Wilson argues, in opposition to earlier sociological work on the African-American family, that the non-intact family supposed to characterize the African-American population in the United States is not the result of slavery, nor a survival of a traditional family form, nor an effect of welfare policies. Rather, it is the result of poverty caused by unemployment among African-American men. 'In the early twentieth century the vast majority of both black and white low-income families were intact' (Wilson 1987: 90). The disproportionate concentration of female-headed, non-intact families in the African-American population is an effect of the relatively greater difficulty African-American men have had in finding employment. 'Given their disproportionate concentration among the poor in America, black families were more strongly affected by these conditions [poverty, high rates of mortality among black men, need of men to travel in search of jobs] and therefore were more likely than white families to be female-headed' (ibid.: 64). The 'good' intact family is damaged by 'bad' conditions. The SNAF code is the key textual structuring device. The movement from a majority of intact to a majority of female-headed families in the African-American population in the United States, is interpreted as a movement from a normal to a deviant or damaged form. A theory of male dominance in family and economy is imported into the analysis without being enunciated. SNAF does its quiet work behind the scenes, generating concepts such as the 'intact' family, with the 'female-headed family' as its deviant form.

The code operates to suppress alternative structuring devices that might, for example, treat men and women in parallel ways; for example, in the context of discussions of unemployment and poverty. When SNAF rules, its constitutive gender differentiation is operative in the text. Wilson's section on the twentieth-century emergence of increasing proportions of defective ('female-headed') families in the African-American population addresses women exclusively. The SNAF code, operating as a set of conventions selecting vocabulary as well as relations posited syntactically, selects women as protagonists of the decline of the intact and the increase in the non-intact female-headed family. Men who separate from their wives disappear from view. Stack's (1974) data might suggest that they continue to have an ongoing relationship with their children, but we do not know. Even when it would be equally appropriate to insert men into the sentences, women are preferred: 'Whereas white women are far more likely to be divorced than separated, black women are more likely to be separated than divorced. Indeed, a startling 22 percent of all married black women are separated from their husbands' (Wilson 1987: 68). The sentence could just as well have been written thus: 'Whereas white men are far more likely to be divorced than separated, black men are more likely to be separated than divorced,' and so on. SNAF ordering procedures govern the selection of women rather than men as the protagonists. By contrast, the section on the contribution made by unemployment to the erosion of the intact family among African-Americans addresses men almost exclusively. The contribution that African-American women's problems of unemployment and low-paid work makes to African-American poverty is not a focus.

In consolidating the SNAF-ordered picture of 'the' African-American family, Wilson relies on statistical data produced by agencies such as the U.S. Bureau of Census and the National Center for Health Statistics. Though these data do not replicate the normative substance of SNAF, they preserve its order in skeletal form. Mary Romero (1992)[10] did an ethnographic study evaluating census data of undocumented immigrants in San Francisco. She compared census data already collected on people living in a census-block of some 105 units in an ethnically mixed though predominatly Hispanic neighbourhood with what she learned in a house-to-house study. Census categories and procedures misrepresented the actual household composition of people living in these units significantly. The typical distortions she describes can be understood as resulting from the application of SNAF-ordered categories, forms, and procedures to situations that were not SNAF-ordered.

The historical effects of SNAF are visible in the requirement that the skeletal equivalent of a head of household be designated. At one time, when a head of household was to be designated, preference was given to men over women. Currently one individual is designated, identified as that person in whose name a unit is owned or rented. The status of other household members must be defined relative to this person. He or she may not in fact be particularly central to the household organization. Since members of the household have to be identified in terms of their relationship to the person accorded this position, extended families sharing residence may be misrepresented. The only category available on the census form for family members who are neither spouse, child, parent, or sibling of the designated head of household would seem to be that of 'boarder.'

Romero found that in some instances, several families shared one unit. Yet only one individual can be accorded the central position, and all others must be related to her or him. Further, the numbers of categories available on the form may not be enough to record all those in residence. And since multi-family residences were in breach of municipal housing regulations (also SNAF-governed?), landlords, fearing that the census data might somehow leak out to the municipal housing authorities, might intervene in filling out census forms to ensure that each unit was represented as inhabited by only one family. Such SNAF-designed data-collection devices generate a representation of the population that reproduces SNAF. I do not mean by this that non-intact families, for example, are represented as intact. Rather, I mean that the data is ordered according to SNAF. Where data *can* be ordered according to SNAF, it will be so ordered; where it cannot, *SNAF ordering generates deviant cases*, as it does for Wilson. Other dimensions of kin relations, such as those described by Stack (1974), wholly escape the census categories and never come into view.

The empirical ground that Wilson relies on is not ethnographic. It is largely census data or data from other government agencies. The studies that he draws on and sites are similarly grounded. The empirical grounding of his argument is thus already SNAF-ordered. Consider, by contrast, a radical alternative to his SNAF-governed narrative put forward by a feminist anthropologist, Henrietta Moore. Female-headed families are not, she suggests, to be seen as the result of poverty (and hence, by implication, as damaged in some way). Drawing on her African experience, she writes: 'some women are choosing not to marry ... and ... significant numbers of married women are choosing to live separately from their husbands' (Moore 1988: 64). Such choices may also be being made by women in North America. Of course, there may be a relation between poverty and such choices. Patterns described by Carol Stack (1974) suggest a good practical economy in women's choices to have several children by different men; apparently, the child's father has an ongoing relationship with his child. Hence a household consisting of a woman with several children broadens its range of kin contacts and consequently its range of potential economic support.[11] Patterns of familial and kin relations that maximize connections among households and among kin make good sense in such conditions. Women's ability to provide for their children and themselves autonomously may be enhanced by avoiding dependence on a particular man and may participate in the relational dimensions of the community that create connections and support among households. It is only when such patterns of domestic economy are re-presented in SNAF-ordered terms that they appear as defects. The very language Wilson uses betrays the normative effect of SNAF.

A SNAF-ordered representation of the patterns described by Stack (1974) might well appear in text as an inter-generational reproduction of defective forms of family. Wilson draws on such studies to sustain his argument. For example:

Hogan and Kitagawa's analysis of the influences of family background, personal characteristics, and social milieu on the probability of premarital pregnancy among black teenagers in Chicago indicates that those from nonintact families, lower social class, and poor and highly segregated neighborhoods have significantly higher fertility rates. Hogan and Kitagawa estimated that 57 percent of the teenage girls from high-risk social environments (lower class, poor inner-city neighborhood residence, *female-headed family, five or more siblings, a sister who is a teenage mother*, and loose parental supervision of dating) will become pregnant by age eighteen compared to only 9 percent of the girls from low-risk social backgrounds. (Wilson 1987: 75; my emphases)

Wilson writes of 'female-headed families' and 'out-of-wedlock births' as forms of dislocation (ibid.: 72). Both of these are SNAF-generated deviant forms. Conceptions of low- and high-risk in the passage above follow this conceptual track. A high-risk social environment, that is, a social environment in which a young woman is at high risk of bearing a child 'out-of-wedlock' is one that includes a 'female-headed family.' But in the actualities of people's everyday living, we might find, rather than dislocation, social organization maximizing the range of reciprocal economic and other benefits under tough conditions. My emphases in the above passage locate items, 'female-headed family, five or more siblings, a sister who is a teenage mother,' that might be SNAF-filtered indicators of such patterns. Note, too, that SNAF equates family and household; so do Wilson, and Hogan and Kitagawa. Hence, inter-household connections are invisible.

We can begin to see how the operation of SNAF in distinct discursive and administrative sites provides for the in-text 'reality' of Wilson's account. Wilson's SNAF-governed theorizing, and that of studies he draws on, relies for the most part on SNAF-generated government statistics and is validated by analyses for which they are a resource. Though the studies and the statistics are independent of one another, the ordering procedure generating both is the same. The government statistics have not been created for Wilson or dovetailed to his study or the studies he cites. Nevertheless, they establish a common empirical ground for the substantial range of studies on which Wilson can call. The operation of SNAF as an ideological code creates a conceptual isomorphy between the data-base, the studies Wilson cites, and Wilson's own argument. The empirical 'solidity' of Wilson's text depends on this. No wonder, then, that Wilson is able to conclude (for this section of his study) that 'available evidence supports the argument that among blacks, increasing male joblessness is related to the rising proportions of families headed by women' (Wilson 1987: 83). Policy implications follow: '... the available evidence justifies renewed scholarly and public policy attention to the connection between the disintegration of poor families and black male prospects for stable employment' (Wilson 1987: 90).

Discussion

I would like to claim this paper as making observations of phenomena of text-mediated social relations, much as biologists may make observations of the operation of genetic codes. Of course, biological observations at the molecular level are mediated by a technology that is not needed here. Yet I want to stress the 'observed' character of what I have described. I propose that we can explore the social organization of a T-discourse and that the procedures coordinating its multiple sites, including the talk relating its texts, can be identified, and their 'effects' analysed. I do not usually use notions like 'effects' because I avoid causal imputations in explicating social organization. Nonetheless, the term seems appropriate here because ideological codes, as I've examined them here, operate largely outside the conscious intention of the researcher or writer. This, I think, is amply demonstrated by Alison's and my experiences with our study of mothering and schooling. Nor do I think Wilson decided on a SNAF-designed version of the African-American family because it served his political project – though it does. The SNAF design was already at hand: in the ongoing controversy about the African-American family that the Moynihan Report (Moynihan 1965) had initiated – a controversy that is through and through SNAF-ordered – and in the extensive literature on the family borne forward in the disciplines of sociology, child development, education, and so on. Presumably such ideological codes become incorporated into our thinking as we participate as readers in the T-discourses they infect.

The coordination of SNAF-governed texts with SNAF-governed representations of the society through statistics collected by and vested in state agencies provides for the in-text production of simulated realities such as Wilson's. I stress here the discursive concerting of independent sites. Ideological codes do more than order discursive productions. They also provide for the kind of interchange relying on conceptual isomorphy. Where the ordering procedures generating terms and sentences are the same, different content can be lined up as Edward Wilson lined up (his version of) the family organization of hunting and gathering societies with (his version of) the family organization of contemporary America in the sociobiological quotation above. In William Julius Wilson's study, his SNAF-ordered thesis about African-American families is directly coordinated with the SNAF-generated data of the U.S. Bureau of Census. The statistics realize and express the thesis; the thesis interprets the statistics.

Such observations of ideological codes rely both on analytic strategies such as those I've used above and on experiences – of doing research or of reading and writing sociology – that analysis explicates. They rely not only on attention to texts as the inert bearers of statements, but also on experience of and in courses of action in discourse, reading texts, such as William Julius Wilson's, and going back and forth between text and research practice, as Alison and I did in our study of mother's work in relation to their children's schooling. I have not stressed the experience of reading Wilson's text in which the analysis above was grounded, but it *was* a distinctive experience of reading in which I found myself both resisting as a feminist the argument put forward and yet not finding in the text the ground for such reservation. This difficulty was compounded, of course, by my being white and hence feeling that I had no right to contend with an African-American man's authoritative account of African-American lives. When I came to see that Wilson's virtual reality was organized by the same schema that invaded Alison's and my research, I could begin to isolate the operation of the same ideological code, SNAF, in both sites.

Chatting with Mary Romero one day while hiking up Mount Pisgah in Oregon contributed observations of the operation of the code in the routine production of government statistical data. SNAF-infected texts are all around us. They give discursive body and substance to a version of The Family that masks the actualities of people's lives and inserts an implicit evaluation into accounts of ways of living together in households or forming economically and emotionally supportive relationships that do not accord with SNAF. The conceptual containment of alternatives may be very important politically. I suspect that speaking and writing may often be governed by ideological codes, even when we dispute their specifics. I had not realized, until I talked to Mary, how a skeletal SNAF still governed the census-data format. SNAF also designs the law for and coordinates the administration of welfare (Abramovitz 1988), generating as a by-product statistical data that affirm the defective character of mother-headed family-households. Thus ideological codes may have a peculiar and important political force, carrying forward modes of representing the world even among those who overtly resist the representations they generate. Like Alison and I, we may, unnoticing, be trapped by our own competences as readers and writers of social science, as participants in a T-discourse, into regenerating a discursive politics to which we are opposed.

9

'Politically Correct': An Organizer of Public Discourse[1]

The Regulation of Public Discourse: Ideological Codes at Work

The evolution of the ruling relations described in chapter 5, their increased interpenetration and interdependence, creates conditions under which control can be exerted by operating within the intertextuality of the medium itself. In the previous chapter, I examined how an ideological code, the Standard North American Family, coordinates representations of families, households, and relationships in the community in multiple sites of the ruling relations. Though there has been direct ideological intervention to reinforce the code of SNAF, I do not think that it originated in that fashion. In this chapter, I explore an ideological code, 'political correctness,' that would appear to have been 'planted' (Weir 1994) and put into circulation to regulate the intertextualities of public discourse, particularly at the points of intersection between universities and social movements.

To control concepts, theories, and ideology and their dissemination in public text-mediated discourse is an important source of power in a society largely organized by text-mediated relations. An article in the *New York Times* (Uchitelle 1993) describes just how effective such control may be. The theory that national economies are revived by reducing the deficit, hence promoting the lower interest rates that encourage investment, is established in public discourse in such a way that it displaces consideration of alternatives. Yet evidence for the theory is lacking; there are leading economists, including Nobel Prize winners, who dissent from it. Despite this, the theory dominates the terms of the debate, locking in even those who do not agree with it. 'Nowhere has deficit reduction been embraced more militantly than in the [U.S.] budget debate. Virtually no one in either party any longer challenges the proposition that deficit reduction will eventually be good for the economy' (Uchitelle 1993: 1). The theory is established as *organizer* of public discourse on the economy; even dissenting views must operate on its terms *and hence reproduce it.*

Ideologies, concepts, and theories are particularly powerful in regulating public text-mediated discourse. By public text-mediated discourse, I mean those relations of discourse to which, in principle, access is unrestricted. Notice that in this approach, discourse is a field of relations and not only of statements (see chapter 7). Discourse *exists* in people's socially organized activities. Ideologies, concepts, theories, etc., are among the organizers of its relations and process, whatever function they may be understood to have when addressed from other analytic stances.

Public text-mediated discourse consists of those relations that have evolved historically, under conditions of contemporary mass communication, from the 'public sphere' that Jürgen Habermas (1989) analyses in his early study. In making text-mediation integral to its definition, I do not mean to suggest public discourse exists only in texts. It includes the mass media in all its forms, as well as the talk that goes on around and about media; political talk and writing; academic discourse, both in print and talk; and so on. Imagine the field of public text-mediated discourse as many ongoing conversations carried on, in part, in print, or as broadcast talk, or as images on television or film, and, in part, in the many everyday settings of talk among people that take up, take off from, or otherwise incorporate ideas or substance from public discourse. They are conversations among people who don't necessarily know one another except through that medium. They are situated in many different places. Some are only readers or watchers; while others – writers, actors, celebrities, politicians, and so on – appear in the parts they play in print and on screen, split off from the actualities of their own lives. Others are writers, film directors, camera people, technicians, and publishers; while yet others work in the vast industrial basis of the text-mediated and text-based relations of public discourse. The textuality of public text-mediated discourse is essential to its peculiar temporal and spatial properties of ubiquity and constancy of replication across multiple and highly various actual situations of watching, reading, or hearing.

Michel Foucault (1980) has taught us to recognize the complex of text-mediated relations as itself an organization of power. He writes of it as 'power/knowledge,' envisaging it as a decentred form of power, distributed over a complex of discursive sites. Creating and reproducing ideology, concepts, knowledge, theory, etc., have been largely the business of an intelligentsia, carried on in multiple sites and a variety of media, but participating in the same, loosely coordinated complex of relations. New conceptualizations and knowledge did not proceed from a determinate source and spread into discourse as its organizers. Rather, the creative sources of change operated in a field of relations from multiple sites of interplay with ongoing discursive concerns. No one position could command. But envisage now this complex of text-mediated relations as lending itself to control from a centre that works with precisely the dispersal of discursive sites, and, importantly, through a command of the concept-, ideology-, and theory-making that organize the production, 'operation,' and reading/watching/hearing of texts.

We have reason to think that this is happening now in the United States and is being extended to Canada. Ellen Messer-Davidow (1993) has explored the manufacture, in right-wing think-tanks, foundations, and so on, of an attack on liberalized higher education. On the basis of field research of such think-tanks, institutes, and foundations, she describes an ideological campaign waged by an apparatus aimed at securing control of the concepts, ideologies, and theories that coordinate multiple sites of power/knowledge generated by the ruling relations. The right wing, representing a powerful section of the capitalist class in the United States, has created information- and policy-generating think-tanks, an institute for training journalists as recruits to replace the predominantly liberal professional journalists of today, and a multi-headed attack on liberal higher education, and particularly on 'multiculturalism' and on the gender and ethnic diversification of the university curriculum. Right-wing control of public discourse through command of concepts, ideologies, and theories has been an objective of right-wing intellectuals and ideologues since the great fright in the 1960s that liberals or, worse, the left had been successful in securing the ideological heights (Blumenthal 1986). Ideological/conceptual/theoretical command of the field of text-mediated relations is immensely powerful, the more so as it is *largely invisible as* power, and the right wing, or perhaps more realistically the U.S. capitalist class, aims at and is increasingly effective in securing it.

I use the term 'ideological code' as in the previous chapter to identify a particular ideological function that travels in the peculiar space-no-space of text-mediated relations, reproducing its distinctive organization in the multiple sites articulated to them, and both in text and in talk about and on the way to text. The neo-conservative version of 'political correctness'[2] (Weir 1994) has travelled in just this fashion. The deployment of the neo-conservative PC was initiated by Richard Bernstein's 'The Rising Hegemony of the Politically Correct,' published in the *New York Times* in October 1990, and promulgated further in President Bush's address to the commencement ceremony at the University of Michigan in March 1991 (Bush 1991).

In the field of public discourse, an ideological code, such as 'political correctness,' operates to structure text or talk. Each instance of its functioning can generate new instances. It reproduces as people 'pick up' its organization from reading it, or about it, or hearing it used, and using it themselves, hence passing it on to readers, watchers, or hearers.

The formal openness of the relations of public discourse has been established against the state's crude efforts to regulate it. In the liberal state, constitutions protect against those in positions of power who would limit people's right to speak and hear others speak in their interests. Freedom of speech has been a principle limiting the powers of the state to repress its citizens and restrict the openness of public discourse. Censorship has traditionally been an issue of governments' attempts to impair that openness. But constitutions do not protect the openness of public discourse against those positioned to regulate public discourse; for example, through control of the mass media. They do not protect against controls through the conscious creation and seeding of ideological codes independently of the state. Ideological codes don't appear directly, as they do in an act of censorship; no one seems to be imposing anything on anybody else; people pick up an ideological code from reading, hearing, or watching, and replicate it in their own talk or writing. They pass it along. Once ideological codes are established, they are self-reproducing.

Thus ideological codes operate as a free-floating form of control in the relations of public discourse. They can replicate anywhere. They organize talk, thinking, writing, and the kinds of images and stories produced on film and television. Listening, reading or watching, people pick them up and reproduce them in their own talk, thinking, and writing. I want to make clear that an 'ideological code' in this sense is not a definite category or concept. Nor is it a formula or a definite form of words. Rather, it is a constant generator of procedures for selecting syntax, categories, and vocabulary in writing and speaking, for interpreting what is written and spoken, and for positioning and relating discursive subjects. It is not as such social organization, but it is a social organizer.

'Ideological codes' may be, and perhaps often are, components of ideological 'master-frames.' They operate as 'outriders' of that frame, carrying it into discursive sites where the ideology itself might not be assimilable. They seem to operate pretty independently as devices, carrying the effects but not the body of the ideology that governed their design. This is their power as discursive devices; this is their utility to the right-wing industries of ideology described by Messer-Davidow and others. People pick them up and use them without realizing the source and the efficacy of meaning they carry with them into the settings of their use; they become an active currency of ruling, operating in the interests of those who set them afloat and may have designed them, but their provenance and ideological 'intention' is not apparent in them. They do not appear as regulatory measures; they are not forms of censorship by the state. Indeed, characteristically, they are spontaneously adopted and reproduced.

The analysis in this paper builds on a method of thinking about the social that addresses knowledge, concepts, theory, ideology, and so on, as people's actual practices, 'occurring' in time and place, and 'active' in coordinating social relations. My interest is in making visible how the ideological code 'politically correct' enters as a method or practice of interpretation into public text-mediated discourse as people's practices, including our own. This means explicating our own practices of ordering and interpreting textual materials. That we 'know how to do it' is a major resource in the analysis that follows.

Foucault (1972: 41) provides an account of the formation of objects within a discourse that calls first for a mapping of the *surfaces* of the emergence. This paper aims to map the *surfaces* of 'political correctness' as an object formed within public discourse. However, Foucault's formulation presupposes – and occludes as part of a conscious theoretical strategy – the interplay of actual practices among people that, within a discourse, constitutes the object. His mapping of the emergence of objects is at the level of statements and concepts, and though he writes of 'formation,' his account is peculiarly static. Working with a conception of discourse as social relations actively produced by people situated as they are and must be in the local actualities of their living calls for a formulation of 'object formation' as an active, *and social*, process. This, of course, continues the exploration in chapter 8 of discourse as social organization, and theory as an organizer of its social relations. Where the constitution of discursive objects is concerned, George Herbert Mead's (1947) account of the capacity of symbolization to bring objects into being within the social act is congenial. For Mead, the existence of objects for a group is accomplished in a social act, and language 'does not simply symbolize a situation or object which is already there in advance; it makes possible the existence' (Mead 1947: 78) of that object for those active in the social act. Here the social act is discursive; the object brought into being, 'political correctness,' comes into discursive existence in people's textual practices. 'Political correctness' is the symbolization that brings into being within the social processes of discourse objects that are there for any of us, regardless of our political views. It provides a generalized procedure for constituting discursive objects in the local settings of public discourse.

In analysing 'political correctness' as an ideological code, I am analysing how it operates, or how it might be entered into the organization of a text in its writing, or as a 'knowing how' to 'read' a text it has organized. My use of the quotes around 'read' is intended to locate the reader's deployment of concepts, schemata, and the like, that catch up the conceptual or schematic organization that the text intends. This is a level of interpretation prior to bringing what we have read (heard or seen) in relation to other settings in which we might be writing or talking about what we have read. I have analysed this relation of reading in an analysis of an account of someone becoming mentally ill (Smith 1990b), in which I show how the structuring of instances making up the account 'fits' a reading of mental illness and can be read by that concept. Hence, the reader can find in the text what it has told her to look for. In the analysis that follows, I've followed a similar procedure. A Canadian Broadcasting Corporation (CBC) radio program is analysed for how it both instructs the listener in the ideological code of 'political correctness' and then provides a series of stories which the code will read. The stories are of episodes that both express and expand the listener's ability to reproduce the code. In this social act of text-mediated discourse, 'political correctness' is constituted as a discursive object.

'Political Correctness' – a Regulator of Public Discourse

Mikhail Bakhtin's (1981) theory of the novel conceives it as a dialogue woven out of the multiple and diverse speech genres of a heteroglossic society. But though public discourse appears formally open, in fact, speaker participation in it has been and is quite powerfully regulated by devices that regulate the authority of speakers. 'Authority is a form of power that is a distinctive capacity to get things done in words. What is said or written merely means what the words mean, until and unless it is given force by the authority attributed to its "author"' (Smith 1987: 29–30). Public discourse is also a social organization of authority, regulating whose voices will count in the making of its topics, themes, concepts, relevancies, etc. The teaching in schools and universities of the literary canon, of nationalist-oriented histories, and established social science generalizes to *all* participants in public discourse as its taken-for-granted background the understandings, speech genres, references, objects, personages, authorities, and so on that reproduce the values, orientations, and standpoints of the established powers in educational institutions. The dominance of these established understandings is sustained by the authority of white men as 'those whose words count both for each other and for those who are not members of this category' (Smith 1987: 30). The authority to speak for themselves as women has been denied to women, and major struggles in the women's movement have focused on gaining entry for women to speak as women in the public discourse. Similarly, non-white speakers have been deprived of authority to speak as members of their social category, to put forward their experience and interests as belonging as of right to the public sphere.

These forms of cultural dominance have been and are currently under attack by the groups they marginalize. 'Political correctness' as an ideological code can be seen in this context as a traditional elite's resistance to loss of an exclusive authority, founded in gender and imperialism, within the sphere of public discourse. Of course, the production and operation of ideological codes is not new, nor is it an exclusively right-wing device. But 'political correctness' is specialized to focus on regulating the authority of participants in public discourse, and hence on restricting who can be part of the making of its topics and relevancies, and hence the social forms of consciousness. Since it is a free-floating code, it can operate independently of the right-wing ideologies that generated it. The code's most recent history (Weir 1994) began with authoritative enunciations, instructing readers in how to operate the code themselves; it was then brought into more general use in settings of conflict within public text-mediated discourse; and has finally been incorporated into that discourse's anyday vocabulary. We should not suppose, of course, that this means necessarily that there has been a sudden rightward shift in the population – though, of course, this may have happened. The PC code has 'caught on.' This is the 'power' of the device.

In the context of the political sectarianism of the 1970s and '80s, the term 'political correctness' was used to extend a political sect's politics to the everyday conduct of its members. It became later a left-wing insider's joke, used ironically. The right-wing 'designer' 'political correctness' code (the PC code), by contrast, is specialized to operate in the field of public text-mediated discourse. It has been reworked to locate initiatives by or on behalf of those excluded from authoritative participation in public discourse to transform their place and their right to insert the topics and relevancies of the groups they represent, particularly into the universities. Its syntax has been transformed: rather than a challenge to bring private behaviour into line with political principle, it operates as a category of deviance; it names the actions it is used to characterize as deviating from principles of freedom of speech. It operates to reaffirm the authority of the established and to discredit the voices of those attempting change.

The CBC Joins the 'Political Correctness' Campaign: Analysis of a Documentary

A Canadian Broadcasting Corporation's *Sunday Morning* radio program on political correctness was broadcast on 28 July 1991.[3] It is a documentary bringing to the listener an account of episodes identified as instances of 'political correctness,' using commentary and passages from interviews to tell the story.

The documentary form is essentially dialogic in ways that lend themselves to analysis following Bakhtin's (1981) conception of the dialogic structure of the novel. According to Bakhtin, it is the novelist's art to bring different genres of speech into active, though not necessarily equal, dialogue with one another. In the documentary, the radio reporter or the film-maker creates a dialogic structure of voices or (in film) images originating in actual events and claiming to represent them to an audience. Thus, unlike the novel, the documentary claims to represent a world beyond its textuality. Its internal dialogic organization relates the listener/watcher to the world it posits beyond itself. V.I. Vološinov's formulation of the dialogic of reported speech applies here: 'Reported speech is speech within speech, utterance within utterance, and at the same time also *speech about speech, utterance about utterance*' (Vološinov 1973: 115). As we shall see, the ideological code of 'political correctness' is both topic and regulator of the dialogic organization of the CBC program. In a sense, the program instructs the listener how to operate the code.

1. Hooking the Intra-institutional into Public Discourse

I have imagined the dialogic organization of the documentary as a set of layered transparencies relating listeners who participate in the public discourse of radio to a series of events or episodes in post-secondary institutions or, in one case, a museum. The layers are a structuring of reported speech: each inscribes messages that overlay those on lower layers; what comes through from lower layers (and hence from the original events) is what subsequent layers allow to surface. The top layer is that of public discourse, where listener interfaces with the documentary in the radio program; at the bottom are the original events, only accessible as they are inscribed in and 'written over' at subsequent layers. The original events or the original controversy do not appear directly. They are 'represented' to listeners, mediated by laminated layers and their top-down dialogic regulation. Listeners hear of the original events only through what participants have to say 'directly,' or in their reported speech, or as the events are described by others (a concealed form of reported speech, relying, as such description must, on a telling of original events by participants).

The image of layered transparencies explicates the layering of the dialogic of reported speech in the documentary. The original events become accessible to listeners through the 'series' of layers and their one-way dialogic. Higher layers comment on and regulate lower layers; lower layers do not comment on or interpret upper layers.

Layer One

The first and topmost layer (layer one) is the *surface* of the documentary, located in and setting the social relational framework of public discourse. All other layers are seen through this surface. The surface isn't wholly in the text itself. It is at the interface between text and listeners. Hence the importance of controlling the framework that listeners bring to their listening. The introduction by *Sunday Morning*'s host, Mary-Lou Finlay, sets up the governing framework for listeners as follows:

1.1 The documentary is identified, and thus authorized, as part of the *Sunday Morning* program.

1.2 Finlay introduces the reporter as '*Sunday Morning*'s Mary O'Connell,' delegating to her the authority of voice that she holds as host of the CBC program. She thereby authorizes the reporter's control of the dialogic of the documentary. This sequence also establishes Mary O'Connell as the connecting link between original and intra-institutional events and the moment of public discourse by telling us that O'Connell has been visiting universities in Canada, exploring 'the world of the "politically correct."'

1.3 Thirdly, and perhaps most importantly, Finlay establishes the narrative theme of the documentary, introducing the concept of PC and a schema that will interpret the stories of what happened and find the coherence of the layering and sequencing of reported speech in the documentary. The schema is set up in two steps. First a question is posed: is political correctness 'the new enlightenment or the new tyranny'? Then the apparent openness of the question is foreclosed by describing O'Connell's investigations as aimed at discovering 'how enlightenment "crosses over" into tyranny.' This schema is operative throughout.

Layer Two
Layer two is wholly the reporter's. She comments on what other speakers say, assigns or withdraws credibility, and ensures narrative coherence by, for example, adding supplementary descriptive material. She produces the overall coherence of the documentary as narrative, but she also creates coherence by locating its different pieces as expressions or instances of the 'crossing over' of 'enlightenment into tyranny' that is the effect of political correctness.

Layer Three
At layer three, participants in the original events speak *about* them. They do not, of course, regulate their own speech; this is accomplished by the reporter functioning as a filter and artfully selecting passages that will intend (or fit) the interpretations of layers two and one. The reporter's voice is also heard at this level in extracts from interviews with speakers from the original events.

In the overall dialogic organization of the documentary, higher layers filter and control the interpretation of speakers appearing on lower layers. In so doing, the original events become expressions of the overall interpretive framework, established first at the level of public discourse (layer one). The documentary as a whole transposes local events arising in specific institutional contexts, within their organization of power, authority, and communication, into the arena of public discourse, with an entirely different organization of power, authority, and communication. Listeners, lacking access to the original site or the original events, are committed, as a course of listening, to the palimpsest of the layered reported speech and its one-way dialogic.

The series of layers structures the telling of a series of episodes in which challenges to the 'normal' (taken-for-granted) course of institutional affairs have been made. Here is a summary of them:

• Members of the student union at the Ryerson Polytechnical Institute in Toronto complain about racist and sexist content in a student union entertainment, and a self-declared schizophrenic demonstrates against the title, 'Loonie Bin,' of a comedy night on the grounds that it demeans people who are mentally ill.

- A complaint of sexism against a rock group made by a woman from the Queen's University Women's Centre results in the Queen's student council cancelling the group's invitation to perform at the university.
- The University of Toronto's student newspaper, *The Varsity*, has an editorial policy that would refuse publication to material inciting violence or hatred towards people, particularly on the basis of their membership in a disadvantaged group.
- A small group of students at the University of Toronto demonstrate against the possibility that courses in the African Studies program may be cut.
- An Afro-Canadian activist argues that African history should be taught by Africans or people of African origin.
- Afro-Canadians demonstrate against the Royal Ontario Museum's exhibit 'Into the Heart of Africa' and later harass Jeanne Cannizzo, an Africanist associated with the design of the exhibit, while she is giving a course at the Erindale campus of the University of Toronto.

What is at dispute? On college and university campuses, students and faculty are going about their normal business: putting on comedy shows, arranging for rock performances, publishing student newspapers, giving lectures in anthropology, arranging museum exhibits, and the like. In so doing, the taken-for-granted 'normal' forms of discourse or performance, embedding the 'normal' gender, racial, and imperialist presuppositions, are reproduced.

These normal forms are subjected to critical challenges by (or on behalf of) members of social groups for whom they reproduce forms of domination that marginalize and subordinate them. In this collection of episodes, challenge takes the form, severally, of appealing to college authorities, action by an elected body, picketing, and direct confrontation in the classroom. In several episodes there is a reversal of established institutional power relations: an ex-mental patient demonstrates against a college-sponsored entertainment; a group of students protest threatened cuts to an African Studies program; an unnamed group of Afro-Canadians demonstrates against a museum exhibit; students in a class challenge a professor. Other than actions by student unions, the initiatives described are from those who lack access to the institutional processes of regulation and change.

2. The Layering of Dialogue in the Episodes

In ways that are perhaps characteristic of radio documentary reporting, listeners are placed in a relation of overhearing comparable to the 'voyeuristic' structure of film. In some instances, extracts from original interviews have been edited to represent direct speech to the listeners. The structuring role of the reporter is concealed, backstage. Thus, those who were active as participants in the original controversies seem to speak, but they are no longer independent subjects, speaking for themselves. Fragments of their talk are used by the reporter to constitute them as subjects, subordinated to her script. They are her fabrications and do her will. The dialogic of each episode has two layers: at layer two, the reporter's narrative and commentary directly address the radio listener. For example, in the Ryerson vignette, the reporter narrates the original events and comments on what speakers who were participants in those events say, assigning value and credibility to those speakers or what they had to say; at level three, segments of speech by participants in the original events appear in two modes of reported speech:

2.1 Segments of original participants' speech are inserted into a dual-level dialogue (layers two and three) with segments of the reporter's commentary – a kind of mock dialogue, which hops back and forth between layer two, where the reporter addresses, listeners and layer three of original participants' speech produced in an interview with the reporter. For example, in the episode of the University of Toronto *Varsity*, the reporter comments on how freedom of speech is coming on university campuses to mean 'freedom to censor.' This is followed by a segment of speech from the *Varsity* editor stating the *Varsity*'s policy. It is structured as if the latter were a response to the former. But, in fact, they are at different dialogic levels, the reporter's 'editorial' comments overlaying the *Varsity* editor's statement. The latter has presumably been extracted from an original interview. Who knows what its context was in the original?

2.2 On layer two, there are snatches of interviews in which the reporter questions or comments and the speaker from the original events responds or makes a statement. In the *Varsity* episode, the dual-level dialogue is followed by a direct interchange in which a statement by the *Varsity* editor is followed by a question from the reporter and a response to it from the *Varsity* editor.

3. The Events as Expressions of PC

The stories of the episodes float the intra-institutional events free of their institutional context, shaping them up to operate as expressions or instances of the overall theme. Exemplification is a powerful device: on the one hand, a schema, in this case of the passage from enlightenment to tyranny; and, on the other, a collection of episodes. The schema is empty without its instances; the instances are merely a collection of stories without the schema that interprets them. The PC code structures how the intra-institutional events are told, so that they will instantiate the schema it governs. A circular procedure is in operation: *listeners are given instructions for finding each episode as an instance of PC; and the telling of each episode is constructed to correspond to those instructions.*

If you listened to these little stories presented without the code as interpreter, you probably would not see them as belonging together. Some PC collections I've listened to on the radio have assembled instances that I have found really strange. For example, a Peter Gzowski panel on this topic included, among more standard representatives, someone speaking on issues of sexual harassment in the university. She was represented as part of the PC movement, not, as might have been conceived, to address sexual harassment as denying women their authority as speakers within the academic community, but as an instance of challenging institutional authority.

So the episodes don't hang together 'naturally' – that is, without interpretive artifice – out of a simple telling of episodes. The coherence of the collection as a sequence has to be complemented by listeners' application of the code as interpreters. Otherwise, the whole thing might fall apart, an effect forestalled by the reiteration of the code for each episode. Coherence is an effect, on the one side, of the structuring of episodes to fit the code as interpreter and, on the other, of the hearer's uses of the code (under instruction) to find how each new episode expresses it. There is a circular process, peculiar to the ideological organization of narratives. The particulars are selected to intend the code as a procedure for making sense of them, and the code finds for the listener or reader just that sense in the particulars.[4]

A variety of strategies are used to produce the episodes as expressions of political correctness. In some, the actions of the challengers are represented as coercive, sometimes as violent and abusive. The culminating story in the CBC program is of the verbal abuse and harassment of Jeanne Cannizzo, the anthropologist who designed the Royal Ontario Museum exhibit that was the focus of Afro-Canadian protest. It casts its shadow backward onto other incidents, such as that of the solitary ex-mental patient picketing a students' comedy night, that otherwise might be hard to assimilate to the frame of 'tyranny' or 'totalitarianism.' Other episodes undermine and invalidate the rationality of what is recommended and the principles that justify the critique. For example, the decision of the student council at Queen's to cancel a rock group's performance is represented as based on irrational and counter-factual interpretations. The reporter's commentary legitimates those speaking for the 'normal' institutional order and discredits those who challenge.

4. The PC code as Regulator of the Dialogue between Original Events and Public Discourse

In their reporting, the original events are lifted out of their local historical contexts and reshaped to the relevancies established for that discourse. The series of levels embedding the intra-institutional events in the relations of public discourse set up a dialogue between the two, but it is a dialogue that is heavily stage-managed: not everyone identified as a participant is given a speaking part; no one gets to choose what part her or his voice will play. That is the reporter's privilege. The participants' voices appear only as reported speech, either embedded in the reporter's narrative or as extracts from interviews.

As we've seen, the PC code organizes a telling that selects and reshapes the intra-institutional issue by embedding it in the relevancies of public discourse. It has been put in place to govern listeners' interpretive practices. To return to my image of laminated transparencies, the code is inscribed at the top layer and is recursively effective in those below. The challenge to the normal course of institutional affairs that each vignette presents *raises issues in terms of principles of human right.* Those challenging are either subordinate to or outside the institutional structure of authority. Generally, they are students, but sometimes they are outsiders altogether, without standing in the institutional process.

In the layered and PC-governed dialogue that brings the challengers' voices forward from the institutional context to the listeners present and on to the terrain of public discourse, this lack of institutional authority to speak is consequential. The authority of their challenge is grounded in principles that are held to have jurisdiction within the institution superordinate to its formal structure of authority. Hence, those lacking institutional authority can assume the authority of the principle, in this case, of human rights. This authority, however, is peculiarly vulnerable to the PC code, which, in the one-way dialogue between public and intra-institutional discourse, displaces *principles of human rights and installs 'freedom of speech' as an exclusive principle.* This displacement undermines students' or outsiders' authority to challenge institutional authority and to speak in the institutional context that has been legitimated with reference to principles of human rights. Deprived of the validation of principle, their challenges to the normal course of institutional affairs appear arbitrary and unwarranted. A retroactive fit is thus created between the stories told and the schema of a passage 'from enlightenment to tyranny' introduced in the opening remarks by Mary-Lou Finlay.

The various devices of reporting speech in the radio documentary medium operate in the program to subordinate the original speakers to the monologic (Gardiner 1992) regime that the PC code sets up in public discourse. The code's structuring of 'reported speech' represses. The voices of those speaking for the 'human rights' issue appear only as expressions or instances of political correctness. Voiding the 'human rights' principle removes authority and credibility from those challenging institutional authority.

Here is a detailed analysis of how this effect operates in the dialogic of reported speech in one episode, that reported of the Ryerson Polytechnical Institute:

- A comedian performing at a Ryerson Polytechnical 'club' ridicules 'political correctness' and 'leftish' students.
- Members of Ryerson's student union complain to the entertainment officer about the racism/sexism of a comedian's performance (presumably, this is the same comedy show as that at which the comedian ridiculing 'political correctness' appears, but this isn't clearly stated).
- They ask the Entertainments Office to adopt a policy that will be in conformity with the human rights code.
- The comedy performance named 'Loonie Bin' is picketed by an ex-student, who claims that its title trivializes mental illness.

Here students pressure for change from the administration. The students' complaint of racism and sexism in the comedian's performance appeals explicitly to principles of human rights as embodied in Canada's human rights legislation. It isn't just a personal matter; it isn't arbitrary. The issue is independent of their particular subjectivities. Reference to 'human rights' principles authorizes their initiative, providing an authority beyond that of the institution itself.

The PC code removes that authorization. At the documentary surface where the reporter is telling the story (layer two), a dialogue internal to a sentence reduces the students' principled claim to the merely subjective and arbitrary. The reporter's account produces a classic instance of Bakhtin's (1981) hybrid sentence, in which two utterances are blended:

What we are calling a hybrid construction is an utterance that belongs, by its grammatical (syntactic) and compositional markers, to a single speaker, but that actually contains mixed within it two utterances, two speech manners, two styles, two 'languages,' two semantic and axiological belief systems. We repeat, there is no formal – compositional and syntactic – boundary between these utterances, styles, languages, belief systems; the division of voices and languages takes place within the limits of a single syntactic whole, often within the limits of a simple sentence. (Bakhtin 1981: 304)

In this instance, the blending is in fact the overlaying of the reporter's interpretation onto the reported speech of the students, so that her interpretation appears as what they said. Here is the sentence:

They said a new policy was needed to ensure that the content of entertainment would not violate the human rights code *or their notions of 'politically correct.'* (My emphases)

The two 'utterances' are both represented as reported speech, as predicates of 'they said.' The duality of language and 'belief system' becomes visible if we break the two utterances out of the hybrid construction. Here they are:

A new policy is needed to ensure that the content of entertainment will not violate the human rights code.

And:

A new policy is needed to ensure that the content of entertainment will not violate our notions of 'politically correct.'

The first utterance is subordinated to the interpretation in terms of political correctness supplied by the second. The blending is done by treating both as reported speech, what 'they said.' The sentence as a whole does indeed contain two 'belief systems,' to use Bakhtin's conception. But they do not stand in an equal relationship in the dialogue created by the hybrid. We see layer three through an inscription at layer two. The statement at layer three is reconstructed to fit the PC code. The reference is no longer to an *objectively* posited human rights code, but to the students' *notions* of politically correct. The students' original proposal appeals to objective principles embodied in Canada's constitution; reworked, the students are represented as seeking to impose their own subjective and, by implication, arbitrary notions of what is politically correct. At the surface, the documentary-listener interface, this story can now be seen as another instance in which, beginning with 'enlightenment,' those who protest end up in 'tyranny.'[5]

The Ryerson story contains two episodes. The second is the story of the former student, the solitary picketer of Ryerson's comedy night protesting its 'Loonie Bin' title. He pickets because he 'thought that [the title] trivialized mental illness.' He is described by the reporter as a schizophrenic. Here, on layer two of the laminated transparencies, is a powerfully recursive concept suspending the credibility of what is reported of someone involved in the original events. Categorization as mentally ill suspends the attribution of agency and hence of responsibility. So the solitary picketer is represented (through the reported speech of the entertainments officer) as a '*victim* of a "politically correct" way of thinking' (my emphases). Somehow a 'way of thinking' has fastened itself onto him and taken him over.

5. Reflections

What puzzled me at first about the program was that in a number of rather obvious ways it departed from what I had come to assume as canons of good reporting. This was particularly so with respect to how the different positions were represented. Perhaps it was my imperfect assimilation of the PC code that permitted this puzzlement since operating the code establishes one side as what is taken-for-granted among participants to public discourse.

In the documentary's final sequence, there is some representation of the 'human rights' issues involved, but in portraying the intra-institutional events, no attempt was made to give the other side a voice. The PC code organizes listeners' relationship to the intra-institutional controversy so that while the offensiveness of the protest to those challenged by it may be fully represented, the nature of the offence to those protesting is either not presented at all or presented in a cursory way, sometimes by those who have been challenged.

The PC code produces a selective hearing of this dispute. The taken-for-granted forms that have given offence are either not described at all or described only to discredit them. We are not told what the students who complained to the administrator at Ryerson found racist and sexist about the student comedy hour; we are not told what kinds of hate material the University of Toronto student newspaper will not publish; we are not told what is problematic about the built-in perspective of an anthropology of Africa created by anthropologists of European origin; we are not given details of what Afro-Canadians found objectionable about the Royal Ontario Museum's African exhibit. When we are told, it is only to trivialize or ridicule. The solitary schizophrenic picketing Ryerson's 'Loonie Bin' comedy show is presented without dignity or textual compensation for the established stigmatizing of the mentally ill; the technical rationality of the male spokesperson for the rock group is contrasted with the (female) 'subjectivity' of the grounds on which its performance was cancelled.

A characteristic of the taken-for-granted is that it is not subject to reflection or reflective revision. Hence, if the listener or reader isn't told what is wrong with the normal institutional forms, she or he will not know how to see it. Apart from the devices described above, challenge and protest are trivialized in the absence of such information: they appear to be about nothing in particular, a fuss about nothing. Whereas, of course, from the side of the group demeaned by them, such normal forms incorporate practices that are acutely painful, silencing, and enraging.[6]

The PC code reproduces the social contours of the normal form. It generates its 'deviant category.' As Durkheim (1960:102) has shown us, the social logic of identifying the deviant is to reinforce the sentiments sustaining the normal form. The rule, here the 'normal' form, does not have to be explicit to be affirmed in the shared repudiation of the deviant; it is affirmed collectively. Hence, the significance of the PC code as a device that positions participants in public discourse so that they are at the centre of what everyone knows and takes for granted, vis-à-vis which the 'politically correct' are 'other.' We, listening, watching, reading, are drawn into the magic circle defined, not by determinate values, but by what it constitutes as other, implicitly, but *not* explicitly, affirming our freedom to continue our taken-for-granted practices of sexism and racism without being subjected to challenge.

Like Theseus entering the labyrinth, listeners are given the thread that will enable them to retrace the maze. We are instructed in the code at the outset (layer one), and the instructions are reinforced as each episode is narrated. The code is thereby established as an interpretive paradigm enabling listeners to find for each episode and for the collection as a whole the lineaments of the transition from 'enlightenment' to 'tyranny.' The listener gets the message. Of course, she doesn't necessarily interpret it in exactly the same way – she may agree or disagree or have a variety of reactions to different episodes – but agreement or disagreement or a variety of reactions presuppose that she has already recognized 'what it's about.' Most importantly, listeners have acquired a device they can deploy thereafter. The code has been enunciated. In listening, our consciousness has participated in it as a practice. We will know how to do it again; we can carry it away for our own future use; we can discover and construct our own PC stories; and we can apply it to situations where we are challenged.

Replicating

Thus the code replicates. Once it is seeded, what came first is not a relevant issue. The listener or reader learns how to operate the code, as teller of a story or as reader/hearer. Recurrent multiple instances from a variety of sources confirm its reality. The narrative structure fitting the schema of tyranny is replicated. The protester or challenger, normally a member or members of a group of relatively low institutional authority, is the initiator; the institutional representative is represented as victim (his/her 'offence' is minimized); a language of violence, force or coercion is used to describe the protest. For example, a *Newsweek* article (Adler et al. 1990) tells of students marching into the classroom of the Berkeley anthropologist Victor Sarich and 'drown[ing] out his lecture with chants of "bullshit."' The article does refer to an article Sarich had published in a campus newspaper arguing that the university's affirmative-action program was discriminatory to whites and Asians. The classroom action, however, is not set in the context of information appearing in the following paragraph, namely, that Sarich holds the view that different races have genetically determined differences in intelligence. Presenting the action of students first, and displacing what might have provided a motivational context for that action, represents it as inadequately motivated and arbitrary. It is fitted thereby to the PC code as a method of reading.

Another PC-coded story in the same article tells how 'students forced [the] withdrawal' of a case on the rights of lesbian mothers that had been assigned to the New York University Law School moot court. The dean of the College of Liberal Arts overrode the decision of the curriculum committee to suspend that session of the moot court. The students' action is described as coercive; the dean's is recorded neutrally and without comment. The telling fits the story to the theme of 'tyranny' established in the CBC program described above. Notice that exercise of institutionalized power and authority goes unremarked, even when it acts to censor or restrict academic freedom. No issues of McCarthyism, tyranny, or censorship are raised. The same *Newsweek* article reports actions by University of Texas administrators to suspend the use of a text for an undergraduate course. No issues of academic freedom or censorship are raised in the article. The text is described as 'a primer of PC thought' (Adler et al. 1990: 52). The structuring of these narratives fits the PC code as the reader's method of making sense of them. As readers, we already have the template; we have only to apply it to find the fit; when we find the fit, there's no experience of incongruity, and no reason therefore to question.

The PC code authorizes representatives of the institutional order to repress and discredit those who challenge it. Characteristically, the device appears in stripped form, without being embedded in a particular ideology and without reference to the conservative political interests from which the device originated. By using descriptive terms that conflate the challenge to the established order with the oppressive use of coercive state power, the code is grafted on to legitimating frames or principles that have public currency, notably the principles of freedom and of 'freedom of speech,' in particular. The original ideological provenance of the device is displaced at the surface by using terms from a vocabulary of liberal politics, particularly terms identified with the anti-totalitarian liberalism of the 1950s. Terms such as 'totalitarian,' 'tyranny,' 'McCarthyism,' and 'storm troopers' (with its reference to Nazi Germany) are used. A memorandum circulating in a Canadian university refers in its topic line to 'an apotheosis of tyranny.'

The original liberal critique of totalitarianism was, of course, a critique of the coercive and arbitrary uses of state power. Detaching the terms from their ideological ground takes advantage of the moral valence they have come to carry, while excising reference to the practices of repression sustained by the state's command of judicial procedure and its monopoly of the legal use of force. To those of us who remember the McCarthy period (even from a distance, as I do), the conjunction is disorienting. But stripped of their theoretical provenance, and resituated, the PC code governs their operation. Hence, critiques of established powers from those in low power positions can be described as tyranny or censorship or the like without any sense of strangeness. An exaggerated power is attributed to them. Metaphors of 'force' are brought into play. The actions or effects of protestors' actions are represented as coercive and repressive

(Adler et al. 1990) or as terrorist. Eugene Genovese, in a *New Republic* article, calls for the firing of 'cowardly' administrators who do not stand up
to 'terrorism' (Genovese 1991: 32). Thus, the solitary picketer, former
student and ex-mental patient, demonstrating against the 'Loonie Bin'
title of Ryerson's comedy night, can be subsumed under the category of
'tyranny,' put in place in the introduction to the topic without arousing,
at least for the writers' of the script, a sense of anomaly.

In the mass media stories that are doing the work of seeding the concept, terms such as these are often positioned prominently in the introductory material, in titles, and in headlines, functioning to announce the
applicability of the PC code even in instances when the story itself
doesn't readily produce a fit. In effect, they instruct the reader how to
interpret what follows. For example, the *Newsweek* issue cited above (24
Dec. 1990) includes an interview with Stanley Fish. Fish speaks against
the teaching of the literary canon in American universities, opposing the
imposition of an orthodoxy and supporting the enjoyment of difference
and diversity. The interview is headlined 'Learning to Love the PC
Canon.' The reader who knows how to apply the PC code will know how
to treat the headline as instructions for a selective reading; s/he will
search the interview for items that can be interpreted as PC, neglecting
those that cannot. It suggests that Fish's commitment to difference and
diversity be understood as imposing a new orthodoxy, the PC, rather
than the traditional, canon.

As it appears in multiple media sources, political correctness comes to
have a discursively constituted reality; it is represented as a definite movement or group. However heterogeneous the actual bases of protest may
be, and they are far from forming even effective political coalitions, the
PC code enables them to be represented as a political entity, threatening
freedom of speech. As such, the code is even replicated and transmitted
by people who would recoil from the right-wing political ideology in
which it originated. Timothy Findley, responding to accusations of racism
in the Canadian literary establishment, identifies the politically correct as
a kind of sectarian cult:

[It] is distressing to imagine how freedom to read might ultimately be affected by
those who believe in what is called political correctness. The politically correct
who have been so well intentioned, so protective of those whom they saw as
defenseless, soon became infected with paranoia. They threw up walls. They created ghettos. We stay in. You stay out, especially where the written word is concerned. (Findley 1994)

'They' take on a virtual reality. In some interpretations, 'their' threat to freedom is more than contingently related to good intentions. 'They,' the 'politically correct,' are represented as embracing an actively repressive philosophy: 'PC is, strictly speaking, a totalitarian philosophy' the *Newsweek* article (Adler et al. 1990) tells us. The circle is drawn; 'we' are inside; 'they' are the other who threatens 'our' freedom. It is a circle drawn in precisely the same way by Arthur Schlesinger, Jr, speaking in May 1994 to a Manhattan audience, who warns that, 'in a bizarre switch of roles,' First Amendment rights are endangered by the movement for political correctness in 'our' (U.S.) universities:

The ideologues of multiculturalism would reject the historic American purposes of assimilation and integration. They would have our educational system reinforce, promote and perpetuate separate ethnic communities and do so at the expense of the idea of a common culture and a common national identity. (Honan 1994)

That his argument replicates Findley's so exactly testifies to the operation of the code as an *organizer* of text-mediated relations. The sentences and language differ from text to text, but the social organization that orders and transmits their ordering is recursively reproduced.

Once effectively seeded, the code reproduces the social organization that draws the circle identifying 'us' with established institutions from 'them,' an enemy who threatens freedom of speech by insisting on being heard, and threatens what 'we' have in common by insisting on the validity of diverse cultural traditions. The generative power of the code reproduces this organization in the diverse and multiple sites of its use. Programs such as the CBC's on 'political correctness' or news stories such as that in *Newsweek* (Adler et al. 1990) have taught us, listeners or readers, the organization generated by the PC code. We know how to take it up, how to practise it. From editorial instructions (introductions, headlines, etc.), and from the stories and their narrative structure, readers/hearers have learnt how to apply the code and how to identify PC-type situations. It is now established as a device through which a politics may be entered into texts and talk without politics or ideology ever appearing. Here are two examples from a recent (to the writing of this paper) issue of the *New York Times Book Review*. The first is from a review of Stephen Birmingham's novel, *Carriage Trade*:

Silas Tarkington has done every merchandising trick in the book to make himself and his store appear Old World Classy. Neither 'Carriage Trade' nor Silas Tark-ington is remotely interested in political correctness. (Wasserstein 1993)

The second is from a review of Allan Bloom's *Love and Friendship*:

Nor did Bloom's social observations strike me as sharply observed. He mocks Smith College for urging students to resist 'lookism' (bias in favor of attractive people), an especially silly bit of political correctness, to be sure, but hardly proof that Americans no longer care about beauty. (Pollitt 1993)

These examples show the term 'political correctness' positioning reader and writer within the circle of the 'normal forms,' and not as among those 'interested in political correctness' or among the 'silly' opposed to a bias favouring 'attractive people.'

When people are criticized for how they have spoken or written of non-whites or women, they can turn the tables on criticism by discrediting it as PC. They are thereby magically positioned in an authoritative and legiti-mating order. Faculty in universities write memoranda identifying pres-sures felt in the classroom as political correctness; students ward off challenges to racist or sexist language; emblematic stories travel as a media-mediated form of gossip and crop up in characteristically formu-laic forms in meetings as accusations against progressive spokespeople or as supportive evidence or comments for right-wing speakers; a newspaper columnist identifies a university dean and vice-president with 'feminist / politically correct forces' because they sought to establish a teaching eval-uation that asked whether instructors used demeaning sexist and racist language in the classroom;[7] even progressive people, finding themselves under attack for racist and sexist practices built into the normal forms they have taken for granted, avail themselves of the PC code.[8] Thus the PC code, as regulator of the social relations of public discourse, sets up a discursive order locating the reading/listening subject within the circle that preserves the 'normal forms' and excludes initiatives for change from those the circle marginalizes. It redraws the time-dishonoured boundaries constituting the centrality of white masculinity to the rela-tions of ruling and the otherness of those who challenge that hegemony.

10

Texts and Repression: Hazards for Feminists in the Academy

Introduction

This chapter explores discourses and the intertextuality of discursive texts, not as literary or philosophical events, but as local practices organizing a sequential social act. Two texts will be examined. They make up a sequence, a kind of 'conversation,' though not by any means a friendly one. The sequence of texts is analysed for how it shapes public debate, articulating particular institutional sites, in this case, a university in Western Canada, into widening circles of debate and controversy. The texts to be explored concern issues of sexism raised in relation to a department of political science at a Canadian university. The controversy or debate that they generated reverberated through Canadian academic institutions, the networks of the women's movement in Canada, and to some extent the mass media, connecting with the larger politics of that counter-movement Sidney Blumenthal (1986) calls the 'counter-establishment' and Susan Faludi (1992), 'backlash.'

This investigation is preoccupied with discourse as it happens in sequences of social action, inseparable from such sequences and as constitutive and coordinating them. Here I am interested in repression as a textual practice and specifically in how an objectifying discourse can subdue the expression of divergent perspectives and experiences generated in the everyday actualities of social organization, supplanting them with an objectified form of 'consciousness.' In general, I want to learn more about how texts coordinate subjectivities or consciousnesses, the latter conceived as 'active' and inseparable from people in their activities, and, in this context, how texts that universalize or objectify, create forms of consciousness that override the 'naturally' occurring diversity of perspectives and experiences. Here, I think, is where the power that Michel Foucault (1980) attributes to knowledge comes into operation. Such universalizing or objectifying discourses operate to coordinate people's diversities of experience, perspective, and interest into a unified frame at the institutional level. They may indeed be constitutive of what we mean by 'institutions.'

The story begins before we have a text to work on in the experiences of women students (graduate and undergraduate) and junior faculty in a department of political science.[1] A committee led by one of the junior faculty made a report (hereafter, the Report) to the department describing, in the familiar itemizing form, the chilly climate that women experience in the department. That is the first text. It was presented and discussed at a faculty meeting in the spring of 1993. The second is a letter (hereafter, the Letter) responding to the Report, written by the tenured men in the department and addressed to the junior member of faculty who chaired the committee. It is copied to the vice-president academic, the president of the faculty association, and all regular faculty (of the department). In the Letter, the tenured male faculty members of the department call on the junior faculty member to withdraw the Report on the grounds that it makes unjustifed accusations of gross misconduct against them. Later, as the controversy widens, involving feminists elsewhere in Canada, academic and political networks among political scientists (many of them on the left politically), and the media, the Letter can be seen, I suggest, as a critical intervention *at the institutional level* that redefines the terms in which the issue will be debated, establishing the hegemony of a juridical discourse, with its language of allegations, evidence, due process, and so forth. The 'application' of the juridical discourse, I suggest, reproduces at the institutional level the forms of exclusion that the notion of 'chilly climate' assembles for women at the pre-predicative level of the gender organization of the university. One of the features of this controversy, of which I too was and am a part (and, of course, this paper as well), is the effectiveness of the juridical discourse of the Letter in redefining the intentions and competence of the Report. In effect, I and others I have talked to were captured by the text of the Letter and came to evaluate the original critique in its terms. Though we might sympathize with the women who wrote the Report, we were also critical of its methodological failings. Writing this in a hotel room in Fredericton, New Brunswick, I've just come from a conversation in which I discussed with friends who live there our experiences of that capture. We talked about how, though the Report spoke of what we'd at various times experienced ourselves, we had also been critical of its failure to measure up to the standards of evidence called for by the male faculty's Letter.

When women in the academy raise issues of sexism and racism or simply when we talk about it, the notion of a 'chilly climate' comes to hand. For us, it fishes up out of our experience an open-ended collection of instances. I've talked to women critical of the 'climate' committee's Report who yet say, 'I know what they're talking about.' So do I. And when I talk about these issues in a public setting, women in the audience are nodding their heads, smiling (maybe grimacing), turning to one another to make whispered comments. I can see that this notion and the kinds of instances it collects calls up experiences of their own that they can recognize as instances belonging in the collection. Sometimes they add to my collection by coming forward at the end of a talk to tell me of them.

This knowing-what-we-are-talking-about does not translate readily into terms that can be recognized and attended to at the institutional level of organization. Somehow what has appeared obvious gets dissolved into a collection of items each one of which by itself can be resolved into 'subjectivity,' or 'Well, it doesn't only happen to women,' or 'So he was bit rude/insensitive,' or 'where's your evidence?' The notion of 'chilly climate' and its ability to collect experiences fails when it comes to raising the issue at the level of the universalizing discourses in which the order of the academy is formulated. I want to understand how it happens that what may be obvious to feminists is not only invisible to the majority of their male colleagues or teachers, but can be so readily suppressed at the level of the institutional order. In analysing the dialogue in texts that initiated a major controversy, I hope to map the social organization of institutional repression in a way that will help us to see how it comes about.

I begin by formulating the kind of social organization of gender in which the experiences recognized by feminist discourse arise. I want to show how it generates different sites of experience for women and men. This is followed by a description and analysis of the 'chilly climate' Report and, very briefly, what happened when it was presented to the faculty meeting of the political science department. Then I describe the Letter written by the eight male tenured faculty and analyse its retroactive reading of the Report.

From the first text to the second text there is (a) a shift in venue from the department to the institutional level of the university; and (b) a repositioning of the issue from the feminist discourse in which the report was framed to a juridical discourse. The latter extends the umbrella of a regulatory order over how the issue is subsequently defined and discussed. The language of allegations, charges, evidence, and due process displaces feminist discourse and the experiences it has enabled women to recognize. It is a language that seems to be incapable of recognizing the kinds of experiences recognized by feminist discourse, depreciating and degrading what we have to report in forcing it into the framework of accusations, charges, allegations, and so forth. Its objectifying practices, vital in defending the freedoms of individuals against the state, come into play in this context to suppress and subordinate. Issues of due process, entitling the accused to identify their accusers and to respond to the specifics of their accusations, take on an oppressive cast where the accused stand in a relation of authority and superior power over those who are their 'accusers.'

Though subsequently withdrawn, the Letter provided the framework for public discussions within and beyond the university. The juridical discourse organizes how issues are represented and how they are addressed, *on both sides*. Its version of what happened also became a resource in the building of a 'backlash' discourse seeking to protect the academic freedoms of university faculty against the threat of 'inclusiveness' (Richer and Weir 1995). In this process, the problems of making changes in the local practices of sexism and racism that are part of the daily working life of universities disappear from view *at the institutional level*.

I am not arguing that this sequence of two texts represents a turning point (though it may have been); rather, it epitomizes an increasingly general deployment of a juridical discourse as a means of defending the *status quo ante* in universities against both feminist and anti-racist critiques. By the time a similar 'affair' had emerged at another Western Canadian university, the regulatory jurisdiction of the juridical discourse had already been established and came to hand in discrediting a critique of both sexism and racism launched by graduate students in that university's department of political science (Marchak 1996; Smith 1997).

A Brief Excursus on Method

Briefly, something about the method of analysis here. I have tried to avoid becoming technical. But I want to mark a difference in a method of reading that I discovered when I was working earlier on two versions of an event that took place in 1968 in Berkeley, California (Smith 1990d). We, I writing and you reading, are people whose work is deeply implicated in reading and writing, pages of print or computer screens. We take for granted the texts before us – that we can move back and forth in them, that we can read them in relation to one another, much as those did who investigated and reported on the Berkeley matter (going back and forth to try to arrive at a 'balanced' view of the matter). In my analysis of the two versions of the Berkeley event, I at first compared one account with the other, looking for differences, for where they converged, and so on. But then I came upon what I have since made into a methodological instruction for myself: investigate/analyse texts as they (might) 'occur' in actuality, namely, in some sequence of action in relation to each other. In the case of the alternate versions of the event in Berkeley, one account was superseded by the other; the second account was, in fact, designed to subsume and displace the first.

In my experience of these texts as a sequential course of reading, I found that the second provided a set of instructions for rereading the first. The retroactive reading was of a particular and interesting kind. It did not contradict the first. Rather, it subsumed it, so that the first-person accounts in the first text could be read as partial observations of what was *really* going on. The second text rewrote the events, supplying a level of organization that reinterpreted the observed events as expressions of an institutional order. The distinctive competence of its 'administrative' language was to subsume the descriptive language of the first. When the two texts I am examining in this chapter are viewed in this manner, analogous processes can be seen to be at work. The Letter reconstructs the feminist critique of the department made in the 'climate' committee's report. It is that reconstruction which is the focus here.

In a sense, the analysis also discovers my own practices of reading. Like others who had taken the part of the 'chilly climate' committee, I had nonetheless adopted the framework supplied by the Letter in looking at the Report as imperfectly researched and lacking the kind of evidence needed to sustain the 'allegations' the Letter instructed us to see it as making. The kinds of criticisms of the methodology of the Report, voiced or unvoiced, that I described above are organized, I think, by taking on the Letter's framework in a retroactive reading. It took the analysis reported in this chapter for me to be able to see how I had been implicated and how the Letter had been active in organizing my consciousness.

Intersections of Gender with the Regimes of University and Discourse

Gender organization is in large part historically sedimented and transmitted through local practices passed on hand-to-hand, so to speak, over generations. For the centuries of their history in Europe, universities have been exclusively for men. For centuries, knowledge and learning were among men, and men spoke to and wrote for other men. Back in 1964, Jessie Bernard (1964) discovered what she called the 'stag' effect: when men were asked to name those they held to be significant in their field, they named only men, even when there were women who had done work considered to be important. Here was a residue sedimented by an exclusively masculine history. I imagine that men took the maleness of their university and discursive colleagues for granted. Excluding women was built into their daily lives. Men's achievements were oriented to work done by other men, aiming for other men's esteem and recognition. Their everyday working lives were lived in a world in which women were never colleagues. If there at all, women were secretaries, research assistants, sessional instructors, cleaners, food servers or students – but never equals and co-participants. At home, there were wives and daughters, irrelevant to their work. I imagine how they talked only to other men about things that mattered, and that the things that mattered were what men talked about. Their camaraderie included men's jokes and comments on the physical attractiveness or otherwise of the women they encountered. They did not think of women students as those who might become colleagues; they sometimes looked at them from within the circle of male collectivity as sexual objects; they were sometimes useful; they were often irrelevant. Occasionally, a male faculty member married a student; there was occasional sex, an occasional affair.

I imagine an ethnography of a contemporary university department that would display the gender organization sedimented in the everyday work processes regulated by the university as a regime. It is this everyday level of social organization that remains largely out of sight. To help us envisage this level of organization, I am helped here by reading Alison Lee's (1996) account of the gender organization of a high-school classroom in which a course in geography was being taught:

[T]he most lasting impression I have of this classroom is of boys' voices ... of male voices physically swamping girls' ... [the boys'] voices were often loud, the physiological difference combining with the classroom spatial arrangements and their apparent sense of freedom to produce their voices in ways which asserted their presence fairly effectively ... there was a marked absence of girls' voices, despite their physical presence in the room. (Lee 1996: 72–3)

How familiar this is to those of us who have been reading the feminist

studies of female-male interaction and have come to be able to observe
what goes on around us! Lee continues:

Boys swamped girls in visible ways as well, through their numbers, the massing of
their bodies in clusters around the room, their occupation of most of the space.
Indeed, there was a strong sense of centre and periphery in the distribution of
bodies in space. Girls sat together in the front left-hand corner and seldom left
this space. Individual boys and groups of boys, on the other hand, moved regularly around the classroom space, visiting each other. (Lee 1996: 73)

Allowing for differences in going from the local to the institutional level,
we can surely find an analogous gender organization in those university
departments still bearing the sediments of their masculinist history.

In the past of the university, women, if present at all in an academic
role – as students, research assistants, researchers, instructors, and occasionally as faculty – were not members of the university on the same foot-
ing with men; their work did not count; they were not people who had
things of significance to say. If a woman were doing valuable work, it
could be appropriated without scruple or acknowledgment. Only men
could be the subjects of scientific sentences since, in the virtual world of
scientific discourse, only men were constituted 'author.' Were a woman
to occupy a position of authority, the contradiction between that position's authority and her subjectlessness as a woman would create uneasiness. A male colleague wrote of a woman university administrator of some
years past that 'she received an elaborate courtesy that was not born of
respect but rather, of unease ... she was not perceived as another academic administrator to be judged on the basis of her competence, but as
a different kind of creature' (quoted in Backhouse, Harris, Michell, and
Wylie 1995: 100). In university classrooms, men oriented (and orient) to
men as those who were or would be legitimate participants in the same
academic world. A collectivity of men could (and can) be activated across
the faculty-student status boundary by telling jokes about women, deni-
grating women's competence, and being sarcastic at women's expense
(particularly, of course, when women are present). A woman physics
major at Duke University in the 1990s tells this story:

On a physics test, her professor included the following example: Starting with the
lungs and using Bernoulli's equation, describe in full physical detail the production
of the sound 'Ohhh' by our lone sophomore female physics major. An anatomical
sketch would be helpful. (Quoted in Sandler, Silverberg, and Hall 1996: 33)

Women's local relationship to the universalized male subject was built into and reproduced by gendered speech genres in which women were excised as subjects, in which they were sexual objects and served as sexualized metaphors for objects, in which the standpoint of (white) men was exclusive vis-à-vis those it constituted as other – women and non-white peoples among them.

I imagine the absolute normality of the regime of masculinity in the university; I imagine it being just the way people lived and worked; I imagine the everyday ordinary language of hallway, cafeteria, bar, and classroom as building in the exclusion of women as subjects/speakers. The everyday working life of a university department is also organized by the discourse or discourses of the discipline the department represents. Here, too, are worlds still largely male-dominated whose authorized speakers (Smith 1987) are mainly male. It is an intellectual tradition largely written from the point of view of the men who made it. It is also an intellectual world that has been assembled from within an exclusively European tradition, which therefore organizes the work of classroom, the resources of library, and the language, objects, and conventions of discourse as a centre defining others who are not represented as subjects or auithorized speakers (Said 1979). The experiences, interests, and associations of men of a certain class and race bled into the paradigms of the humanities and social sciences, and even into the natural sciences (Spanier 1995: 149). In going to work in the library, listening to lectures, taking notes, working on papers, or taking tests, a woman student would not find a discourse in which, as a woman, she could appear as subject. Women or students from histories or cultures that were and are discursively excluded as subjects, and who may today be finding themselves as subjects and speakers in specialized programs (Women's Studies, Native Studies, and so on), are still absent or marginalized in mainstream discourse.

Projected into the present, this past has never been disavowed. The relations of discourse authorize and affirm the historically sedimented local organization of race and gender in the everyday worklife of faculty and student. Still today the majority of faculty are white men. In the local regime of a particular university, they are the authorized speakers and teachers of the discourses of their discipline. They are the authorized regulators of classrooms and assigned readings and those authorized to judge students' products. In the classroom, and the graduate classroom in particular, women and men are taught by men who can enter the discourses they teach without an experience of denial of presence, voice, and subject position. A self-insulating, self-reproducing system created in the past is decanted into the everyday ordinariness of the present.

The Feminist Critique

For women students and faculty in the university, a feminist discourse named what we had experienced but had not known how to speak. To women who know enough of feminist discourse to know how to name and see what is going on around them in the university, the taken-for-granted everyday practices of a male-dominated society display an ordinary, and pervasive, sexism. This is the reason the phrase 'a chilly climate for women' resonates. It originated in a report written in 1982 by Roberta Hall and Bernice Sandler (1982), where it was used to describe 'the myriad small inequities that by themselves seem unimportant, but taken together create a chilling environment' (Sandler, Silverberg, and Hall 1996: 1). An unsystematically assembled list drawn from my own experience, from interviews with women faculty in departments of political science in Canada, and from reading yields the following:

- Visitors to the department meeting you in the hallway ask for information or directions (are you a secretary?).
- You feel strangled in faculty meetings.
- You practise speaking complete sentences and paragraphs, rather than handing the completion of your meaning over to another by devices such as 'you know.'
- Your colleague in the next-door office stops by on his way to lunch with 'the boys' (your colleagues) and doesn't ask you to come along.
- You are junior faculty, untenured, working at night in your office, and the chair of the department drops by for a chat which has no purpose or point — is he going to make a pass?
- When an assistant dean comes to address the sociology faculty to emphasize the importance of toughening up grading, his language is inclusive only of men — 'you young men,' he says, 'get hot under the collar ...'
- When you try to raise issues of gender equity in hiring in a departmental search committee meeting, the chair shouts at you.
- When you have protested first to your chair, then to the dean, about being harassed by male students in an introductory sociology course in which you have made women a topic, nothing is done and you know you have only succeeded in exhibiting yourself as someone who cannot manage her classroom.

- When a distinguished woman scholar in your field is invited to give a lecture, none of the men in the department come – 'But I don't do feminist theory,' they say when asked why.
- In seminars and meetings, the men interrupt or ignore you; when you raise an issue, it's hard to get it discussed by them; and so on.

These are instances from the faculty side. A similar list could be written based on the experience of women students; and, from either side, of the experience of racism or homophobia.

The notion of climate does not define specific acts or kinds of behaviour; it locates the generalized character of a regime that is vested in the routine and everyday and in the ordinary as well as the technical languages which regenerate the local orderliness of the everyday work of a university. It is all around us and nowhere in particular, like the weather. Analogously the exclusions of non-white people, organized *variously* through state and economic organization, are articulated as the taken-for-granted local practices of universities.

When women students and a junior member of the faculty of the University of Victoria (Canada), constituted as the Committee to Make the Department More Supportive of Women (set up a year earlier), the 'climate' committee for short, made a critique of sexism in the Department of Political Science, they appealed implicitly to principles of rational discourse fundamental to the university. They sought to correct barriers, which feminist discourse has enabled us to recognize, to their full and equal participation in the academic discourses that the university sustains.

The historically sedimented masculine university creates major gender asymmetries. A symmetry of presence of women and men as subjects for each other has been lacking in the discourses it houses. Among other practices deforming the symmetry of presence in academic contexts is men's orienting to women in an exclusively sexual mode: 'Call me fussy,' said one woman student, 'I just object to someone staring at my bust all the time' (President's Advisory Committee on the Status of Women, University of Saskatchewan 1995: 186). Attending to a woman as a sexual object *in a professional context* displaces her as subject in a professional mode. Within the discourses of the sciences and humanities, men have been subjects for women, but women have not been subjects for men; and, until this women's movement, perhaps not even for each other or themselves.

Feminist discourse has developed categories that name, specify, and collect what it is about men's taken-for-granted and everyday working practices and modes of relating in the university that undermines women's participation as full equals in the discourses of the sciences and humanities. The concept of a 'chilly climate' is one. It expresses the pervasiveness of the problem, rather than specific acts.

Beginning in people's experience presupposes divergent perspectives and different interpretations. People bring to any moment of activity the deposits of their idiosyncratic biographies. But differences are also structured in the social organization of their everyday activities with others, and these, though modified by what individuals bring to the situation, are not idiosyncratic. Women can join in finding and recognizing experiences we have in common.

Men are situated differently in these historically sedimented gender relations and, for the most part, do not participate in a discourse that enables recognition of what it is that feminists are pointing to when we say: 'This is sexist.' 'One of the hardest things about working in my Faculty is that they don't know they have a problem. The majority of my Faculty would say they don't discriminate. Yet they make such obvious sexist comments' (woman faculty member, quoted in Backhouse, Harris, Michell, and Wylie 1995: 120). While feminists have no difficulty in recognizing in the Report written by the 'climate' committee of the University of Victoria's Political Science Department the lineaments of barriers we have experienced, men generally seem not to do so. Feminists who read the Report may say, as I did when I first read it, 'Well, it may not be put together as effectively as it might, but I know just what they're talking about.' We are reading as knowledgeable practitioners of the discourse within which the Report is written. It is familiar ground. It is clear that it has not been at all obvious to the male faculty who respond to it.

Men, however, are for the most part not competent readers, if readers at all, of feminist discourse. Nor are they sensitized by experiencing the uneasiness, dismay, anxiety, sometimes anger, which women may experience and which feminist discourse recognizes. The feminist critique does not raise issues for them at the level of academic discourse, where criticism is a familiar hazard, but at the level of their taken-for-granted and largely unreflective ways of doing things and of the very normality of the ways in which they relate to one another and to women.

The Report of the 'Climate' Committee

The report of the 'climate' committee was presented to the Department of Political Science in the spring of 1993. The members of the committee identified in the final paragraph of the Report were two graduate and three undergraduate students, and its chair, a junior faculty member (untenured). The Report is not in highly formalized form. It is not on letterhead paper; it is typed, but not expertly formatted (the format of subheadings displaces levels); it is not paginated. The date appears to have been added in a different typeface (I suspect it was typewritten onto an original computer-generated text). This does not create a problem of authenticity since there is no question about when it was delivered. It is identified in the first paragraph as the work of a committee that the Department of Political Science set up the previous year in response to concerns 'regarding the discouraging and unsupportive environment experienced by ... women students' that surfaced during the report of the department's Graduate Review Committee (Department of Political Science, minutes, 11 May 1992). The Report is thus clearly located as departmental business, authorized by the department.

The Report is, it says, 'preliminary.'[2] There is no extended account of its method of production. In the introductory paragraph, it is said that the Report 'emerg[ed] from discussions with ... women students.' The final paragraph refers to the committee's method of proceeding. '[It] has consulted widely with the student body and the Political Science Women's Caucus of the Course Union,[3] and through a variety of meetings, forums and exchanges.'[4]

The introductory section of the Report places the responsibility for change with the department as a whole, noting that it has already recognized its responsibilities in this respect by recent hirings aimed at rectifying its gender imbalance. However, concerns are expressed that the Report may meet with 'hostility, indifference, and the calling into question of women's credibility and right to participate in and make representation to the department on issues of equity.' These concerns had arisen because, earlier in the year, the Women's Caucus of the Political Science Course Union had made representations with respect to the hiring process then under way in the department and had been sharply rebuffed.

The general format of the Report is as follows: there are five major headings, under each of which instances of departmental 'practices' are described, followed by recommendations for change; the headings are 'Teaching,' 'Class Content,' 'Funding,' 'Sexual Harassment and Everyday Hostility,' and 'Hiring.' The Report concludes with a section titled 'Further Recommendations,' which is followed by the paragraph referred to above.

The sections display a regular structure. Each opens with a general statement about 'barriers' faced by women in the area designated by the heading. This is followed by several descriptive items that provide specific illustrations of the general statement. The descriptive items are mixed in character. Some refer to particular incidents, for example, under the heading 'Teaching': 'faculty comments such as "feminism is just Marxism in a skirt" and "feminism is just political puff."' Others generalize across a range of incidents, clearly relying on the feminist discourse on the academy for the concepts that assemble them: 'professors do not interrupt men who are dominating seminars or class participation, and do not encourage and support women speaking.' Still others make use of such categories of feminist discourse as 'sexist' without further specification: 'professors often refuse to allow women students to respond to extremely sexist and anti-feminist comments made in class by male students.' All sections conclude with recommendations for measures the department should take to remedy the situations they describe. These add up to a comprehensive program of change. In a sense, the Report is a hybrid, formulating its issues in an objectifying style, avoiding the identification of particular individuals, and attributing the problems to the department as a whole rather than to the individuals who were originally involved in the incidents described. At the same time, it has relied throughout, in generating its examples, on what feminist discourse recognizes in women's experience.

The Male Faculty Response

The Letter from the eight male tenured faculty is the second text. Addressed to the junior member of faculty who chaired the 'climate' committee, it was written some days after a departmental meeting at which the Report was discussed. Written on letterhead paper and 'professionally' formatted (though there are a number of minor typographical errors), it was accompanied with a memorandum informing the junior faculty member that copies of the Letter had been sent to the dean, the academic vice-president, and to the president of the faculty association, as well as to all regular faculty members (presumably of the department).[5] Using departmental letterhead appropriates for the Letter the authority of the institutional site. Copying the Letter to officers in the administrative hierarchy repositions the issues, at least as the Letter formulates, taking them from the departmental level to the level of the university at large, and thereby opting out of the collegial process in the department.

The Letter denies that the Report 'reflect[s] the reality' of the department. It asserts that the Report makes 'two utterly false statments [*sic*],' and that these are so damaging to the reputations of male faculty in the department that discussion cannot be pursued until they are withdrawn.[6] The Letter then quotes from the section of the Report headed 'Sexual Harassment and Everyday Hostility' as follows: 'Female staff and students experience harassment and hostility. The range of behaviours that women experience include the following: sexist and racist treatment of students in the class and during consulations [*sic*] ... sexual advances at social gatherings by male faculty members to students' (quoted in Bilson and Berger 1994: 12–13). These statements indicate, they claim, 'a pattern of corrupt and repugnant behaviours' and are 'so obviously damaging' to their reputations that they must be retracted. The formulation of statements as generalities implies that 'there have been many instances' of sexism and that 'more than one faculty member has made sexual advances to more than one student on more than one occasion.' It is their belief, they state, that 'there are no incidents whatsoever of the behaviours described;' the events described in the Report have never happened. The Letter then challenges Professor Brodribb to provide evidence supporting the statements made in the Report 'to the proper university authorities,' using the university's procedures for investigating sexual harassment, and to agree to abide by the results of the investigation. If, however, she cannot 'provide credible evidence to substantiate the assertions,' then they 'demand an unqualified apology and retraction' (Bilson and Berger 1994: 40) by a date six days from the date of the Letter. Collegial discussion, the Letter indicated, cannot be resumed until the matter is resolved. If credible evidence is not produced and no apology and retraction made, 'then it will be necessary ... to take further steps to protect our reputations.' This clause has been widely interpreted, including by the external reviewers (Bilson and Berger 1994: 41), as a threat to take legal action.

Reconstructing the 'Climate' Report

Michel Foucault's theory of discourse (Foucault 1972; 1981) proposes that the categories, concepts, theories, epistemologies, and methods of positing the objects and relations of discourse are constituted in its rules and conventions. The discourse on which the Letter relies is juridical. It is a discourse with the power to reorganize and subordinate other discourses. It is a particular practice of this power that is examined here in an analysis of how the Letter interprets and retroactively redefines the Report.

Central to the Letter is the construction of its discursive objects – assertions 'alleging sexist and racist behavior [sic]' and 'suggesting gross sexual misconduct,' indicating 'a pattern of corrupt and repugnant behaviours [sic].' The imposition of a juridical template over the Report generates these objects. It is useful to follow Stanley Fish's (1967) recommendation to analyse a text as a course of reading in which its meaning is built sequentially. I have taken his advice in analysing the Letter's 'conversation' with the Report as a sequence of steps, or perhaps devices, each next one of which relies on previous steps.

Step 1

The juridically relevant segments of the Report, namely its references to sexual harassment, sexism, and racism, are brought into focus; the remainder is discarded. The effect is to displace the Report as an account of a generalized 'climate' in the Department of Political Science. The section 'Sexual Harassment and Everyday Hostility,' which contains these references, is reproduced below in its entirety (the numbering is for purposes of referencing and does not appear in the original):

1. SEXUAL HARASSMENT AND EVERYDAY HOSTILITY:
2. Subtle (and not so subtle) forms of sexual harassment are a
3. significant barrier to women's full and equal participation in the department.
4. Female staff and students experience harassment and hostility. The range of
5. behaviours that women experience include the following:

6. – comments about the 'feminist imperialists'
7. – comments like 'I'm not going to be evaluated by the feminist police'
8. – sexist and racist treatment of students in the class and during consultations
9. – sexual advances at social gatherings by male faculty members to students
10. – pitting women against each other during class (eg. calling upon a devout
11. anti-feminist woman to argue it out with a feminist)
12. – interruption or blocking of conversations and exchanges between women,
13. especially when these seminar discussions focus on feminism
14. – the general silencing of women in seminar classes
15. – disparaging scholarship on women, or ridiculing material that deals with
16. women's perceptions or [sic] in class and informally (eg. derogatory
17. comments about 'the feminists' and 'feminism')
18. – sexist humour as a classroom device

19. *We recommend that this behaviour stop.

20. *We also recommend that faculty, staff and students who are addressing
21. issues of sexual harassment receive departmental support.
22. *We recommend that the Department take leadership in formulating a serious
23. and unequivocal policy against sexual harassment. This policy may serve as
24. an example to other sections of the University community.
25. *We recommend that an effective and serious approach to women's safety
26. become part of the mandate of Traffic & Security.

Step 2

The objectionable 'assertions' are extracted from the surrounding text of the original for quotation in the Letter. Two passages are selected (lines 4–5 and 8–9) and reassembled to make up the following passage:

Female staff and students experience harassment and hostility. The range of behaviours that women experience include the following: sexist and racist treatment of students in the class and during consulations [sic] ... sexual advances at social gatherings by male faculty members to students. (Quoted in Bilson and Berger 1994: 12–13)

Stripping away the context and adjusting the continuity produces a passage representing the Report that is fitted to the Letter's account of the offending assertions, as follows:

(a) The first sentence (lines 2–3 above) of the section is omitted. It defines the significance of sexual harassment as a barrier to women's 'full and equal participation in the department.' Omitting it removes any indication of the Report's claimed intention to treat the behaviours described as attributes of the department rather than to focus on the behaviour of individual members of the department. Omitting any reference to the Report's recommendations regarding the department's role in making change (lines 19–26) has a similar effect.
(b) The first two items (lines 6–7) in the list of the 'range of behaviours' are omitted. This omission is not noted in the letter. The remainder of the items (lines 10–18) illustrating the theme are also omitted. Thus, any passages incompatible with the Letter's reading of the Report as making 'allegations' of 'corrupt and repugnant behaviours' have been eliminated.

In reading the Report, I found the use of the concept of 'sexual harassment' equivocal. I think this is because it locates an intersection of discourses. As formalized procedures for dealing with complaints of sexual harassment have been established in universities, sexual harassment has come to be juridically defined and to be restricted increasingly to specifically sexual forms of harassment. The 'Report of the Review Committee into the Political Science Department,' written by Beth Bilson and Thomas R. Berger, cites a judicial decision formulating just such a restricted definition (Bilson and Berger 1994: 22). There is, however, a feminist usage that defines it more broadly to include behaviour that expresses hostility towards women or denigrates them as women. This usage is still current in the feminist literature and tends to survive institutionally where universities have harassment procedures which also take up racial harassment.[7]

As I start to read this section of the Report, its introductory paragraph (lines 2–5) tells me to discard the first of these interpretations (i.e., the juridical). The 'range' of the examples (lines 6–18) confirm the second, broader interpretation.[8] In omitting all but two of the items, the Letter restricts interpretation of 'sexual harassment' to the juridical, ruling out the broader feminist interpretation.

Step 3

Tracing a course of reading through the Letter, the reconstructed segment attributed to the Report can be seen as the object referred to in the Letter's next move – the construction of the 'assertions' as 'obviously damaging to our reputations.' 'Obviously' instructs the reader to register the reputational damage as what anyone could see. We have seen in step 2 how the groundwork for this has been laid. The next move is to articulate the 'objects' within the framework and juridical language of the Letter. The items illustrating 'sexual harassment and everyday hostility' can now be read as 'unfounded assertions' 'alleging sexist and racist behavior' and 'suggesting gross sexual misconduct,' together 'indicat[ing] a pattern of corrupt and repugnant behaviours.'[9]

Step 4

The course of reading that the Letter sets up for the reader upgrades the rhetorical value of references to 'sexist behavior':

(a) The original wording of the Report is reconstructed in a juridical language: 'sexual advances at social gatherings' (the Report) becomes 'gross sexual misconduct' (the Letter). An intertextual tie is set up between the 'assertions' and grounds for dismissal of faculty that may be written into disciplinary clauses of faculty-university contracts and/or into the formalized sexual harassment procedures of the university.[10] There are implications, therefore, that more than reputation could be at stake.

(b) Stripping away all other items except the reference to sexist and racist treatment of students has had the general rhetorical effect of enhancing the offensive value of the assertions. I found the jump from 'sexual advances at social gatherings' to 'gross sexual misconduct' rather startling. It is a rhetorical shift in the offensive value of the item as it appeared in the Report; but accomplished, as it is, in step-by-step fashion, the reader does not necessarily recognize how steep the shift has been.

In later texts, further along in the widening controversy, there are further upgradings. These are also filtered through the ordinary process through which one text refers back to another, which refers back to another, and so on. Readers, however, don't generally lay the texts side by side to compare them. Being accused of making sexual advances to students at parties would hardly warrant the formality of the Letter's indictment. Upgrading the offence brings it to a level commensurate with the outrage the Letter expresses. Here is the groundwork for further upgradings, first in an informally distributed paper written by one of the signatories to the Letter (who refers to 'allegations' of 'truly corrupt and violent behaviour') (Magnusson 1993: 5); and, later, John Fekete performs a further upgrading – 'sexual advances' by faculty to students at social affairs become 'sex-crimes' (Fekete 1994: 294).

Step 5

Juridical discourse is objectifying. It pre-empts diversities of consciousness and experience. Its procedures subdue such differences to methods of dispelling ambiguity, of the determination of what constitutes good evidence, and so forth. Categories must have a determinate reference to events, states of affairs, and so on, independent of the statements that use them. The wording of the Report must be reshaped into formulations of definite acts performed by actual and identifiable individuals. Once defined as charges or accusations, they must meet crititeria of proper evidence. Determination of truth and falsity is a project integral to the practice of objectivity and to arriving at an account capable of overriding what you think, what I think, what she thinks. In the first two paragraphs of the Letter, a falsehood/reality contrast is introduced: the Report 'provides a portrait of our Department which, in our view, does not reflect reality'; and 'there are two utterly false statments [*sic*] in the report ...' The sequence I have analysed as a course of 'construction' follows. Only then can the junior faculty member chairing the 'chilly climate' committee be challenged to produce 'credible evidence' for 'the proper university authorities.' The insistence on a retraction if credible evidence is lacking relies on a whole course of construction that has transformed the Report's delineation of a 'climate' into allegations of determinate and improper acts committed by definite people on definite occasions for which evidence must be brought to if their truth or falsity is to be assessed.

To my count, the Report lists twenty illustrative items; the Letter focuses on only two. Some of these items describe students in class being treated, either by the instructor or by other students, in ways that should surely be considered as less than the best professional practice, regardless of whether women or men are involved. Instructors are described as treating women students and what they put forward with contempt; as allowing, even encouraging, 'harassing' behaviour from male students in class that is continued outside class; as allowing male students to dominate classroom discussions; as making 'patronizing and demeaning comments on work submitted'; and so on. These are not made an issue in the Letter. Nor are the questions the Report raises about the lack of feminist content in mandatory political science courses and of feminist and Native instructors. In stripping down the Report to fit the juridical frame, the Letter disables the Report's attempt to make visible a taken-for-granted gender order that deformed the conditions of women's full and equal participation in the discourse of political science.[11]

At what point does criticism become accusation? At what point does the detailing of critique become 'charges' and 'allegations'? The theory of symbolic interaction and its echoes in ethnomethodology tell us that it is the response to the act that gives the latter its determinate character. Here we see an act, the Report, given definition in the terms, syntax, and methods of juridical discourse. The institutional character of the Letter elevates the Report to its own status. It was publicized in an article in the *Globe and Mail* (Wilson 1993), which appeared shortly after the date of the Letter. Its interpretation comes to dominate the debates that followed, including the issues focused on by the external review (Bilson and Berger 1994). In a sense, the Letter *produces the accusations of which it complains.* The external reviewers observed: 'It is all very well to say that the purpose

of the report of the Chilly Climate Committee was not to indict individuals. Yet that is its effect' (Bilson and Berger 1994: 55). It is an effect that
the Letter itself creates in its retroactive reconstitution of the Report as a
formalized and public or semi-public document, reinterpreted in a juridical mode.[12]

Juridical Discourse and Institutional Debate

The social organization of the everyday in which the women's experiences originated were worked up into the text of the Report in meetings
and discussions among them. The Report is entered into a departmental
sequence of action: it originated when the committee was set up by a
decision of a departmental meeting in the previous year; it is delivered at
a departmental meeting; is discussed; further work on it is called for. Faculty at the meeting did not welcome the Report, and, at the male faculty's
request, it was forwarded to the equity office of the university. No move
had been taken by that office by the date of the Letter, which lodged the
'accusations' at the institutional level by 'copying' the letter to the dean,
the vice-president (academic), and the president of the faculty association. The projected, but incomplete, departmental sequence of producing, reading, and responding to a text that attempts to describe typical
aspects of women's experiences in the department is abruptly pre-
empted by the men's Letter. The latter launches the issue into institutional space not only of the university but also, implied in the threat to
take 'further steps to protect our reputations,'[13] of law and state. It establishes the discourse that will regulate debate, providing schemata, terms,
discursive objects, an epistemology (positivist), and methodological conventions for determining the truth-value of propositions. The external
review written by Beth Bilson and Thomas Berger, despite its generally
sympathetic treatment ot the issues raised by the 'chilly climate' Report,
clearly adopts its problematic from the Letter.[14]

To read is to expose oneself to capture. It is to risk being entered by an
organization of language and making it ours. The power of a text bearing
the marks of authority when it is launched into public space is considerable. As readers are captured, it comes to provide the terms of discussion
with others similarly caught. I have referred to my own experience of
such capture earlier. In setting the terms and schemata of debate, the
Letter establishes a shift in focus from the issues about women's situation
in the department to the damage to the male faculty's reputations and
issues of due process. As debate engages, the terms and schemata that will

organize it have already been put in place,[15] a powerful and ordinary feature of the regulation of public discourse.

Thus the juridical interpretation and the texts it organizes are foundational to the debate that follows. Reviewed from the standpoint established by the Letter, the Report is evaluated in terms of evidential requirements which an internal critique of the department would not have called for. As an internal document, the Report could be taken to be *pointing out* what could be observed by any member of the department; indeed, some of my interview data suggests that what the committee intended was to make concrete and explicit issues which had been left vague and ambiguous in a previous report to the department on this and related topics. The Letter, however, relocates the Report at the institutional level as well as subduing it to juridical discourse.

Juridical discourse organizes subsequent criticisms of the Report. The Report is treated as if it had been intended originally as a public text launched at the institutional level. The 'Report of the Review Committee into the Political Science Department' (Bilson and Berger 1994), the last and most authoritative of a series of reviews of the events, is fully in the juridical mode. Though generally favourable to the Report, it criticizes its methodology, drawing on a critique by a distinguished feminist sociologist who had been consulted by members of the 'chilly climate' committee (Bilson and Berger 1994: 17–19); it deplores the Report's ambiguous use of terms such as 'sexism' and 'harassment' (ibid.: 24), supplying its own authoritative and unidimensional definitions, based on a judicial decision; criticizes the Report's reliance on women's experience; and is particularly critical of the violations of due process in the 'accusations' it makes against the men. Once it is launched into public space, the Report is examined for methodological standards of objectivity which are not normally required of internal departmental documents, particularly those that are preliminaries to departmental discussion. It is called to this level of accountability in the process of being redefined and recast through the steps taken by the senior male faculty of the department.

The Letter's reading of the Report establishes a template that can be distilled from later stories, reviews, and so on: *women make serious accusations of sexism or sexual harassment against men, damaging their reputations and putting them at risk of serious penalties. It turns out, however, either that there are no objective grounds for their accusations or that the behaviour they describe is trivial.* This template structures how this or similar controversies are reported in the public media: male faculty at universities are unjustly accused, and false or misleading allegations are made; professors are accused of serious, even criminal, misconduct that, upon investigation, is seen to be trivial and/or unsubstantiated; universities fail to observe due process and proceed to 'punish' the professors before allegations have been substantiated. The stories are produced out of a sequence of actions mandated by a juridical discourse. The analysis above has displayed the substructure of one such story. We can see how an internal criticism of a department once read juridically and transposed into a public arena can be read as an 'accusation' of 'wrongdoing.' Once 'normal rules of justice and due process' are applied, the issue becomes the wrong done to the professors, rather than the women's critique.

John Fekete's (1994) critique of what he calls 'a new authoritarianism' (198) in universities describes 'professors on trial.' Among them are those whose Letter is under examination here. His account of the Report of the 'climate' committee relies on the Letter's productive work as well as on a later contribution (Magnusson 1993) to the bitterness of the debate. He tells us that the Report 'suggests ... a pattern of corrupt and violent behaviour' (289) and that 'sex-crime charges' were made (294). The *Alberta Report* (1995) describes the 'climate' committee's Report as making 'baseless' accusations 'of fostering academic bigotry and sexually harassing female undergrads' against 'unnamed male professors'(38). The introductory paragraph of a front-page article in the *Globe and Mail*[16] (Saunders 1995) presents a critique of what is described as the use of sexual harassment codes to discipline professors 'for ironic comments, passing glances and lectures that students or fellow faculty find upsetting' (A1). The article argues that '... for professors accused of wrongdoing, the normal rules of justice and due process frequently do not apply' (A1). Citing the case examined here as an example, the article suggests that some universities have allowed 'individual professors – or even entire departments, through so-called "chilly climate" investigations – to be disciplined for a wide range of actions that stop short of genuine sexual harassment ...' (A3). At another university, a move by the administration to suspend graduate admissions to a department of which criticisms of racism and sexism had been made, becomes, when it is interpreted by the juridical discourse's mandated course of action (Smith 1990d), punishment dealt out without due process. Interpreted otherwise, say, in terms of a university administration's responsibilities to its students, the administration's edict would have read, not as punishment improperly applied, but as an appropriate administrative intervention in a department that it had judged to have rather serious problems with its graduate program.

The 'wide range of actions' that constitute the body of the Report's critique become, when this template is imposed, only a resource for demonstrating the frivolous nature of the 'accusations' that the women have made. Instances drawn from the feminist critique, particularly those that go back to the issues of 'climate,' are represented as groundless or trivial – the *Globe and Mail* article has the subhead 'Ruffled Feathers on Campus' (Saunders 1995: A3). In a later and analogous episode at another Western Canadian university, the Civil Liberties Association reviewing a report on the situation prepared by a lawyer, commented 'that in the thirty-two pages of repetitive allegations, the preponderance were "minor in nature" and did "not obviously provide a basis for a claim of racism or sexism"' (Marchak 1996: 114). The same structure generates the stories travelling the gossip channels among academics involved in a movement identifying itself with 'academic freedom' and opposing those who raise issues of gender or racial inequities in universities. I heard some of these stories at the 1997 conference 'Academic Freedom and the Inclusive University' at the University of British Columbia. For example: a story of women who went on a packaged tour and brought a case under the Human Rights Code for sexual discrimination against the tour operator because he arranged for them to be served croissants for breakfast; the story of one of the professors involved in the case I have discussed here as having been accused of sexual harassment by one of the student members of the 'chilly climate' committee *when,* the teller of the tale reported with some pleasure, *they had never even met.* Michèle Le Doeuff, quoted in the introduction to the Report, writes that as a philosopher, on the one hand, she faces 'fierce opposition' and, on the other hand, is told that 'you are making a lot of fuss about nothing' (Le Doeuff in Climate Committee 1993).

Discussion

I have wanted to write this not as a micro-sociology that addresses only the local setting in which it arises, but to make a sociological investigation of a particular local sequence of action as it participates in a general institutional level of organization. Generalized and generalizing discourses participate in the organization of local sequences of text-mediated action and hence in the ongoing reproducing of the university as a regime co-ordinating local resources of funding, personnel, real estate, teaching responsibilities, and so on, with discourses organized extra-locally and hooking up with other universities and other institutions.

Reproduced at the level of the public text-mediated relations of discourse, the juridical offers devices that can be used to pre-empt the recognition of experientially based criticisms of sexism or racism in institutional settings.[17] The analysis shows a passage from women's experience into an objectifying discourse as a locally organized sequence of action that is from the outset coordinated with extra-locally organized discourses. In a sense, the sequence of two texts is a sequence of discourses in which the juridical is successful in suspending the efficacy, at least for this sequence, of a feminist discourse specifically aimed at giving expression to experience, even providing generalized forms in which it can be objectified (made independent of particular subjectivities). The method of analysis explores texts as they are entered into and are integral to the organization of sequences of action. The organizing or regulating operation of texts allows us to see how the unfolding and open-ended character of actual people's activities achieves what can be described as 'organization' or 'institution.' Printed and published, texts supply *a standardized, replicable form of words*, detachable from the particular local setting in which the original sequence of action occurred. Texts can be thought of as supplying one part in a conversation, but a part that can be standardized across multiple conversations in different local settings and at different times. Analysis, therefore, of texts as constituents of particular local sequences of action discovers the extra-local organization of discourse and, in a sense, how it can be described as discourse and hence as something existing independently of particular sites of reading and talk. What Michel Foucault (1981) calls 'the order of discourse' organizes, even *regulates*, particular text-reader conversations and particular sequences of action.

In the sequence I have described and analysed here, the order of juridical discourse can be seen also as having the 'capacity' to supersede or subsume other discourses. It relies on an epistemological 'theory,' built into the notion of 'evidence,' that there is a reality knowable in the same way by anyone, against which statements about it can be tested. Its procedures are objectifying, displacing particular perspectives and experiences. A single version of events or deeds has to be produced that is independent of its experiential, and hence necessarily partial, ground. It constructs a determinate event or act for which evidence can be produced and hence relies on what is describable and knowable independently of particular viewpoints. It operates with something like an 'override' device which subdues diverging perspectives. It does not know how to handle different experiences of *one event* other than by discarding one or even both, in favour of an 'objective' version – what really happened.

The issues raised by feminist 'chilly climate' discourse are not readily fitted to such a discourse. Gender organization at the level of the every-day is necessarily reciprocal. It is not the same for women as for men. Alison Lee's description of the interactions of boys and girls in a high-school geography class illuminates these reciprocities. Experiences arising in these relations will diverge *systematically*. *Hence it may be difficult to align stories told by women and stories told by men of the 'same' situation*.[18] The problems that the 'chilly climate' discourse enables women to recognize do not readily resolve into specific acts, let alone acts describable as 'corrupt and repugnant' (the Letter). Imagine the girls in Lee's geography class making their feminist critique. It would be full of those 'myriad small inequities that by themselves seem unimportant' (Sandler, Silverberg, and Hall 1996: 1). Feminists writing on the topic commonly refer to problems of specifying just where the problems they encounter lie and how to describe them. Susan Prentice writes:

... climate is pervasive and systemic, the result of compounded effects, it becomes difficult to pinpoint exactly what initiatives would 'warm' or remedy the climate ... Paula Caplan has pointed out that women faculty and students experience the climate as a 'ton of feathers.' (Prentice 1996: 3)

For the juridical order of discourse, the everyday social organization of gender relations presents problems: it is not easy to produce systematic descriptions of acts or categories of acts that can be identified and recognized again; the acts themselves are embedded in and part of a social organization that generates systematic differences and reciprocities of experience for women and men.

Objectifying discourses have a special status in institutions. They may, indeed, provide for what we mean by 'institution.' Patricia Marchak (1996) sees the critiques of racism and sexism as a threat to the universality and objectivity that are foundational to the university and the authority of its faculty to teach and judge. In speaking from women's experience, women are speaking from one side of an historically normalized organization of social relations in which men, and not women, have represented and derived their authority from the objectified order. Public challenge to the gender order of domination threaded into the texture of faculty–faculty and faculty–student relationships threatens what Joan Landes describes as 'the masquerade through which the (male) particular was able to posture behind the veil of the universal' (Landes 1995: 98). 'Chilly climate' discourse exposes the masquerade and puts in question the authority that relies on the objectified order.

The 'chilly climate' Report, aimed at changing a department's practices, was brought to the 'governing' body of the department as a step in initiating change. It performed an act of judgment, evaluating the department, criticizing its gender order and, either directly or by implication, the men occupying the institutionally defined positions of power and authority within it. An act of judgment constitutes the authority of those who judge. Here are women judging men, students and junior faculty judging senior faculty. For the men to respond by accepting the validity of the critique would imply acceptance of the authority of those who judge in this matter, reversing the institutional standing of the male tenured faculty vis-à-vis junior faculty and students and, in making visible 'the male particular behind the veil of the universal,' putting their authority as faculty in question. The Report claims implicitly, under principles of symmetry and reciprocity, the right to judge the judges. The Letter redresses the balance of authority to judge in the direction of the established gender regime. *It restores the coincidence of gender and formal institutional hierarchies that is challenged by the Report.* The eight male faculty, signatories to the Letter, are constituted as subjects within juridical discourse; they appropriate its authority in challenging the feminist critique.

At the surface constituted by the texts, the local settings of the course of action of which they were originally part do not appear. In the ensuing controversy, it is the texts that define the issues. They are all that ascend from the particular local setting into the strata of discourse. They do not travel with the debris of actuality. The social organization supplied by the texts themselves admit only the categories written into them. In the Letter, the parties to the sequence appear as equals (notice that the Letter is addressed to the junior faculty member alone and does not include the students as addressees; nor does it identify the differences in status). The signatories have been 'accused'; due process requires that they should have an opportunity of confronting their accuser and the particulars of the accusation so that they can defend themselves. The local setting has disappeared, including the gendered character of the university's regime and the relative positions of participants in it. That these are senior male faculty with tenure, including the chair of the department, confronting women students and a junior faculty member undergoing tenure review, is not admissible to the discourse it contains. Invisible also at the surface of these texts is the fact that these are men who have played their part in the university at large, been present on its senate, participated in its faculty association, served on committees, been present on formal occasions, and met less formally in a variety of settings with other members of faculty. Some had direct connections with the provincial government then in power, and all, or most, have extensive connections with political scientists in other parts of Canada. In short, they are men who are widely respected and known; men of substance and standing within the institutional order. In writing the Letter and circulating other documents in support of their position, they had taken for granted, as the writers of the Report had not, that they could command university resources, such as the worktime and skills of departmental support staff, as well as departmental technologies of producing and reproducing documents; they had taken for granted that their Letter could be properly produced on official departmental stationery, be distributed by departmental staff, and later, when they feared that the Report had been distributed widely throughout the country, that they could mail the texts of their rebuttals to faculty members in universities across the country. Though the students active on the committee were not directly addressed by the Letter and the Report carries no names, they had been present at the departmental meeting at which the Report was discussed and were known to male faculty. All members of the committee were potentially exposed to direct or indirect penalties by those with various forms of power over them, including command over resources of the university to use against them. These aspects of what was happening as the sequence of texts originally unfolded are missing from the textual surfaces and *become inadmissible* to the text-reader conversations to which they articulate elsewhere or elsewhen.[19] The connection of the sequence of texts to the everyday gender order of the university is disrupted. *The validity of the critique rather than its substance becomes the issue to be debated.*

Jürgen Habermas's (1970) formulation of the ideal speech situation as foundational to an ethic of rational discourse offers, I suggest, principles by which universities could take up critiques of sexism and racism as legitimate issues. He holds that rationality, truth, and justice rely on the principles of the ideal speech situation in which speakers seek to be understood, to tell the truth, in terms of their own feelings as well as what they know of the world beyond their own subjectivity, and to be accepted by the other as speaking in terms of norms and values they share. The relationship is reciprocal. Each party is both speaker and hearer and recognizes the other as such; there is full mutual recognition of each participant as a subject and a symmetry of the presence of subjects for each other; no one participant is privileged in the performance of dialogic roles, with the implication that though one may teach, the other too is recognized as a subject who may argue and question. Theorizing an ideal speech situation as foundational to rational discourse enables identification of sources that 'deform' its realization. Deformations may arise from 'the social structure on the basis of asymmetries in the performance of dialogue roles' (Habermas 1970: 144). Rationality, for Habermas, is a form of life free from the deformations of arbitrary domination.

The concept of the ideal speech situation offers a foundation for rationality other than Landes's 'masquerade of objectivity' that is uncovered when other subject positions are granted admission. It extrapolates from the very existence of speech and from the intention to understand and be understood built into it. In its ideality, it entails symmetry and reciprocity among subjects in the relationship. It offers not a description but a measure against which the actual can be evaluated. It is specifically attentive to deformations of its ideality arising from the 'social structure' in which the speech situation is set, particularly those that are not fully conscious.

Gender and race are deformations of the ideal speech situation that have been taken for granted in the work life of universities. To criticize these is not to undermine the very fabric of the university by undermining the claim to objectivity and objective judgment on which the authority of its faculty is based, as Marchak (1996) suggests. On the contrary, it is to discover deformations that injure the university's commitment to rationality and truth and its claims to universality. Furthermore, a dialogue conducted under 'rules' of symmetry and reciprocity implicit in the 'ideal speech situation' would proceed very differently from that which ensued from the 'chilly climate' Report. The problem of the gender organization of the everyday – that what women experience is not what men experience and vice versa – would be recognized from the outset. Both parties would have been committed to listening each other. Both parties would be committed to the possibility of being changed in the course of dialogue. The women might say, 'Listen, here are some of the things that we have experienced in classrooms as students or in meetings and hallways and offices as faculty: we have been silenced, ridiculed, ignored, depreciated.' And the men would say: 'We don't know what you're talking about.' And the women say: 'Just listen, just be prepared to believe that this is what we experience in our relationships with you.' White feminists have entered into just such dialogues with women of colour in which we (white feminists) have learned something of what it is that we (white people) may be doing that silences, marginalizes, and depreciates women of colour. To take such critiques seriously means examining them, not as accusations, but rather as a realization of the university's commitment to rationality and truth that calls for a reappraisal of its taken-for-granted everyday practices.

Far from threatening the foundations of the university, critiques of racism and sexism are better understood as committed to removing deformations that have been historically sedimented in the everyday working life and the intellectual practices of universities in North America. Those who make the critique can be seen as measuring a university against an implicit ideal of fully reciprocal and symmetrical dialogue as foundational to universities' claims to universality and commitment to rational discourse.

11

Conclusion

Marx wrote of the theoretical categories of economics as the expressions of the social relations of production.[1] Implied is the notion that theories reflect social relations and that hidden behind the discursively constituted object is an actuality of people's coordinated activities. Various contemporary theories reflect, I think, the actualities of social relations I have described above as the ruling relations. Post-structuralism theorizes the objectification of language and discourse, taking over from structuralism its shift of meaning from signs that 'come to hand' as tools for the speaker's or writer's use to meaning as generated by the interrelations of a system of signs that constitute subjects. Sociology's organizational theory is expanded by a new 'institutionalism' (Scott 1995) beyond the boundaries of discrete organizations into 'complexes of cultural rules' (ibid.: 30). The same presence is the veiled object of James Beniger's (1988) conceptualization and historical treatment of control through communication.

From varying theoretical standpoints, we are locating the same object. There is a real beast there. My own conception of the 'ruling relations' is not intended strictly as theory but as ostensive, that is, as pointing to the beast and providing a preliminary formulation to be filled out, stretched and changed progressively as we discover more about it. We know and can know these relations, as indeed anything else we know, from within as their practitioners. When I put forward the notion of an insider's sociology (Smith 1987), I meant that however we conceptualize the social, we can in fact only find it from within the practices/activities of our own everyday/everynight living.

Taking the standpoint of women in exploring the social has meant for me, among other things, opening up inquiry from that insider's positioning. I am, of course, a participant in the ruling relations. I know them from the inside. Apart from the two papers in the section on theory, the papers in this collection have been driven, for the most part, by various experiences of uneasiness arising from that participation. As I wrote in introducing them (chapter 1), they have been motivated by a sense that I have some difficulty here, some problem, some discomfort with the thinking I know how to do as participant. The women's movement had taught me something that I did not know I was learning, namely, to refuse disjunctures between who I am in the everyday actualities of my living and my relationships with others and my participation in the objectified discourses of my working life. This, of course, has been a perpetual engagement, one that is never complete. It is this engagement that has been translated in most of these essays into inquiries that explicate these discomforts as discourse. What is it about the academy that undermines and reworks the project of reclaiming it for women in general? Where is the inner flaw in the discourse of political economy that marginalizes women? How are the theoretical commitments of established sociology at work in reproducing patriarchy? And in the papers collected as chapters in the final third of this book, I develop analyses that have learned from the theoretical papers in the middle section that what I am exploring are the local practices of the social relations of the objectified discourses of ruling.

In contexts too numerous to identify in a concluding chapter, sociologists have been preoccupied with the problem of articulating micro- with macro-sociologies. I have in any case no interest in entering the debates on this topic. But I want to mark a difference in my own work that comes from having appropriated from Marx and Engels a way of conceptualizing people's active being in social relations that displaces that dichotomy from the outset:

Individuals always started, and always start, from themselves. Their relations are the relations of their real life. How does it happen that their relations assume an independent existence over against them? And that the forces of their own life overpower them? (Marx and Engels 1973: 30)

I have taken this formulation as the theoretical blueprint for exploring the everyday/everynight world as the problematic of a feminist sociology (Smith 1987). Of course, taking women's standpoint gives a different cast to this project because it finds people's starting place in real life as the local actualities of our everyday/everynight living. Applied in the region located by the notion of ruling relations, it directs us, or has directed me, to focus on the ways in which we are active in producing and reproducing the social relations of discourse or large-scale organization, and, inversely, the ways in which those social relations overpower our lives. Our local practices are both determined by and contribute to the social relations with which they are coordinated. I am reformulating thus the linguistic or discursive formulations of post-structuralism as social relations in which people are active.

In the papers collected in the last section of the book, I have been exploring sites of my own uneasiness in these overpowering relations so as to make visible the local practices that coordinate them *as relations*. I keep in mind, though I have not explored here, the problematic of the dynamic that emerges out of the objectified complex of these relations, with their strange mixing of forces and power – the forces that arise out of conjunctions that no one intends or controls, conceptualized in literary theory as 'intertextuality,' and the power generated by an organization of consciousnesses that is objectified and subject to continual redesigning and reworking.

Though their focus is on detail, I want these last papers to be taken seriously as investigations into the sociology of the ruling relations. The blind scholars who have hold of the different parts of the elephant, one a leg, another the trunk, another the tail, and so forth, each have a different theory of the beast they cannot see as a whole. Though they were talking to one another, they stuck to their independently conceived theories, frustrating the possibility of discovering more about the beast that organizes their experience of it. I have taken up a rather different project here. It has been to write sociological studies at the conjunction of scholar and the piece of the beast that she has hold of and that gives determination to her experience of it. I have made, I think, discoveries. They have come out of conjoining discourse and the actualities of my local practices, drawing on theory and concepts, such as Mikhail Bakhtin's theorizing of speech genres and the dialogic of the novel, and working on and with them to formulate my local practices as aspects of the social organization of the ruling relations. This is to work with theory and concepts to make visible these relations, our elephant (and all too white), and to pursue the project enunciated in chapter 6 of 'telling the truth after postmodernism.' A discourse that makes the social its object is never independent of the social it explicates and discovers for us as phenomena (see chapter 6). In writing the social, we are always writing of what is beyond the discursive practices in which it is represented; at the same time, our discursive representations can only be brought into play in coordinating the direction of our attention to the aspects of the social they intend.

I do not remember whether the story of the blind scholars and the elephant has a happy ending. Did they discover the beast they had in common? Probably they were left, since the story mocks scholars, forever arguing over whose theory is correct. The moves I am making in this volume project a rather different kind of argument in which theory does not confront theory, but rather is brought into play in discovering and making discursively explicit the piece of the beast each has hold of and putting theory to the test of communicating what we are discovering so that others can recognize and attend to it in the hope that together we can find out how it relates us to each other. In that process, we have to return to the piece of the beast under our hands to check the adequacy of formulations to communicate what we experience. I do not imagine that we can find this 'beast' as a whole. For one thing, it is always developing, and, at this time, with the radicalizing technologies extrapolated from their basis in computers, it is being rapidly reorganized. For another, built into and pre-occupying its distinctive forms of consciousness and agency is the dynamic of capital's relations of production. As is suggested in chapter 5, the ruling relations *organize* contemporary forms of exploitation. They *organize* the regime of accumulation, that system of institutions organizing and regulating the social to sustain the processes of capital accumulation. It is an organizing that has to be continually renewed as the dynamic of accumulation disrupts and disorganizes transitory stabilities.

The chapter on the ruling relations attempts a preliminary mapping, a sketch of the terrain to be explored and written, with sections that are beginning to be filled in and others that are largely empty, awaiting the explorations that change the outline at the same time as they work up the detail. I do not imagine that the intimacies of the studies assembled in the last section of this book under the heading 'Investigations' are the only discovering project, nor are they the only project that I am at work on or that others working with an approach we have come to call 'institutional ethnography' are developing. They do represent, however, an insistence on discovering and writing the social as the everyday and everynight coordinating of people's actual activities and hence as always in motion. They open up that site where our own activities as participants in discourse enter into and contribute to forces that stand over against us and overpower our lives.

Notes

1: Introduction

1 Social constructionism (Berger and Luckmann) can be seen as an attempt to remedy this.

2 Here is the passage in which the phrase occurs: 'A social phenomena [*sic*] may be generically defined as an *interorganism behavior regularity* – that is, as a non-random coincidence in time and/or space of two or more organisms' behaviors' (Wallace 1988).

3 A collection of their work is to be found in Campbell and Manicom 1995. The following are among those who have been companions and co-workers in this project: Himani Bannerji, Marie Campbell, Gerald de Montigny, Marjorie Devault, Tim Diamond, Kamini Grahame, Peter Grahame, Alison Griffith, Ann Manicom, Liza McCoy, Eric Mykhalovskiy, Nancy Naples, Ellen Pence, Marilee Reimer, George Smith, Karen Swift, Susan Turner, and Yoko Ueda.

2: Contradictions for Feminist Social Scientists

1 Originally published under the title 'Contradictions for Feminist Social Scientists in the Academy,' in Heidi Gottfried, ed., *Feminism and Social Change: Bridging Theory and Practice* (Urbana: University of Illinois Press, 1996), pp. 46–59. Thanks to the University of Illinois Press for permission to publish it in this book.

3: Feminist Reflections on Political Economy

1 I am indebted to Nancy Jackson's exceptionally intelligent and critical reading.

2 It is true, of course, that if we'd read Simone de Beauvoir's *The Second Sex* more attentively, we might have become aware of this sooner. Perhaps because we were first necessarily preoccupied with the problems of developing a discursive space among women, we did not attend to the realities of the power relations within which our enterprise was undertaken.

3 See Marilyn Frye's marvellously lucid discussion of 'sexism' in her *Politics of Reality* (1983); and Sandra Harding's treatment of rationality in her essay 'Is Gender a Variable in Conceptions of Rationality? A Survey of the Issues' (1982).

4 Albert Chandler Jr's *The Visible Hand: The Managerial Revolution in American Business* (1977) is a remarkable study of this transition.

5 See David Noble's study of the emergence of the engineering profession in the United States at this period, *America by Design: Science, Technology and the Rise of Corporate Capitalism* (1979).

6 Thorstein Veblen's *The Higher Learning in America* (1957), should be seen in 'performative' terms as contributing to prying universities free from local controls and organizing them at an extra-local level. Veblen wrote at a watershed point in these developments, and his *Absentee Ownership* (1967) is also preoccupied with them, though it was never taken up in the same way as was *The Higher Learning in America*.

7 See Ben Bagdikian's *The Media Monopoly* (1983) for a very useful account of the relation between the re-siting of newspapers and the institutionalization of objectivity in reporting.

8 In chapter 4, on sociological theory as methods of writing patriarchy, I explore sociological theory as a set of conventions for writing this standpoint into sociological texts.

9 The reference here is to children's books by Maurice Sendak, about Mother Bear and Little Bear. In one book, Little Bear wishes for, or to be, fantastic things. To each one, Mother Bear replies, 'You can't have that wish, Little Bear!' until at last Little Bear finds a wish that she can grant. Mother Bear is definitely a realist.

10 Indeed it can be argued that Marx's method takes advantage of this in proposing that the very categories capable of displaying the properties of political economic relations awaited the development of capitalism, for only capitalism differentiates, and hence makes visible, the effects addressed by political economy.

11 See George W. Smith 1988.

12 Joan Acker (1987) has made precisely the same point in a paper that must have been in the writing at the same time as this. (We have a history of such happy coincidences in our work, speaking for an intellectual and political

companionship, though at a distance, of long-standing.) She writes of the job as a specific property of contemporary formal organization and of how structural accounts of class using notions of positions or places would seem to be grounded in that form of the organization of power in contemporary capitalism.

13 The 'main business' is not intended to carry a particular theoretical weight. It is a tentative conceptual locating of aspects of contemporary social relations which have some of the dynamic that class had in Marx's time, but which cannot in a simple way be reduced to class since they are properties of a complex organization of ruling relations. It is important in this context because it is helpful in making visible some of the problems women have in becoming full political subjects in contemporary capitalist society.

14 Hewlett continues: 'She was a kind woman and followed this up with a piece of personal advice: You know, if I were you, I would drop this whole project. You are an economist who has had enough sense to build a career in serious fields such as development economics. Why risk all that by getting everyone 's back up? The most depressing thing about her response was that I knew enough about her personal history to understand that she herself had encountered difficulties in bearing children mid-career. If she wouldn't take these issues seriously, who would?' (Hewlett 1986: 370).

15 See Sterling and Khouri 1979 on the Keynesian presuppositions of national economic statistical measures, such as the GNP.

16 Malnarich and Smith 1983.

17 Examples of work that goes beyond established relevancies are Diane Elson's strikingly original 'Socialization of the Market' (1988) and Nicky Hart's equally striking analysis 'Gender and Class in England' (1989).

18 In Marx's (Marx and Engels 1976) critique of the ideological practices of the German ideologists, we can find a preliminary isolation of some of the conceptual practices that are now integral to the organization of the ruling relations.

19 We wouldn't like the plumbing either.

4: Sociological Theory: Methods of Writing Patriarchy into Feminist Texts

1 I've worked in a preliminary way on this topic first in a presentation to Judith Baker's course in philosophy at Glendon College, York University, in the spring of 1988; then in a paper called 'Writing Sociology: The Feminist Contradiction,' presented at the conference 'Feminist Transformations of the Social Sciences,' at Hamilton College, Clinton, New York, in April 1988 (Smith 1988); and finally at the American Sociological Association meetings

in Atlanta in the same year in a session organized by Ruth Wallace. I am appreciative of these opportunities to try out a rather complex argument. The paper was finally published as 'Sociological Theory: Writing Patriarchy into Feminist Texts,' in Ruth Wallace, ed., *Feminism and Sociological Theory* (New York: Sage Publications, 1989), pp. 34–64. Thanks to Sage Publications for their permission to publish it here.

2 I use the term 'discourse' to encompass more than statements or the concepts, frameworks, and methodologies of a discipline. We are talking about the same world as we inhabit and our knowledge of it: our share in its ongoing accomplishment is the basis on which we can claim to know and speak of it. Sociology known in this way isn't just ideas in people's heads but a complex of sites: communications, printed texts, teaching in classrooms; practices of inquiry, including thinking, ideas, and concepts; multiple settings of organized talk – workshops, conferences, annual meetings – all of which imply, involve, are accomplished by, and exist only in people's actual activities, of which thinking is one moment. I use the term 'discourse' to identify these socially organized complexes of actions and material conditions, of course, including the texts and statements they bear. I've adapted my use of the term from Michel Foucault's use (Foucault 1972, 1981) to describe the actual organization of social relations coordinating multiple sites through the reading and writing of texts. As I use it, the term 'discourse' refers exclusively to what I have distinguished here as 'textually mediated discourse.'

3 Note that this is not an epistemological issue. It is not an issue of realism, positivism, interpretive sociology, or the like. Sociological epistemologies, for the most part, presuppose the sociological relations that I'm attempting to delineate here.

4 Indeed my dissertation supervisor compared me favourably to other women who had dropped out of the PhD program at Berkeley (largely, I believe, because of the systematic but impalpable discouragement we experienced), telling me that the difference between myself and other women graduate students was that I was 'responsible.'

5 For a fuller exposition of this approach, see chapter 3 of my *The Everyday World as Problematic: A Feminist Sociology* (1987). It is a method developed from the insights of the women's movement in a consciousness-raising practice that was foundational to the development of a feminist discourse, and a conjoining of the materialist method developed by Marx and Engels (1976) and Garfinkel's ethnomethodology (Garfinkel 1967). In different ways, all of these ground inquiry in the ongoing activities of actual individuals. For Marx and Engels, society and history come into being only as the ongoing actual activities of individuals and the material conditions of those activities, and not otherwise.

Although there are, of course, important divergences, notably in the siting of Marxist materialism in labour – the ongoing productive work that both produces and is the very form of social existence – as contrasted with the siting of ethnomethodology in micro-social contexts in which activities in language are the differentiated and virtually exclusive mode, Garfinkel's work opens up distinctively the site of concerted social activities and practices in the textually mediated organization of management, professions, government agencies, and so on, to inquiry conforming to the stipulations of a materialist method, which requires a focus on actual ongoing practices in definite actual settings. It is this aspect of his method and thinking that I have brought into relation to Marxist materialism as interpreted above (developed as a feminist method of inquiry here and in other publications such as *The Everyday World as Problematic* and *The Conceptual Practices of Power* [1990]).

6 See Hayden White's analysis of this form (White 1976).

7 This view of theory is developed more fully in chapter 7 below.

8 Indeed, it could be argued that sociology has been peculiarly subject to theorizing that makes primarily constitutional claims.

9 My interest here is in the constitutional dimensions of theories that organize the objectification of society in the discourse and, in so doing, organize the discourse. I am not concerned with epistemological issues such as positivism. This is not a critique of positivism, but an exploration of the social organization of discourse.

10 Thus Durkheim: 'We use the word "function," in preference to "end" or "purpose," precisely because social phenomena do not generally exist for the useful results they produce. We must determine whether there is a correspondence between the fact under consideration and the general needs of the social organism, and in what this correspondence consists, without occupying ourselves with whether it has been intentional or not. All these questions of intention are too subjective to allow of scientific treatment' (Durkheim 1964: 95).

11 Thus Parsons in *The Structure of Social Action*: 'The unit of reference which we are considering as the actor is not this organism ["a spatially distinguishable separate unit in the world" as studied by the biologist or "behaviouristic" psychologist], but an "ego" or "self." The principal importance of this consideration is that the body of the actor forms, for him, just as much part of the situation of action as does the "external environment"' (Parsons 1968: 47).

12 This is a term originating in Marx that has been given theoretical weight in the work of Louis Althusser.

13 That, as Garfinkel has instructed us (Garfinkel 1967), such a universe of dis-

course is always necessarily indexical does not preclude the existence of conventions that constitute a claim to self-subsistence.

14 I was recently reading Peter Gay's (1973) collection of 'Enlightenment' texts
and was struck by the absence of many of the devices I'm describing here in
the writings of the Scottish philosophers (represented in Gay's collection by
David Hume, Adam Ferguson, and Adam Smith). The possibility of producing
the social as agent independent of actual individuals seemed, in general, not
available to them. Typically, generalized properties of societies were handled
by treating larger units as collectivities resolvable into individual members replicating properties assigned to the collectivity (this would seem to be the origin of the 'national character' type of thinking that was still popular up to
twenty years ago), or as typifications or personifications (the use of typal concepts such as Man, species concepts such as Mankind, or personifications such
as Nature). Collective terms were handled pronominally in the plural, so that
at the point of action they were resolved into individual actors. These devices
were most prominent in the excerpts from Adam Ferguson's *A History of Civil
Society*. It is interesting that excerpts from Adam Smith's *The Wealth of Nations*
showed more instances of causal relations posited between abstract properties
of economy and society, notably quantifiable (in principle) entities such as
wealth and population growth.

15 Schutz (1962), a major proponent of such commitment to keeping faith with
subjects, nonetheless destined subjects' constructs to form the motivations of
homunculi, representing those motivations and their effects in pure form –
presumably after the model of economic reasoning. See also my comments on
Max Weber's method of *verstehen* in chapter 3 of *The Everyday World as Problematic* (Smith 1987).

16 I have used this example because it claims a method which is in many ways
that recommended by feminist sociology, though, in fact, there are distinctly
masculinist dimensions to it. A major problem is the treatment of a story
about young men as a story about youth. I wondered, as I read, about the relations of young women to these groups and in the situations described. I
thought that an account from their viewpoint might result in a considerably
less sympathetic interpretation. I think the same of Paul Willis's *Learning to
Labour* (1977). The formulation of general statements as statements about
youth in general and a youth subculture is extremely problematic in pre-empting textually the experience of young women.

17 This is the 'cultural dopes' procedure that Harold Garfinkel has criticized,
though on other grounds. It is also a procedure foundational to contemporary cultural theory, one put in place in party by structuralism, but more strikingly by the constitutional procedures developed by Jacques Lacan to treat the

subject as a property of discourse (in a sense inclusive of but broader than my usage here).

18 Contrast the extraordinary ethnographic clarity of Lawrence Wieder's (1974) work in insisting that the notion of rules in ethnographic contexts be restricted to situations in which 'rules' are actually talked about by members of the setting in the ordinary course of its and their business. Much of ethnomethodology avoids sociology's constitutive conventions, although as it develops on from its startling and revolutionary founding impetus, some of it has reassumed them as its concealed working practices.

19 Paul Willis's *Learning to Labour* (1977) is again an example. He was close to the young men whose lives in school and out were the source of his enthnography, but strikingly, when he asked them to read it, as he reports (honourably) in an appendix, they could only read the bits about themselves, although they tried (Willis 1977: 195). Perhaps this was simply a problem of the language in which it is written, but, as we have seen, in sociology the language is precisely the problem that is the concern. Contemporary Marxist sociology has been quite as much governed by the founding conventions of sociology as any other.

20 Indeed, Patricia Hill Collins may be skipping over a textually concealed contradiction between *observing* Afro-American women and their experience as *they* tell it.

21 Since this was originally published, Patricia Hill Collins has made, of course, a substantial contributon to changing this situation in her remarkable *Black Feminist Thought* (1990).

22 Arthur Stinchcombe writes: 'As a discipline, sociology as a social structure leads toward scholasticism. But fortunately scholars are not allowed to construct monasteries, so there is a constant stream of empirical pollutants that threaten the scholastic structure. The reason we go to such effort and have some venom behind our pejoratives for those who upset the cultural system of the discipline by letting in undisciplined facts is because they are serious threats. There are enough general intellectuals, enough people who take what they say about sex and ambition in the classroom seriously in their scholarly life, to supply the materials for a constant tension within the sociological community. The thing that keeps our scholastic structure from being perfect and eternal is that we keep having our attention called to social facts that we cannot yet manage without it turning into "high class journalism" or "catering to the students' interest." This threatens the discipline, yet it keeps it alive. The disorganized flow of empirical social reality is the only thing that creates problems difficult enough to make it worthwhile to have a discipline trying to tame the flow into theoretically and methodologically unimpeachable sociology' (Stinchcombe 1983: 10).

23 'Philosophers,' she writes, in contrast to feminists, 'continue to hope to find the pure, general, universal point of view. Thus, feminists readily admit to bias in their perspective, while philosophers continue to assume bias should and can be avoided' (Sherwin 1988: 20).

5: The Ruling Relations

1 For example, see Jameson 1989 and Mowitt 1992.
2 Property relations subordinated a woman's wealth and person to the jural person of her husband (see Davidoff and Hall 1987). As capital accumulated beyond the stretch of kinship, property-owning institutions independent of the family were developed. Albie Sachs and Joan Hoff Wilson (1978) have argued that late-nineteenth-century changes in matrimonial property laws in both Britain and the United States enabling women to hold property separately from their husbands are related to the emergence of such objectifying forms of ownership. In Britain the limited or joint stock company and in the United States the corporation differentiated the finances of the company from the personal finances of its owners, a transformation in the social relations constituting capital celebrated by Berle and Means (1968), perhaps rather belatedly, as a separation of ownership from control.
3 See my discussion of the social organization of textual reality in *The Conceptual Practices of Power: A Feminist Sociology of Knowledge* (Smith 1990).
4 Its origins, however, are most probably in a reorganization of state and capital rather than in science and 'culture.' In these respects, the ruling relations need examination in terms of how they are organized by and organize class. I hope to go into this at a later stage of the work projected in this paper, but such an undertaking would make a book of a paper that is already too long.
5 Correspondence theory may have had its day as a metaphysic, but, opened up through the use of Harold Garfinkel's (1972) notion of operationalizing rationality as members' practices, it directs investigation to how the technical standardization of events complements replicable texts carrying instructions, interpretations, rules, accounts, etc.
6 I am indebted to Liza McCoy for the research that located the sources on which this passage is based and for the discussions in which I learned their significance.
7 In the situation Westwood describes, the introduction of new accounting practices, by requiring a standardization of local productive practices, actually disrupts the local shop-floor regime which workers have achieved. In Westwood's account, the previous production regime had allowed women to associate with one another cooperatively and on a friendly basis; the new system created

competitive relations among them and a context in which they became fearful of being downgraded if they did not maintain adequate and consistent levels of productivity. That the introduction of the new system transformed work relations on the shop-floor is systematically irrelevant to capital. The categories of accounting cannot translate workers' unhappiness into effects on capital, unless the new regime results in a decline of productivity, and productivity does not necessarily decline when workers are unhappy (see Perrow's [1986: 98–112] review of the literature relating worker satisfaction and dissatisfaction to productivity).

8 Though, indeed, many of the formerly independent functions of public discourse are increasingly substructed and organized by capital.

9 See, for example, Perrow 1986 and Scott, Meyer, et al. 1994. The latter have developed a theory of institutions as the environment of large-scale organization.

6: Telling the Truth after Postmodernism

1 This paper was originally published in *Studies in Symbolic Interaction* 19, no. 3 (1996): 171–202. My thanks to JAI Press for permission to include it in this volume. I am also indebted to the reviewers of the journal for their critique of the first draft of this paper that I ventured to submit. Their thoroughness and thoughtfulness were valuable to me in rewriting. It has not been practicable for me to respond to those of their suggestions that were directed towards enhancing its references to symbolic interactionism. Though deeply influenced by the work of George Herbert Mead, originally introduced to me in Tamtosu Shibutani's brilliant course at the University of California at Berkeley in the late 1950s, my history in sociology has not been in symbolic interaction, and I cannot redirect it at this point. I did, however, rework the paper to develop its dependence on Mead more fully, and I hope that this will compensate for the deficits they found. I am also very appreciative of the critical thought and eye of my friend and colleague Liza McCoy.

2 Discourse is an ambiguous term, coming into use in the 1960s in linguistics as that discipline redefined its phenomenal universe from the single sentence to stretches of talk or writing (Schiffrin 1994: 23). As Diane Macdonnell (1986) defines discourse, it resembles Bakhtin's 'speech genres,' and in fact she refers to Vološinov (1973) in introducing the concept of discourse. 'Discourse is social,' she writes, '... The kind of speech proper to the shop-floor of a factory conflicts with that of the boardroom. Different social classes use the same words in different senses and disagree in their interpetation of events and situations.' There is a distinction to be made, at least for the sociologist, between

speech genres which are characteristic of definite forms of work organization – the shop-floor or the boardroom – and those of the social relations mediated by texts that I've called 'the relations of ruling.' Bakhtin (1986) deploys the notion of primary and secondary speech genres to make this distinction – secondary speech genres corresponding closely to the latter. Foucault, particularly in his 'The Order of Discourse' (1981), uses the term in a rather more specialized sense, as those extended text-mediated conversations which constitute 'a conceptual terrain in which knowledge is formed and produced' (Young 1981: 48). The last has been most influential in raising issues of knowledge and truth as effects exclusively within the rules and practices of inclusion and exclusion that determine truth for a given historical period (Foucault 1981: 60).

3 George Herbert Mead's work (1938, 1947, 1992) belongs to a family of ontologies of the social which understand the social as an ongoing creation of actual people and hence as actually happening in real time and in real settings. He indeed influenced at least some of the members of this family, notably, of course, Herbert Blumer (1969), whose formulation of 'the methodological position of symbolic interactionism' has been of such significance to symbolic interactionism. Somewhat more distant are Peter Berger and Thomas Luckmann (1966), whose theory of the social construction of reality focuses on the dynamic of interaction among people in institutional creation; and Harold Garfinkel (1967, 1972), whose radical and brilliant innovations in this general ontological family propose that sociology's notions of order, facticity, sense, etc., be operationalized as people's ongoing accomplishments in the local settings of which they are members. These ontologies have bypassed or rejected theoretical realizations of the social as system or structure and have contrived to retain it as a lived actuality among people.

Mead's ontology is, in my view, congenial to Marx and Engels's (1976) premises for a new materialism to be based, not on concepts, but on actual individuals and their activities under definite material conditions. Marx's treatment of the 'systemic' properties of economic relations, at least as formulated in *The German Ideology*, is grounded in an ontology which problematizes how individuals who always start from themselves, themselves produce the powers that stand over against them and overpower their lives. Economic relations, for Marx, are indeed relations among people that appear as if they were relations between things – money and commodities – and have a dynamic beyond people's intentions and control.

My own development of these sociological ontologies diverges in two respects: one is in insisting on beginning in the local actualities of people's lives and relying on their experience as *point d'appui*; and the second is in shifting focus from actions as 'attached' to individuals to the concerting or relating *between* people's activities – closer in this respect to some varieties of ethnomethodology, particularly those, such as Charles Goodwin's (1981), that displace the individuated subject as centre.

4 I recognize that this term is imprecise. I use it to identify a rather general current of thinking that has developed in North America and is based upon thinking originating in France and associated with the work of Michel Foucault, Jacques Lacan, Julia Kristeva, Jacques Derrida, Jean-François Lyotard, Jean Baudrillard, and others. These theorists differ greatly. What they have in common, in addition to the period and its political movements, is chiefly their problematizing of traditional epistemologies, particularly those foundational to the Marxisms of post–Second World War France, but in North America they have come to be foundational to influential intellectual movements in the humanities and social sciences. I note that Judith Butler and Joan Scott use the term in a similar way in their introduction to their edited volume, *Feminists Theorize the Political* (1992).

5 Ann Game, introducing her 'deconstructive sociology,' says she's 'been greeted with a certain puzzlement on the part of people in the humanities: Why bother with sociology?' (Game 1991: ix).

6 Derrida writes: '*There is no sense* in doing without the concepts of metaphysics in order to attack metaphysics. We have no language – no syntax and no lexicon – which is alien to this history; we cannot utter a single destructive proposition which has not already slipped into the form, the logic, and the implicit postulation of precisely what it seeks to contest' (Derrida 1970: 250; emphases in original).

7 Barthes writes: 'The difference is as follows: the work is concrete occupying a portion of bookspace (in a library, for example); the Text, on the other hand, is a methodological field' (Barthes 1979: 74).

8 Flax's formulation traces Lyotard's of 1988. See Flax 1992: 60–1, in particular.

9 Of course, their proposal looks suspiciously like a meta-narrative of another kind, a retroactive theoretical validation of what has all along been fundamental to the women's movement, namely difference, conflict, alliance, etc. It sets up a universalized subject as the meta-narrator or philosophical legislator of multiple subject positions, none of which can lay claim to the position it has itself commanded. Perhaps most problematic, in multiplying theory, it calls into question theory itself. Who needs theory if anything goes?

10 Richard Rorty goes further: 'When the notion of knowledge as representation goes, then the notion of inquiry as split into discrete sectors with discrete subject matters goes. The lines between novels, newspaper articles, and sociological research get blurred' (Rorty 1994: 58).

11 In this respect there is continuity between post-structuralism and Frege's (Dummett 1981) conception of the objectivity of meaning, overriding individual subjectivities. Christopher Norris (1991: 106) suggests that post-structuralism is an updating of Frege's theorizing of language.

12 Though Jeffrey Alexander has not retreated from modernity, indeed is fighting a vigorous rearguard action, he has given a new centrality to interpretation in his recent work: 'Perhaps it is wise to acknowledge that it is a renewed sense of involvement in the project of universalism, rather than some lipid sense of its concrete forms, that marks the character of the new age in which we live. Beneath this new layer of the social top soil, moreover, lie the tangled roots and richly marbled subsoil of earlier intellectual generations, whose ideologies and theories have not ceased to be alive. The struggles between these interlocutors can be intimidating and confusing, not only because of the intrinsic difficulty of their message but because each presents itself not as form but as essence, not as the sense of the world. Each of these worlds does make sense, but only in a historically bounded way. Recently, a new social world has come into being. We must try to make sense of it. For the task of intellectuals is not only to explain the world; they must interpret it as well' (Alexander 1995: 47).

13 It is pervasive in contemporary theorizing of language and discourse, and not only in post-structuralism/postmodernism. John Searle's (1969) 'speech act' theory is deeply constrained by the assumption of the individuated subject.

14 Indeed, reading Derrida's critique of Husserl against Mead's theory of mind suggests to me that Derrida's grand project is a struggle to recognize, while not admitting, the social from within the epistemological boundaries of the traditional philosophic conception of the individuated subject.

15 As a constitutional theory for cultural theorizing, it is powerful, allocating both conscious and unconscious regions to its determinations; as a foundation for a politics of change, as feminists have proposed (Mitchell and Rose 1982), it follows the course Marx so long ago disdained as a revolution in language only; as an account of the development of children as social beings, it is pitiful.

16 Salecl (1994) as well as Mitchell and Rose (1982) claim that Lacan's theorizing posits an empty genderless subject who becomes committed to gender in his or her procession through the Lacanian version of the Oedipal complex. This view neglects how gender has already entered into the process as the dumb and invisible mother and the Father arrogating language and law.

17 See also Colette Soler's account in her essay 'The Subject and the Other (I)' (Soler 1995).

18 Stripped of the rhetoric of power and effectivity, Butler's account has much in

common with Berger and Luckmann's in *The Social Construction of Reality* (1966).

19 The invisibility of the social to Searle's philosophy reaches an apotheosis of systematic ignorance in his 1995 book, *The Construction of Social Reality*.

20 In many ways, as those of us who are old enough to remember other graduate students asking, 'But are we really only a bunch of roles?' the contemporary theorizing of the subject as a position in discourse has an odd familiarity. It has been odd, too, to read in Lacan and sometimes in Derrida awkward and extraordinarily inert accounts of self and other when some fifty years earlier Mead was writing a subtle and dialectical account of self and of mind as self-reflection which constructs the individuated subject inherited from Descartes's *cogito* as arising in and inseparable from an ongoing social process.

21 Michel Foucault's conception of self-formation has some parallels with Mead's conception of the self, involving attention to or awareness of the subject's experiencing in everyday activities – 'care of the self is the care of activity,' he says (Foucault 1988: 25). But self-formation is conceived as a kind of moral discipline, involving bringing principles to bear on the individual's activities. Mead's conception of self, however, is of a capacity to participate in social organization, which is *prior* to the level of organization Foucault explicates.

22 Mead was committed to the development of 'a behavioristic account of the self, mind, and reflective intelligence' (Mead 1992: 106). His use of the term 'response' had not yet been appropriated by the stimulus-response theory he opposed (1992: 112–15), a use which contaminates our contemporary reading of Mead. Now we might want to introduce the concept of 'interpretation' into the act-response sequence to reclaim Mead's insistence on the active part an organism plays in the constitution of the object to which it 'responds:' 'The form creates objects towards which it responds and within which it acts: it creates its environment' (Mead 1992: 115).

23 Though Mead's conception of the self is of a dialectic arising with and coordinating the individual's consciousness within the social act, his version of the subject or self is fully within the tradition of the unitary subject of the Enlightenment. For Mead, science, scientific rationality, and discovery are extrapolations of the self-reflective self – in a sense, Mead's theory of mind and self can be seen as a social account of the Cartesian subject. For example, consider the following passage from his essay 'The Nature of Scientific Knowledge,' which is chapter 3 in *The Philosophy of the Act* (1938):

> ... the world that is there includes and surrounds the problem [that leads to discovery] in the sense that the problem is also there within the field of conduct ... When these problems pass into the field of reflection, they are so formulated that they would occur in any experience, that is, they take on a

universal form. Such a formulation is essential to the reflective process of their solution. Their actual occurrence, however, in the world that is there awaits the advent of the conflict of responses in the experience of some individual; and the solution as well, inasmuch as it departs from the common or universal habits of the community, must be an individual achievement before it can become the attitude of all and be thus universalized. Mead's 'science' lacks a sense, let alone an analysis, of its institutional and hence 'power' dimensions. By contrast, Michel Foucault's work has provided us with an understanding of science as discourse which makes Mead's idealization of science as a community of reasoning individuals look seriously inadequate. At the same time, Mead's struggle to find the concerting of the individual consciousness and of individual experience with science as a conversation directs us towards dimensions of scientific discourse which Foucault's theory obliterates. His dialectic between experience as arising in an individual's consciousness and the universalizing of (what presumably becomes at this juncture) 'the problem' in a (scientific) community, could contribute usefully to the feminist debates on the status of experience in knowledge.

24 Charles Morris's (1955) semiotics, which drew in part on Mead's conception of symbolic communication, does not advance a solution in this respect since in his theory it is the individual subject whose concerns and interests drive discourse, and language is expressive of his intentions. Typical is Morris's discussion of 'religious discourse':

> The adequacy of religious discourse itself depends upon whether or not it appeals to given individuals in a given cultural milieu as a way in which their lives can be satisfactorily focused and directed. When this is not the case, new prophets appear to proclaim a mode of life which they have found significant, and if other individuals find the new way to be significant for themselves, a new religion and religious literature arises which will seek its esthetic embodiment, its appropriate techniques, and its critical defense. The complicated human self has need of some focal attitude to give it orientation, and the significance of religion lies in its attempt to meet this need. (Morris 1955: 148)

25 When I first discovered the Oxford philosophers, notably Gilbert Ryle and J.L. Austin, and tracked back to their inspiration in Ludwig Wittgenstein, I was immensely attracted to the notion of exploring philosophical issues by, as Wittgenstein (1953: 48) put it, 'bring[ing] words back from their metaphysical to their everyday use.' I thought their analyses of 'specimens' of people's everyday language practices were a model for sociology. In working on the problem of how to conceive of language in the concerting of people's activities, that is, as social, I have followed their example in making collections of specimens – I call it 'botanizing' in another context (Smith 1990: 165–7).

26 I notice now that small children, before they can name, learn to point and that pointing brings the other's look to orient in the direction of pointing.

27 This may be another version of the loss of reality that, Lacan argues, is entailed by entry to the symbolic order, although, in this view, 'reality' comes into being only in the social act constitutive of the world in common among diverse consciousnesses.

28 Before that moment, she was what she called a 'Phantom' (Keller 1956: 37). She walks away from the well-house recognizing herself as Helen and her teacher as Teacher (Keller 1956: 40).

29 See Jean Piaget's brilliant ethnography *The Child's Construction of Reality* (1958).

30 An old husband's tale?

31 I was reminded in developing this analysis of its application to the telling of a story which is of a 'reality' inaccessible to most of us (Alfred Schutz might have included it as a member of his 'multiple realities' [Schutz 1962b]). Black Elk's vision as told to John Neihardt is recounted as if it had an everyday reality. This effect is, I think, achieved because the divine beings which people his vision are represented as consciousnesses positioned differently from him who may therefore involve him in the social act of referring to and constituting the presence of an object in common – making Vološinov's 'inter-individual territory.' For example:

> Now suddenly there was nothing but a world of cloud, and we three were there alone in the middle of a great white plain with snowy hills and mountains staring at us; and it was very still; but there were whispers.
>
> Then the two men [his mythical Grandfathers] spoke together and they said: 'Behold him, the being with four legs!'
>
> I looked and saw a bay horse standing there, and he began to speak.
> (Black Elk 1972: 22–3)

This has the same grammatical structure as the story of Karen, her mother, and the cat. The Grandfathers are seeing what Black Elk does not yet see. They tell him to look: 'Behold him, the being with four legs!' they say. *Then* Black Elk looks and sees the bay horse (which begins to speak). He recognizes and affirms what they have indicated.

32 See Lucy Suchman's *Plans and Situated Actions* (1987) for an examination of the problems of producing generalized instructions to direct actions in multiple and particular local settings.

33 Some of these may have arisen, of course, as objects in social acts exclusively in and of discourse.

34 Mead's conception of experience and its relation to knowledge is not of an individual subject's unmediated access to a reality independent of the social.

That is the version of experience that has been criticized by feminists (see Mohanty 1995). From the latter viewpoint, recognizing that discourse mediates experience invalidates claims that women's experience provides a privileged source or ground of knowledge (it is seldom clear who actually makes such claims). In contrast to a model of experience assuming the individuated subject as the ground of knowledge, Mead understands experience as conjoining current consciousness with organization laid down in the course of an individual's biography. Hence, experience is socially mediated. Since, in Mead's view, knowledge is social, experience, as essentially of the individual, can only be a moment in the social act in which knowledge comes about, though Mead seems to have held that scientific discoveries arise at the intersection between individual experience and science as a community in conversation.

35 Some of Mead's later writing suggests that the 'objectness' (identity, persistence, continuity, etc.) of an object is itself an accomplishment of an ongoing course of action. See, for example, his account of how we can 'speak of the fruit as existing throughout the whole process of preparing it for the table' (Mead 1938: 143). It would seem that Mead's account of the object and of the possibility of reference and representation bypasses altogether Derrida's critique (see, in particular, Derrida's *Speech and Phenomena and Other Essays on Husserl's Theory of Signs* [1973] and Rodolphe Gasché's *The Tain of the Mirror: Derrida and the Philosophy of Reflection* [1986].

36 Mead uses the term 'conversation' (1938: 52–3).

37 See Bruno Latour and Steve Woolgar's *Laboratory Life: The Construction of Scientific Facts* (1986) for an ethnography of this sequence.

7: Exploring the Social Relations of Discourse: Sociological Theory and the Diaologic of Sociology

1 Based on a paper prepared for the annual meetings of the Canadian Sociology and Anthropology Association, Montreal, 1995.

2 There is another level of dialogic organization in the sociological text on which this paper does not focus: other sociologists appear as characters in the text; they are cited as authorities, attributed theoretical positions, attacked, quoted to support a position taken by the writer, or to illustrate the writer's interpretation. The sociological text positions itself intertextually within the discourse, locating and relying on formulations, theories, positions, and methodological procedures of the discourse; it may draw similarly on related discourses, such as those of cultural theory or philosophy.

3 Indeed there is a fundamental ambiguity in Bakhtin's concept of monologism, since in his view utterances are intrinsically dialogic.

4 I do not mean that all sociologists share the same theory, though it is generally true that courses in sociological theory, covering a pretty standard array of sociological theorists, are required for undergraduate majors and graduate degrees in sociology. However, variants of sociological theory that are foundational to particular sociological enclaves, such as symbolic interactionism, claim general discursive status and are exclusive in the sense that they do not 'recognize' other monologic standpoints.

5 '... some of the ways in which the differences between them [the two frames of reference] are displayed in antenatal consultations and women's experience of having a baby' (Graham and Oakley 1981: 52).

6 Other theorists in other fields have made analogous formulations, suggesting that all are pointing to the same beast, like the six blindfolded Jains holding different parts of an elephant. Mead argues that the 'significant symbol' always presupposes a 'universe of discourse' as the field within which it has significance. His notion of a universe of discourse is not of a purely conceptual object, but as 'constituted by a group of individuals carrying on and participating in a common social process of experience and behavior' (Mead 1938: 89). Wittgenstein uses the term 'a form of life' to emphasize how 'meaning' is embedded in and arises as it comes to mean in the contexts of its use. Bologh (1979) has developed Wittgenstein's thinking as the basis of a phenomenological sociology. She writes:

> ... language must be understood actively as a form of life and not passively as a totality of names for things that exist independently of subjects. A form of life, or language-game, may be understood in terms of unspoken rules or presuppositions for knowing an object. These rules constitute a 'game,' a purposive activity, within which acts and words, like moves in a game, come to make sense. Only within the game are the moves or words intelligible as such. (Bologh 1979: 2)

7 A form of 'hybrid' utterance, to use Bakhtin's term (Bakhtin 1981) – dialogue embedded in a covert secondary dialogue, the overhearing – characteristic of Shakespeare's comedies.

8: The Standard North American Family: SNAF as an Ideological Code

1 The first version of this paper was prepared for a session on the family organized by Jay Gubrium for the meetings of the American Sociological Association in Cincinnati in 1991. It was completed while I was visiting scholar in the Center for the Study of Women in Society, University of Oregon, and was published as 'The Standard North American Family: SNAF as an Ideological Code,' *Journal of Family Issues*: 14, no. 2 (1993) 50–65. special issue, ed. Jay

Gubrium, 'Rethinking Family as a Social Form.' I am grateful to Sage Publications Inc. for permission to reprint the paper here. The research by Alison Griffith and myself referred to in the text was supported by grant #410–84–0450 from the Social Sciences and Humanities Research Council of Canada.

2 For a more fully developed account of this way of conceiving of text-mediated discourse, see my essay 'Femininity as Discourse,' in *Texts, Facts, and Femininity: Exploring the Relations of Ruling* (Smith 1990b).

3 See my paper 'K is Mentally Ill: The Anatomy of a Factual Account,' in Smith 1990b.

4 Properly speaking, SNAF as an ideological code cannot be identified with any particular formulation such as this. Rather, it is the capacity to generate formulations.

5 Perhaps down the line, such initiatives and the kinds of changes that are already taking place in family organization and are becoming visible through government censuses and surveys, may eventually displace SNAF. It may be that the sociobiologists, attending to the increasing percentage of women-headed families represented in these statistics, may turn from baboons or the mythic version of hunting-gathering society popular in the sociobiology of the Edward Wilson era, to chimpanzees, who seem to be organized in matricentred familial groups.

6 This was, in fact, one among a number of problems that arose for us because we were still working with some of the standard sociological research procedures. Though we had been clear that we were *not* studying a population of mothers with children in elementary schools, we nevertheless in many ways continued to treat the respondents as a sample – as, for example, by attempting to develop typologies enabling us to describe *all* our cases.

7 One teacher in a class I taught told me that she could tell a child from a single-parent family in her first encounter with a new class at the beginning of the school year.

8 Harold Garfinkel's (1967) use of the concept of the documentary method of interpretation is based on Mannheim's but is significantly different.

9 There were one or two interesting exceptions to this.

10 I am also indebted to conversations with Mary Romero for some of the information that follows.

11 Connections may also be extended inter-generationally with similar effect. A study by Michael Young and Peter Willmott (1986) of a working-class neighbourhood in East London in the 1950s shows the importance of mother-daughter relations in providing economic and emotional supports when special strains were placed on a household by events such as childbirth or periods of unemployment. Such extra-household familial linkages create a kind

of distributive domestic economy that cannot be identified with a particular household. We could expect African-American communities to have similar inter-generational connectedness. The presence of these kinds of links, however, depends on a sufficient degree of historical continuity in the community and its patterns of settlement. Unfortunately, SNAF inhibits research that would explore the actual forms of social organization and the conditions of their viability.

9: 'Politically Correct': An Organizer of Public Discourse

1 A number of people have helped me, particularly by introducing me to sources and examples. I am particularly indebted to Andree Stock in this respect. I am also generally indebted to the members of my 'Social Organization of Knowledge' course in 1991, whose discussions of the CBC program on political correctness analysed in this paper were invaluable in the development of my thinking. Ellen Messer-Davidow provided valuable critical comments.

   This paper originally appeared in Stephen Richer and Lorna Weir, eds, *Beyond Political Correctness: The Future of the Canadian Academy* (Toronto: University of Toronto Press, 1994). Thanks to the University of Toronto Press for permission to reproduce it in this volume.

2 See Lorna Weir's (1994) excellent history of the uses of the term. She describes a shift taking place in the 1980s from the use of the term as a critique internal to social movements to an external critique, culminating in what she calls the 'neoconservative PC.'

3 All references in this section are to 'Politically Correct,' *CBC Sunday Morning,* 28 July 1991.

4 I have made a detailed analysis of ideologically generated accounts in chapters 6 and 7 of *The Conceptual Practices of Power* (Smith 1990a).

5 The course of hearing is more powerful in its effects than the course of reading. In the latter both statements appear as alternatives so that the substitution of the second for the first is weakened. But in the hearing, the second simply supersedes the first; the first doesn't hang around for comparison with the alternative version that follows it.

6 This problem is explored further in chapter 10.

7 The example refers to a column by Trevor Lautens in the *Vancouver Sun* of 29 March 1994. His opening remarks (characteristically for this type of writing) set the PC frame. 'What's the tamest word? Rebuke. The University of B.C. administration, specifically the feminist / "politically correct" forces widely identified with dean of arts Patricia Marchak and academic vice-

president Dan Birch, has been rebuked.' The effect of the PC code as organizer of the story that he goes on to tell is substantial. When I first read the column, I assumed that dean and vice-president had been 'rebuked' by those higher in the administration than they. In fact, the dean and vice-president had been criticized by some faculty members for the inclusion of the items in question in the proposed teaching evaluation. It is the PC code that transforms 'criticism' into 'rebuke' by according the critics overriding institutional authority.

8 Or members of the related complex of terms that the PC code appears to have drawn into play along with it, such as 'McCarthyism.' My impression is that that epithet came into play in this new form (detached from any reference to state censorship) attached to and as an elaboration of 'political correctness.'

10: Texts and Repression: Hazards for Feminists in the Academy

1 The research basis for this story consists of extensive documentary materials I have collected from a variety of sources, supplemented by resources housed in the Special Collections of the University of Victoria's Macpherson Library (thanks to Jane Turner for help in locating these). I have also interviewed participants, though perhaps not as widely as I might have (this research has been pursued without funding). My interviews have been mainly focused around the documentary materials, particularly the Report and the Letter. These interviews have been for background only, and I have not quoted or made direct use of what I was told (though I would have liked to). All the statements about events or processes relating to the sequence of two texts I analysed are based on interview material and/or other documentary materials (such as an article written by members of the 'chilly climate' committee; see Brodribb et al. 1996). I cannot, however, claim impartiality. I have not interviewed any of the senior male faculty who signed the Letter analysed in this chapter. Though only indirectly, I came to be involved in the controversy, and I am still too angry.

2 In a record of the meeting based on a compilation of notes made by participants supporting the Report, members of the 'climate' committee make it clear that it had been intended as a basis for dialogue and was preliminary. There was discussion of assigning a work-study position to it (minutes of the Political Science Department meeting, 29 March 1993: 10).

3 A union of students taking courses in the department.

4 In addition, the archives of the University of Victoria library contains a substantial package of materials, which apparently were used by the 'climate' committee in preparing its Report. These materials include the Hall and

Sandler pamphlet (Hall and Sandler 1982), which introduced to feminist discourse the concept of the 'chilly climate,' as well as other papers and reports on the situation of women in universities.

5 It was accompanied by a lengthy document entitled 'Gender Equity in the Department of Political Science,' which rebuts the Report in lauding the department's record of hiring women. It raises issues of academic freedom with respect to some of the other aspects of the Report. I have not addressed this here because I am focusing on the traces of the interpretive schema of juridical discourse inserted by the Letter and how it can be seen as organizing subsequent texts and talk. Issues of academic freedom become more prominent in a later controversy, arising from a critique of sexism and, in this instance, also racism, in the Department of Political Science at the University of British Columbia. I hope to address this in another analysis later.

6 See the article of 19 April 1993 in the *Globe and Mail* (Wilson 1993).

7 In a sense, the success of the women's movement in installing sexual harassment procedures as part of the disciplinary machinery of the university has created its own problems. The intervention of faculty associations, properly concerned with the interests of members charged under these rules, has moved such procedures in a more strictly legalistic direction. They become less flexible and hence less effective as a means of dealing with the kinds of generalized 'asymmetries' that women experience and are named by the feminist 'chilly climate' discourse. I note that Professor Hester Lessard's (of the university's Faculty of Law) report to the president as chair of the Equal Rights and Opportunities Committee charged with reviewing the university's harassment procedures 'urges that climate complaints be differentiated from individual complaints of harassment' and that a new procedure for the former be set up (reported in Bilson and Berger 1994: 29). I can't find that this suggestion was ever followed up.

8 However, the recommendations (lines 19–26 of the passage from the Report), particularly the reference to women's safety in the last (lines 25–6), return me to an equivocal reading since they seem to refer to 'sexual harassment' in the current institutional sense.

9 Two spellings of 'behaviour' appear in the Letter.

10 I have not, as yet, had an opportunity to find out whether this is a reference to the University of Victoria Faculty Association contract with the university.

11 It would be a mistake to think that these moves succeeded in suppressing the Report of the 'climate' committee. After the Letter had been received, the Report and the Letter appear to have circulated widely, though largely through informal networks. The repressive effects of the Letter are largely in deflecting or displacing the substantive issues raised by the Report.

12 Examples of the problems of translation from 'preliminary' to formal public document substruct many passages in the external reviewers' report (Berger and Bilson 1993). In one instance, they write:

> Professor Brodribb says that the word 'staff' as used in the report was not intended to include support staff, that it meant faculty. But Professor Brodribb and the members of the committee have never advised the staff that the report was not intended to refer to them. (Berger and Bilson 1993: 20)

Such problems are read very differently when the document is seen as a draft, rather than a final, document. The assumption that the Report is in final published form makes important differences in how it is read. Four years later, at a conference on academic freedom and the inclusive university at the University of British Columbia (April 1997), one of the external reviewers, Thomas R. Berger, told the audience that the Letter was a response to a report *that had already been published*. The review he wrote with Beth Bilson appears to presuppose such a move throughout. A subsequent letter from the chair of the Department of Political Science dated 23 April 1993, addressed to colleagues and circulated, according to my information, across Canada to political science departments, accuses the 'chilly climate' committee of distributing its Report to academics across Canada and 'to the local and national media.' I cannot find that there was any distribution of the Report, other than informally, before the Letter was received by Professor Brodribb. The materials I've examined and the interviews I've done with people involved support the view that the Report was not made public until the male faculty's rebuttals had been widely circulated, although both Letter and Report were summarized in the *Globe and Mail* news item of 19 Apirl 1993. My best information is that the Report was available to students in the women's caucus of the course union of the department at the time of the meeting. This is evidenced by the letters of support that were written by a number of them. I've also heard that the Report did get informal distribution elsewhere in the university as students brought it to the attention of women faculty as a critique that could be made in other departments. It is, of course, entirely possible that the Report travelled on student networks to other departments of political science in Canada. However, it seems clear that the Report was never formally distributed until after the Letter was received; nor did the 'climate' committee have access to the departmental resources which enabled the male faculty to produce and distribute their materials.

13 The first break into the news was on 19 April 1993, eleven days after the date of the Letter, in a *Globe and Mail* news item (Wilson 1993), in which this passage is glossed a threat.

14 Particularly in its treatment of the Report as if it were a formal public docu-

ment, in its preoccupation with the methodology of the Report, and in its foregrounding of the reputational damage to the male faculty and hence to issues of due process.

15 The report of the external reviewers (Bilson and Berger 1994) provides an example of how the discursive schema set in place by the Letter captures the terms in which the issue can be discussed. A woman member of faculty reports insisting to male colleagues that the Report dealt with discrimination that was systemic, while they were adamant that the individual men were personally accused of 'these acts' (Bilson and Berger 1994: 35).

16 A business-oriented newspaper, the *Globe and Mail* is the only Canadian newspaper with national circulation.

17 I notice in how I have written these sentences that I have used phrases ascribing actions to the texts. 'The Letter reclaims ...,' I wrote above. These phrases point to dimensions of the operation of these texts in this institutional setting that have not yet been explored. I have drawn attention to them when I was describing how the juridical discourse of the Letter 'captures' the reading subject when she returns to the Report. But this, of course, is only one particular moment in a complex controversy. The texts were read and participated in other courses of action or interaction; other texts were generated. Beyond the first publication of the Letter and the Report, there were letters and articles published in university newspapers, investigations, reviews initiated by the university administration, private debates between women and men, discussions in the Canadian women's movement, an e-mail network raising issues in the women's movement internationally, mass media features, letters to the editor, columns, and so on, on both sides of the issue (it would be particularly interesting to see how or whether the juridical discourse has contaminated those supporting feminists). I have also, for largely political reasons (for I am not impartial and my time is limited), not explored parallel mass media writing on the feminist side.

18 Janet Bing and Lucien Lombardo (1997) have described three different frames at work as people 'talk past' each other about sexual harassment. One frame, which they call the 'judicial,' clearly corresponds to what is here called 'juridical' discourse. The other two are the diverging frames in which, on the one hand, women's experience is expressed and, on the other, is dismissed by men.

19 As they are, for example, in the external review (Bilson and Berger 1994).

11: Conclusion

1 'Economic categories are only the theoretical expressions, the abstractions of the social relations of production' (Marx 1973: 95).

Bibliography

Abramowitz, Mimi. 1988. *Regulating the lives of women: Social welfare policy from colonial times to the present.* Boston: South End Press.

Acker, Joan. 1987. Hierarchies and jobs: Notes for a theory of gendered organizations. Paper presented at the meetings of the American Sociological Association, Chicago.

Adler, Jerry, et al. 1990. Taking offense: Is this the new enlightenment on campus or the new McCarthyism? *Newsweek,* 24 Dec., pp. 48–55.

Alberta Report. 1995. A banished complainer: The University of Victoria suspends a 'harassed' feminist professor. *Alberta Report,* 27 March, p. 38.

Alexander, Jeffrey C. 1995. *'Fin de siècle' social theory: Relativisim, reduction, and the problems of reason.* London: Verso.

Althusser, Louis. 1971. Ideology and ideological state apparatuses. In *Lenin and philosophy and other essays,* 127–86. New York: Monthly Review Press.

Austin, John Lanshaw. 1962. *How to do things with words.* London: Oxford University Press.

Backhouse, Constance, Roma Harris, Gillian Michell, and Alison Wylie. 1995. The chilly climate for faculty women at Western: Postscript to the *Backhouse Report.* In *Breaking anonymity: The chilly climate for women faculty,* ed. the Chilly Collective, 97–132. Waterloo, Ont.: Wilfrid Laurier University Press.

Bacon, Francis. 1900. *Novum organum.* New York: Colonial Press.

Bagdikian, Ben. 1983. *The media monopoly.* Boston: Beacon Press.

Bakhtin, Mikhail M. 1981. The *dialogic imagination: Four essays.* Austin: University of Texas Press.

– 1986a. *Speech genres and other late essays.* Trans. Vern W. McGee. Austin: University of Texas Press.

– 1986b. The problem of speech genres. In *Speech genres and other late essays,* trans. Vern W. McGee, 60–102. Austin: University of Texas Press.

Bannerji, Himani, 1987. Introducing racism: Notes towards an anti-racist feminism. *Resources for Feminist Research: A Canadian Journal for Feminist Scholarship*
16(1) [special issue on immigrant women, edited by Roxana Ng, Joyce Scane,
Himani Bannerji, Didi Khayatt, and Makeda Silvera]: 10–12.

– 1988. The politics of representation: A study of class and class struggle in the
political theatre of West Bengal. Ph.D. diss., University of Toronto.

– 1995. Beyond the ruling category to what actually happens: Notes on James
Mill's historiography in *The History of British India*. In *Experience, knowledge, and
ruling relations: Explorations in the social organization of knowledge*, ed. Marie
Campbell and Ann Manicom, 49–64. Toronto: University of Toronto Press.

Barrett, Michele, and Roberta Hamilton, eds. 1987. *The politics of diversity: Feminism, Marxism and nationalism*. Montreal: The Book Centre.

Barrow, Clyde W. 1990. *Universities and the capitalist state: Corporate liberalism and the
reconstruction of American higher education, 1894–1928*: Madison: University of
Wisconsin Press.

Barthes, Roland. 1977. From work to text. In *Image-music-text: Essays*. Selected and
translated by Stephen Heath. Glasgow: Fontana/Collins.

– 1979. From work to text. In *Textual strategies: Perspectives in post-structural criticism*, ed. Josué V. Harari, 73–81. Ithaca, N.Y.: Cornell University Press.

Baudrillard, Jean 1994. *Simulacra and simulation*. Trans. S.F. Glaser. Ann Arbor:
University of Michigan Press.

Becker, Gary S. 1981. *A treatise on the family*. Cambridge, Mass.: Harvard University
Press.

Beniger, James R. 1988. *The control revolution: Technological and economic origins of the
information society*. Cambridge, Mass.: Harvard University Press.

Berger, Peter, and Thomas Luckmann. 1966. *The social construction of reality*. New
York: Doubleday.

Berger, Thomas R., and Beth Bilson. 1993. Interim report of the review committee, September 29, 1993. *The Ring* 19(18): 4–5.

Berle, Adolphe, and Gardiner C. Means. 1968. *The modern corporation and private
property*. New York: Harcourt, Brace and World.

Bernard, Jessie. 1964. *Academic women*. New York: New American Library.

– 1973. My four revolutions: An autobiographical history of the ASA. In *Changing
women in a changing society*, ed. Joan Huber. Chicago: University of Chicago Press.

Bernstein, Richard. 1990. The rising hegemony of the politically correct. *New York
Times*, 28 Oct., pp. 1, 4.

Bilson, Beth, and Thomas R. Berger. 1994. Report of the review committee into
the Political Science Department. Prepared for the President of the University
of Victoria, 21 January.

Bing, Janet M., and Lucien X. Lombardo. 1997. Talking past each other about sexual harassment: An exploration of frames for understanding. *Discourse and Society* 8(3): 293–311.

Black Elk. 1972. *Black Elk speaks: Being the life story of a holy man of the Oglala Sioux, as told through John G. Neihardt.* Lincoln: University of Nebraska Press.

Blumenthal, Sidney. 1986. *The rise of the counter-establishment: From conservative ideology to political power.* New York: Times Books.

Blumer, Hebert. 1969. *Symbolic interactionism: Perspective and method.* Berkeley: University of California Press.

Böhme, Gernot. 1977. Cognitive norms, knowledge-interests and the constitution of the scientific object: A case study in the functioning of rules for experimentation. In *The social production of scientific knowledge,* ed. Everett Mendelsohn, Peter Weingart, and Richard Whitley, 129–41. Dordrecht-Holland: D. Reidel Publishing Co.

Bologh, Roslyn Wallach. 1979. *Dialectical phenomenology: Marx's method.* London: Routledge and Kegan Paul.

Bourdieu, P., and J.P. Passeron. 1977. *Reproduction in education, society and culture.* Beverly Hills, Calif.: Sage.

Brockholdt, James L. 1983. A historical perspective on the accountant's role: The early experience of the American railroads. *Accounting Historians Journal* 10(1): 69–96.

Brodribb, Somer, with Sylvia Bardon, Theresa Newhouse, and Jennifer Spencer, and the assitance of Madia Kyba. 1996. The equity franchise. *Women's Education / Education des femmes* (Canadian Congress for Learning Opportunities for Women / Congrés canadien pour la promotion des études chez la femme) 12(1): 12–20.

Burrough, Bryan, and John Helyar. 1991. *Barbarians at the gate: The fall of RJR Nabisco.* New York: Harper Collins.

Bush, George. 1991. Remarks at the University of Michigan commencement ceremony in Ann Arbor. *Weekly Compilation of Presidential Documents: Administration of George Bush* 27(19): 557–96.

Butler, Judith. 1990. *Gender trouble: Feminism and the subversion of identity.* London: Routledge.

– 1993. *Bodies that matter: On the discursive limits of 'sex.'* New York: Routledge.

– 1994. For a careful reading. In Seyla Benhabib, Judith Butler, Drucilla Cornell, and Nancy Fraser, *Feminist contentions: A philosophical exchange,* 127–43. London: Routledge.

Butler, Judith, and Joan W. Scott. 1992. Introduction. *Feminists theorize the political,* ed. Judith Butler and Joan W. Scott, xiii–xvii. New York and London: Routledge.

Callahan, Marilyn (School of Social Work and advisor to the Vice-President Academic on faculty women's issues), and Andrew Pirie (Faculty of Law and the Centre for Dispute Resolution). 1993. Findings of the review of the situation in the Department of Political Science at the University of Victoria, 11 May.

Campbell, Marie. 1984. Information systems and management of hospital nursing: A study in the social organization of knowledge. Ph.D. diss., University of Toronto.

– 1995. Teaching accountability: What counts as nursing education. In *Experience, knowledge, and ruling relations: Explorations in the social organization of knowledge*, ed. Marie Campbell and Ann Manicom, 221–33. Toronto: University of Toronto Press.

Campbell, Marie, and Ann Manicom, eds. 1995. *Experience, knowledge, and ruling relations: Explorations in the social organization of knowledge*. Toronto: University of Toronto Press.

Carr, E.H. 1964. *What is history?* Harmondsworth, Middlesex: Penguin Books.

Cassin, A. Marguerite. 1990. The routine production of inequality: A study in the social organization of knowledge. Ph.D diss., University of Toronto.

Chandler, Albert, Jr. 1977. *The visible hand: The managerial revolution in American business*. Cambridge, Mass.: Harvard University Press.

Climate Committee of the Department of Political Science. 1993. Report of the Climate Committee to the Department of Political Science, University of Victoria, 23 March.

Coleman, James S., et al. 1966. *Equality of educational opportunity*. Washington, D.C.: Department of Health, Education and Welfare.

Collins, Patricia Hill. 1986. Learning from the outsider within: The sociological significance of black feminist thought. *Social Problems* 33 (Oct./Dec.): S14–S32.

– 1990. *Black feminist thought: Knowledge, consciousness, and the politics of empowerment*. Boston: Unwin-Hyman.

Craft, Maurice. 1970a. Family, class and education: Changing perspectives. In *Family, class and education: A reader*, ed. M. Craft, 3–27. London: Longman.

– ed. 1970b. *Family, class and education: A reader*. London: Longman.

Davidoff, Leonore, and Catherine Hall. 1987. *Family fortunes: Men and women of the English middle class 1780–1850*. Chicago: University of Chicago Press.

Davis, Kingsley. 1967. Myth of functional analysis as a special method in sociology and anthropology. In *System, change and conflict*, ed. N.J. Demerath and R.A. Peterson, 379–402. Glencoe, Ill.: Free Press.

De Montigny, Gerald A.J. 1989. Accomplishing professional reality: An ethnography of social workers' practice. Ph.D. diss., University of Toronto.

– 1995a. The power of being professional. In *Experience, knowledge, and ruling relations: Explorations in the social organization of knowledge*, ed. Marie Campbell and Ann Manicom, 209–20. Toronto: University of Toronto Press.

– 1995b. *Social working: An ethnography of front-line practice.* Toronto: University of Toronto Press.

Department of Political Science, University of Victoria. 1992. Minutes of departmental meeting, 11 May.

– 1993. Minutes [note: these are notes compiled subsequent to the meeting, rather than formal minutes] of the Political Science Department meeting, 29 March.

Derrida, Jacques. 1970. Structure, sign, and play in the discourse of the human sciences. In *The structuralist controversy: The language of criticism and the sciences of man,* ed. R. Macksey and E. Donato, 247–72. Baltimore: Johns Hopkins University Press.

– 1973. *Speech and phenomena and other essays on Husserl's theory of signs.* Evanston, Ill.: Northwestern University Press.

DeVault, Marjorie L. 1986. Talking and listening from women's standpoint: Feminist strategies for analyzing interview data. Paper prepared for the annual meeting of the Society for the Study of Symbolic Interaction, New York.

– 1987. Writing women's experience / writing sociology. Paper presented at the annual meeting of the Society for the Study of Social Problems, Chicago.

Diesing, Paul. 1982. *Science and ideology in the policy sciences.* New York: Aldine Publishing Co.

Dimen, Marcia. 1989. Power, sexuality, and intimacy. In *Gender/body/knowledge: Feminist reconstructions of being and knowing,* ed. Alison M. Jaggar and Susan R. Bordo. 34–51. New Brunswick, N.J.: Rutgers University Press.

Douglas, J.W.B. 1970. Parental encouragement. In *Family, class and education: A reader.* ed. M. Craft, 151–7. London: Longman.

Dummett, Michael. 1981. *Frege: Philosophy of language.* Cambridge, Mass.: Harvard University Press.

Durkheim, Emile. 1960. *The division of labour in society.* Glencoe, Ill.: The Free Press.

– 1964. *The rules of sociological method.* New York: Free Press.

Eisenstein, Elizabeth L. 1979. *The printing press as an agent of change: Communication and cultural transformations in early modern Europe.* Cambridge: Cambridge University Press.

Elson, Diane. 1988. Socialization of the market. *New Left Review* 172 (Nov./Dec.): 3–44.

Faludi, Susan. 1992. *Backlash: The undeclared war against American women.* New York: Doubleday.

Feagin, Joe R., Hernan Vera, and Nikitah Imani. 1996. *The agony of education: Black students at white colleges and universities.* New York: Routledge.

Fekete, John. 1994. *Moral panic: Biopolitics rising.* Montreal and Toronto: Robert Davies Publishing.

Felman, Shoshana. 1987. *Jacques Lacan and the adventure of insight: Psychoanalysis in contemporary culture.* Cambridge, Mass.: Harvard University Press.

Findley, Timothy. 1994. Daring to wake up at the gates of the politically correct. *Vancouver Sun,* 11 March, p. A19.

Fish, Stanley. 1967. *Surprised by sin: The reader in 'Paradise Lost'.* New York: St Martin's Press.

Flax, Jane 1990. *Thinking fragments: Psychoanalysis, feminism, and postmodernism in the contemporary West.* Berkeley: University of California Press.

– 1992. The end of innocence. In *Feminists theorize the political,* ed. Judith Butler and Joan W. Scott, 445–75. London: Routledge.

– 1993. *Disputed subjects: Essays on psychoanalysis, politics and philosophy.* London and New York: Routledge.

Foucault, Michel. 1970. *The order of things: An archaeology of the human sciences.* London: Tavistock.

– 1972. *The archaeology of knowledge and the discourse on language.* New York: Pantheon Books.

– 1979. *Discipline and punish: The birth of the prison.* New York: Vintage Books.

– 1980. *Power/knowledge: Selected interviews and other writings, 1972–1977.* New York: Pantheon Books.

– 1981. The order of discourse. In *Untying the text: A poststructuralist reader,* ed. Robert Young, 51–78. London: Routledge.

– 1988. Technologies of the self. In *Technologies of the self,* ed. Luther H. Martin et al. London: Tavistock.

Fraser, Nancy, and Linda Nicholson. 1994. An encounter between feminism and postmodernism. In *The postmodern turn: New perspectives on social theory,* ed. Steven Seidman, 242–61. Cambridge: Cambridge University Press.

Frye, Marilyn. 1983. *The politics of reality.* Trumansburg, N.Y.: Crossing Press.

Game, Ann. 1991. *Undoing the social: Towards a deconstructive sociology.* Toronto: University of Toronto Press.

Gardiner, Michael. 1992. *The dialogics of critique: M.M. Bakhtin and the theory of ideology.* New York: Routledge.

Garfinkel, Harold. 1967. *Studies in ethnomethodology.* Englewood Cliffs, N.J.: Prentice-Hall.

– 1972. Remarks on ethnomethodology. In *The ethnography of communication,* ed. Dell Hymes and John J. Gumperz, 309–24. New York: Holt Rinehart and Winston.

Garfinkel, Harold, Michael Lynch, and Eric Livingston. 1981. The work of a discovering science construed with materials from the optically discovered pulsar. *Philosophy of the Social Sciences* 11: 131–58.

Gasché, Rodolphe. 1986. *The tain of the mirror: Derrida and the philosophy of reflection.* Cambridge, Mass.: Harvard University Press.

Gay, P., ed. 1973. *The enlightenment: A comprehensive anthology*. New York: Simon and Schuster.

Genovese, Eugene D. 1991. Heresy, yes – sensitivity, no: An argument for counter-terrorism in the academy. *New Republic*, 15 April, pp. 30–5.

Giddens, Anthony. 1987. *Social theory and modern sociology*. Stanford: Stanford University Press.

Goodwin, Charles. 1981. *Conversational organization: Interaction between speakers and hearers*. New York: Academic Press.

Graham, Hilary, and Ann Oakley. 1981. Competing ideologies of reproduction: Medical and maternal perspectives on pregnancy. In *Women, health and reproduction*, ed. H. Roberts, 50–74. London: Routledge and Kegan Paul.

Grahame, Peter R. 1991. Finding the reader: Early consumer activism and the project of consumer literacy. *Continuum: The Australian Journal of Media and Culture* 5: 215–27.

Gramsci, Antonio. 1971. *Selections from the prison notebooks*. Trans. and ed. Quinton Hoare and Geoffrey Nowell-Smith. London: Lawrence and Wishart.

Griffith, Alison. 1984. Ideology, education and single parent families: The normative ordering of families through schooling. Ph.D. diss., University of Toronto.

– 1986. Reporting the facts: Media accounts of single parent families. In *Resources for Feminist Research: Issues of the Decade* 15: 32–43.

– 1995. Mothering, schooling, and children's development. In *Experience, knowledge, and ruling relations: Explorations in the social organization of knowledge*, ed. Marie Campbell and Ann Manicom, 108–22. Toronto: University of Toronto Press.

Griffith, Alison, and Dorothy E. Smith. 1987. Constructing cultural knowledge: Mothering as discourse. In *Women and education: A Canadian perspective*, ed. Jane Gaskell and Arlene McLaren, 87–103. Calgary: Detselig.

– 1990a. Coordinating the uncoordinated: Mothering, schooling and the family wage. In *Perspectives on social problems, vol. 2*, ed. Gale Miller and James Holstein, 25–43. Greenwich, Conn.: JAI Press.

– 1990b. What did you do in school today? Mothering, schooling and social class. In *Perspectives on social problems, vol. 2*, ed. Gale Miller and James Holstein, 3–24. Greenwich, Conn.: JAI Press.

Grinnell, Frederick. 1987. *The scientific attitude*. Boulder: Westview Press.

Grosz, Elizabeth. 1990. *Jacques Lacan: A feminist introduction*. London: Routledge.

Gubrium, Jaber F., and James A. Holstein. 1990. *What is family?* Mountain View, Calif.: Mayfield Publishing Co.

Habermas, Jürgen. 1970. Toward a theory of communicative competence. *Inquiry* 13: 114–47.

– 1989. *The structural transformation of the public sphere: An inquiry into a category of bourgeois society*. Trans. Thomas Burger and Frederick Lawrence. Cambridge, Mass.: MIT Press.

Hagedorn, Robert. 1990. *Sociology.* Toronto: Holt, Rinehart and Winston.

Hall, Roberta, and Bernice R. Sandler. 1982. *The classroom climate: a chilly one for women.* Washington, D.C.: Project on the Status and Education of Women, Association of American Colleges.

Haraway, Donna. 1985. A manifesto for cyborgs: Science, technology, and socialist feminism in the 1980s. *Socialist Review* 15: 65–108.

Harding, Sandra. 1982. Is gender a variable in conceptions of rationality? A survey of the issues. *Dialectica* 36(2/3): 226–42.

– 1986. *The science question in feminism.* Ithaca, N.Y.: Cornell University Press.

Hart, Nicky. 1989. Gender and class in England. *New Left Review* 175 (May/June): 19–47.

Hempel, Carl G. 1966. *Philosophy of natural science.* Englewood Cliffs, N.J.: Prentice-Hall.

Hewlett, Sylvia Ann. 1986. *A lesser life: The myth of women's liberation in America.* New York: Warner Books.

Honan, William H. 1994. Arthur Schlesinger Jr. assails campus speech codes: A historian denounces 'ideologues.' *New York Times,* 27 May.

Huber, Joan. 1995. Centennial essay: Institutional perspectives on sociology. *American Journal of Sociology* 101: 194–216.

Hurston, Zora Neale. 1986. *Their eyes were watching God: A novel.* London: Virago.

Isenberg, Daniel. 1984. How senior managers think. *Harvard Business Review* (Nov.–Dec.): 81–90.

Jack, Dana Crowley. 1991. *Silencing the self: Women and depression.* Cambridge, Mass.: Harvard University Press.

Jackson, Nancy. 1995. 'These things just happen': Talk, text, and curriculum reform. In *Experience, knowledge, and ruling relations: Explorations in the social organization of knowledge,* ed. Marie Campbell and Ann Manicom, 164–80. Toronto: University of Toronto Press.

Jameson, Fredric. 1989. *Situation of theory.* Vol. 1 of *The ideologies of theory: Essays 1971–1986.* Minneapolis: University of Minnesota Press.

Kasper, Anne S. 1986. Women's consciousness and a feminist methodology. Department of Sociology, George Washington University.

– 1994. A feminist, qualitative methodology: A study of women with breast cancer. *Qualitative Sociology* 17(3): 263–81.

Keller, Helen [Adams]. 1909. *The story of my life. With her letters (1887–1901) and a supplementary account of her education, including passages from the reports and letters of her teacher, Anne Mansfield Sullivan [Anne Sullivan Macy].* By John Albert Macy. New York: Grosset and Dunlap, 1909.

– 1956. *Teacher: Anne Sullivan Macy; A tribute by the fosterchild of her mind.* Garden City, N.Y.: Doubleday.

Kinsman, Gary. 1995. The textual practices of sexual rule: Sexual policing and gay men. In *Experience, knowledge, and ruling relations: Explorations in the social organization of knowledge*, ed. Marie Campbell and Ann Manicom, 80–95. Toronto: University of Toronto Press.

Kittler, Friedrich A. 1990. *Discourse networks 1800–1900.* Trans. Michael Metteer and Chris Cullens. Stanford: Stanford University Press.

Kolb, David. 1986. *Critique of pure modernity: Hegel, Heidegger and after.* Chicago: University of Chicago Press.

Kovel, Joel. 1982. *Age of desire.* New York: Harper Colophon.

Lacan, Jacques. 1977. *Écrits: A selection.* New York: Norton.

Laclau, Ernesto. 1980. Populist rupture and discourse. *Screen Education* 34: 87–93.

Laclau, Ernesto, and Chantal Mouffe. 1985. *Hegemony and socialist strategy.* London: Verso.

Landes, Joan B. 1995. The public and the private sphere: A feminist reconsideration. In *Feminists read Habermas: Gendering the subject of discourse*, ed. J. Meehan, 91–116. New York: Routledge.

Latour, Bruno. 1990. Drawing things together. In *Representation in scientific practice*, ed. Michael Lynch and Steve Woolgar, 19–68. Boston: MIT Press.

Latour, Bruno, and Steve Woolgar. 1986. *Laboratory life: The construction of scientific facts.* Princeton: Princeton University Press.

Lautens, Trevor. 1994. Fair and square: Profs fire rebuke at dean. *Vancouver Sun*, 29 March, p. A15.

Lee, Alison. 1996. *Gender, literacy, curriculum: Re-writing school geography.* London: Taylor and Francis.

Lee, John E. 1991. Language and culture: The linguistic analysis of culture. In *Ethnomethodology and the Human Sciences*, ed. Graham Button, 196–226. Cambridge: Cambridge University Press.

Lemert, Charles C. 1994. Post-structuralism and sociology. In *The postmodern turn: New perspectives on social theory*, ed. Steven Seidman, 265–81. Cambridge: Cambridge University Press.

Lizardo, Rubén. 1993. Building bridges, demolishing divisions. *Crossroads* 34 (Sept.): 11–14.

Lyotard, Jean-François. 1984. *The postmodern condition.* Minneapolis: University of Minnesota Press.

– 1988. *Peregrinations: Law, form, event.* New York: Columbia University Press.

Macdonnell, Diane. 1986. *Theories of discourse: An introduction.* Oxford: Basil Blackwell.

Magnusson, Warren. 1993. Feminism, McCarthyism and sexist fundamentalism. Department of Political Science, University of Victoria.

Malnarich, Gillies, and Dorothy E. Smith. 1983. Where are the women? Paper presented at the Conference on the Centenary of Marx's Death, University of Manitoba, Winnipeg.

Manicom, Ann. 1988. Constituting class relations: The social organization of teachers' work. Ph.D. diss., University of Toronto.

– 1995. What's health got to do with it? Class, gender, and teachers' work. In *Experience, knowledge, and ruling relations: Explorations in the social organization of knowledge*, ed. Marie Campbell and Ann Manicom, 135–48. Toronto: University of Toronto Press.

Mannheim, Karl. 1971. On the interpretation of Weltanshauung. In *From Karl Mannheim*, ed. K. Wolff. New York: Oxford University Press.

March, Peter, Elizabeth Rosser, and Rom Harré. 1978. *The rules of disorder.* London: Routledge and Kegan Paul.

Marchak, Patricia M. 1996. *Racism, sexism, and the university: The political science affair at the University of British Columbia.* Montreal and Kingston: McGill-Queen's University Press.

Marko, Ksynia. 1994. Materials and weaving. In *The atlas of rugs and carpets*, ed. David Black, 13–19. London: Tiger Books.

Maroney, Heather Jon, and Meg Luxton, eds. 1987. *Feminist and political economy: Women's work, women's struggles.* Toronto: Methuen.

Marx, Karl. 1955. *The poverty of philosophy.* Moscow: Progress Publishers.

– 1973. *Grundrisse: Introduction to the critique of political economy.* Trans. Martin Nicolaus. New York: Random House.

Marx, Karl, and Friedrich Engels. 1973. *Feuerbach: Opposition of the materialist and idealist outlooks.* London: Lawrence and Wishart.

– 1976. *The German ideology.* Moscow: Progress Publishers.

– 1988. *The communist manifesto.* London: Verso.

Maurer, David W. 1964. *Whiz mob: A correlation of the technical argot of pickpockets with their behavior.* New Haven, Conn.: College and University Press.

– 1981. The argot of pickpockets. In *Language of the underworld*, ed. Allan W. Futrell and Charles B. Wordell, 234–56. Lexington: University of Kentucky Press.

McCoy, Liza. 1991. Accounting as inter-organizational organization. Paper presented at the annual meetings of the Society for the Study of Social Problems, Cincinnati, Ohio.

– 1995. Activating the photographic text. In *Experience, knowledge, and ruling relations: Explorations in the social organization of knowledge*, ed. Marie Campbell and Ann Manicom, 181–92. Toronto: University of Toronto Press.

McDermott, R.P., and Henry Tylbor. 1986. On the necessity of collusion in conversation. In *Discourse and institutional authority: Medicine, education, and law*, ed.

Sue Fisher and Alexandra Dundas Todd, 123–39. Norwood, N.J.: Ablex Publishing.

McEwen, Joan I. 1995. *Report in respect of the Political Science Department of the University of British Columbia.* Vancouver: University of British Columbia.

Mead, George Herbert. 1938. *The philosophy of the act.* Ed. Charles W. Morris. Chicago: University of Chicago Press.

– 1947. *Mind, self and society : From the perspective of a social behaviorist.* Ed. Charles W. Morris. Chicago: University of Chicago Press.

– 1992. *The individual and the social self: Unpublished work of George Herbert Mead.* Ed. with an introduction by David L. Miller. Chicago: University of Chicago Press.

Merleau-Ponty, Maurice. 1962. *Phenomenology of perception.* London: Routledge and Kegan Paul.

Merton, Robert K. 1967. *On theoretical sociology.* London: Collier-Macmillan.

Messer-Davidow, Ellen. 1993. Manufacturing the attack on liberalized higher education. *Social Text* 36 (Fall): 40–79.

Meyer, John W., John Boli, and George M. Thomas. 1994. Ontology and rationalization in the Western cultural account. In *Institutional environments and organizations: Structural complexity and individualism,* ed. W. Richard Scott, John W. Meyer, et al. Thousand Oaks/London/New Delhi: Sage.

Mintzberg, Henry. 1973. *The nature of managerial work.* New York: Harper Row.

Mitchell, Juliet, and Jacqueline Rose, eds. 1982. *Feminine sexuality: Jacques Lacan and the école Freudienne.* London: Macmillan.

Mohanty, Chandra Talpade. 1995. Feminist encounters: Locating the politics of experience. In *Social postmodernism: Beyond identity politics,* ed. Linda Nicholson and Steven Seidman, 68–86. Cambridge: Cambridge University Press.

Moore, Henrietta L. 1988. *Feminism and anthropology.* Minneapolis: University of Minnesota Press.

Morris, Charles W. 1955. *Signs, language and behavior.* New York: George Braziller.

Mowitt, John. 1992. *Text: The genealogy of an antidisciplinary object.* Durham, N.C.: Duke University Press.

Moynihan, Daniel P. 1965. *The negro family: The case for national action.* Washington, D.C.: U.S. Department of Labor, Office of Policy Planning and Research.

Mueller, Adele. 1987. Peasants and professionals: The social organization of women and development knowledge. Ph.D. diss., University of Toronto.

– 1995. Beginning in the standpoint of women: An investigation of the gap between *cholas* and 'Women of Peru.' In *Experience, knowledge, and ruling relations: Explorations in the social organization of knowledge,* ed. Marie Campbell and Ann Manicom 96–107. Toronto: University of Toronto Press.

Murdock, George P. 1949. *Social structure.* New York: Macmillan.

Murphy, George J. 1980. Some aspects of auditing evolution in Canada. *Accounting Historians Journal* 7(3): 45–61.

– 1984. Early Canadian financial statement disclosure legislation. *Accounting Historians Journal* 11(2): 40–59.

Musgrove, F. 1970. The 'Good Home.' In *Family, class and education: A reader*, ed. M. Craft, 184–202. London: Longman.

Naylor, Tom. 1975. *The banks and financial capital.* Vol. 1 of *The history of Canadian business 1867–1914*. Toronto: James Lorimer.

Ng, Roxana. 1990. Immigrant women: The construction of a labour market category. *Canadian Journal of Women and the Law* 4: 96–112.

– 1995. Multiculturalism as ideology: A textual analysis. In *Experience, knowledge, and ruling relations: Explorations in the social organization of knowledge*, ed. Marie Campbell and Ann Manicom, 35–48. Toronto: University of Toronto Press.

Noble, David. 1979. *America by design: Science, technology and the rise of corporate capitalism*. Oxford: Oxford University Press.

Norris, Christopher. 1991. *Spinoza and the origins of modern critical theory*. Oxford: Basil Blackwell.

Oakley, Ann. 1981. Interviewing women: A contradiction in terms. In *Doing feminist research*, ed. Helen Roberts, 30–61. London: Routledge and Kegan Paul.

Paget, Marianne A. 1987. Unlearning to not speak. Paper presented at the meetings of the Society for the Study of Social Problems, Chicago.

Parsons, Talcott. 1968. *Marshall. Pareto. Durkheim.* Vol. 1 of *The structure of social action*. New York: Free Press.

– 1982a. The role of theory in social research. In *Talcott Parsons on institutions and social evolution*, ed. L.H. Mayhew, 65–75. Chicago: University of Chicago Press.

– 1982b. The superego and the theory of social systems. In *Talcott Parsons on institutions and social evolution*, ed. L.H. Mayhew, 129–44. Chicago: University of Chicago Press.

Pengelly, Beth. 1996. Introducing the classics: A case study of the introductory work to translations of Max Weber and Georg Simmel. Ph.D. diss., Murdoch University.

Perrow, Charles. 1986. *Complex organizations: A critical essay*. Glenview, Ill.: Scott, Foresman and Co.

Piaget, Jean. 1958. *The child's construction of reality*. London: Routledge and Kegan Paul.

Pollitt, Katha. 1993. This just in: We're not as wise as Plato: Allan Bloom has departed, leaving behind his indictment of American cultural life. Review of *Love and Friendship*, by Allan Bloom. *New York Times Book Review*, 8 Aug. 1993, p. 9.

Prentice, Susan. 1996. Addressing and redressing chilly climates in higher education. *CAUT Bulletin* [status of women supplement] 43(4): 7–8.

President's Advisory Committee on the Status of Women, University of Saskatchewan. 1995. Reinventing our legacy: The chills which affect women. In *Breaking anonymity: The chilly climate for women faculty*, ed. the Chilly Collective, 171–210. Waterloo, Ont.: Wilfrid Laurier University Press.

Radstone, Susannah. 1992. Postcard from the edge: Thoughts on the 'Feminist Theory: An International Debate' conference held at Glasgow University, Scotland, 12–15 July 1991. *Feminist Review* 40 (Spring): 85–93.

Rapp, Rayna. 1978. Family and class in contemporary America: Notes towards an understanding of ideology. *Science and Society* 42: 278–300.

Reimer, Marilee. 1988. The social organization of the labour process: A case study of the documentary management of clerical labour in the public service. Ph.D. diss., University of Toronto.

– 1995. Downgrading clerical work in a textually mediated labour process. In *Experience, knowledge, and ruling relations: Explorations in the social organization of knowledge*, ed. Marie Campbell and Ann Manicom, 193–208. Toronto: University of Toronto Press.

Reinharz, Shulamit. 1983. Experiential analysis: A contribution to feminist research. In *Theories of women's studies,* ed. G. Bowles and R. Duelli Klein, 162–91. London: Routledge and Kegan Paul.

Richer, Stephen, and Lorna Weir, eds. 1995. *Beyond political correctness: The future of the Canadian academy.* Toronto: University of Toronto Press.

Romero, Mary. 1992. Ethnographical evaluation of behavioral causes of census undercounts of undocumented immigrants and Salvadorans in the Mission District of San Francisco, CA. Report submitted to the Center for Survey Methods Research, Bureau of the Census, Washington, D.C.

Rorty, Richard. 1994. Method, social science, and social hope. In *The postmodern turn: New perspectives on social theory*, ed. Steven Seidman, 46–64. Cambridge: Cambridge University Press.

Rosenau, Pauline Marie. 1992. *Post-modernism and the social sciences: Insights, inroads and intrusions.* Princeton, N.J.: Princeton University Press.

Rothenbuhler, Eric W. 1990. The liminal fight: Mass strikes as ritual and interpretation. In *Durkheimian sociology: Cultural studies*, ed. Jeffrey C. Alexander, 67–87. Cambridge: Cambridge University Press.

Rousseau, Jean-Jacques. 1979. *Emile; or, on education.* Introd. and trans. Allan Bloom. New York: Basic Books.

Rubin, Iakov Izrailevich. 1973. *Essays on Marx's theory of value.* Montreal: Black Rose Books.

Ryan, Mary P. 1993. Gender and public access: Women's politics in nineteenth-century America. In *Habermas and the public sphere*, ed. Craig Calhoun. Cambridge, Mass.: The MIT Press.

Saber, Mostafa, and Mansour Hekmat. 1992. Labour law against workers' rights: A critique of labour law. *Labour Solidarity*, Jan./Feb., p. 4.

Sachs, Albie, and Joan Hoff Wilson. 1978. *Sexism and the law: A study of male beliefs and judicial bias in Britain and the United States*. New York: Oxford University Press.

Said, Edward W. 1979. *Orientalism*. New York: Vintage Books.

Salecl, Renata. 1994. *The spoils of freedom: Psychoanalysis and feminism after the fall of socialism*. London: Routledge.

Sandler, Bernice R., Lisa A. Silverberg, and Roberta Hall. 1996. *The chilly classroom climate: A guide to improve the education of women*. Washington, D.C.: National Association for Women in Education.

Saunders, Doug. 1995. Ruffled feathers on campus. *Globe and Mail*, 1 July, pp. A1, A3.

Saussure, Ferdinand de. 1959. *A course in general linguistics*. New York: Philosophical Library [originally published in 1916].

Schatzmann, Leonard, and Anselm Strauss. 1966. Social class and modes of communication. In *Communication and culture: Readings in the codes of human interaction*, ed. Afred G. Smith, 442–55. New York: Holt, Rinehart and Winston.

Schiffrin, Deborah. 1994. *Approaches to discourse*. Oxford: Blackwell.

Schrecker, Ellen W. 1986. *No ivory tower: McCarthyism and the universities*. New York: Oxford University Press.

Schutz, Alfred. 1962a. Commonsense and scientific interpretations of human action. In *Collected papers, vol. 1*, 3–47. The Hague: Martinus Nijhoff.

– 1962b. On multiple realities. In *Collected papers, vol. 1*, 207–59. The Hague: Martinus Nijhoff.

Scott, Joan W. 1992. Experience. In *Feminists theorize the political*, ed. Judith Butler and Joan W. Scott, 22–40. New York: Routledge.

Scott, W. Richard. 1995. *Institutions and organizations*. Thousand Oaks, Calif.: Sage.

Scott, W. Richard, John W. Meyer, et al. 1994. *Institutional environments and organizations: Structural complexity and individualism*. Thousand Oaks, Calif.: Sage Publications.

Scully, Samuel E. 1993. Memorandum to all regular faculty members. Department of Political Science, University of Victoria, 26 May.

Searle, John R. 1969. *Speech acts: An essay in the philosophy of language*. New York: Cambridge University Press.

– 1995. *The construction of social reality*. New York: The Free Press.

Seidman, Steven. 1992. Postmodern social theory as narrative with a moral intent. In *Postmodernism and social theory*, ed. Steven Seidman and David G. Wagner, 47–81. Oxford: Blackwell.

- 1994. The end of sociological theory. In *The postmodern turn: New perspectives on social theory*, ed. Steven Seidman, 119–39. Cambridge: Cambridge University Press.

Shapin, Steve, and Simon Schaffer. 1985. *Leviathan and the air pump: Hobbes, Boyle, and the experimental life.* Princeton, N.J.: Princeton University Press.

Sherwin, Susan. 1988. Philosophical methodology and feminist methodology. In *Feminist perspectives: Philosophical essays on method and morals*, ed. L. Code et al., 13–28. Toronto: University of Toronto Press.

Sloan, Albert. 1964. *My years with General Motors.* New York: Doubleday.

Smith, Dorothy E. 1987. *The everyday world as problematic: A feminist sociology.* Boston: Northeastern University Press; Toronto: University of Toronto Press.

- 1988. Writing sociology: The feminist contradiction. Paper presented at the conference 'Feminist Transformations of the Social Sciences,' Hamilton College, Clinton, N.Y.

- 1989a. Women's work as mothers: A new look at the relations of family, class and school achievement. In *Perspectives on social problems. Vol. 1*, ed. Gale Miller and James Holstein, 109–25. Greenwich, Conn.: JAI Press.

- 1989b. Sociological theory: Writing patriarchy into feminist texts. In *Feminism and sociological theory*, ed. Ruth Wallace, 34–64. Newbury Park, Calif.: Sage Publications.

- 1990a. *The conceptual practices of power: A feminist sociology of knowledge.* Boston: Northeastern University Press; Toronto: University of Toronto Press.

- 1990b. *Texts, facts, and femininity: Exploring the relations of ruling.* London: Routledge.

- 1990c. The active text. In *Texts, facts and femininity: Exploring the relations of ruling*, 120–58. London: Routledge.

- 1990d. Femininity as discourse. In *Texts, facts and femininity: Exploring the relations of ruling*, 159–208. London: Routledge.

- 1992a. The out-of-body subject: Contradictions for feminism. Paper presented at the meetings of the American Sociological Association, Cincinnati.

- 1992b. Sociology from women's experience: A reaffirmation. *Sociological Theory* 10: 88–98.

- 1993a. High noon in textland: A critique of Clough. *Sociological Quarterly* 34(1): 183–92.

- 1993b. The Standard North American Family: SNAF as an ideological code. *Journal of Family Issues* 14(2): 50–65.

- 1995. Texts and the ontology of large-scale organization. Unpublished paper, Ontario Institute for Studies in Education.

- 1997. Review of *Racism, sexism and the university: The political science affair at the University of British Columbia*, by Patricia Marchak. *Canadian Journal of Higher Education* 27 (2/3): 252–6.

- 1998 (forthcoming). The underside of schooling: Restructuring, privatization, and women's unpaid work. *Journal for a Just and Caring Education.*

Smith, Dorothy E., and Alison Griffith. 1990. Coordinating the uncoordinated: Mothering, schooling and the family wage. In *Perspectives on social problems, vol. 2,* ed. Gale Miller and James Holstein, 25–43. Greenwich, Conn.: JAI Press.

Smith, Dorothy E., Liza McCoy, and Paula Bourne. 1995. *Girls and schooling: Their own critique.* Toronto: OISE, Centre for Women's Studies in Education Publications Series.

Smith, George W. 1988. Occupation and skill: Government discourse as problematic. Occasional Paper, no. 2. The Nexus Project: Studies in the Job Education Nexus, Toronto.

- 1990. Political activist as ethnographer. *Social Problems* 37: 401–21.

- 1995. Accessing treatments: Managing the AIDS epidemic in Ontario. In *Experience, knowledge, and ruling relations: Explorations in the social organization of knowledge,* ed. Marie Campbell and Ann Manicom, 18–34. Toronto: University of Toronto Press.

- 1998 (forthcoming). The ideology of 'fag': Barriers to education for gay students. *Sociological Quarterly.*

Soler, Colette. 1995. The subject and the other (I). In *Reading seminar XI: Lacan's four fundamental concepts of psychoanalysis,* ed. Richard Feldstein, Bruce Fink, and Maire Jaanus, 39–44. Albany, N.Y.: State University of New York Press.

Spanier, Bonnie B. 1995. *Impartial science: Gender ideology in molecular biology.* Bloomington: Indiana University Press.

Stacey, Judith. 1988. Can there be a feminist ethnography? *Women's Studies International Forum* 11: 21–7.

Stack, Carol B. 1974. *All our kin.* New York: Harper and Row.

Stanley, Liz, and Sue Wise. 1983. *Breaking out: Feminist consciousness and feminist research.* London: Routledge and Kegan Paul.

- 1993. *Breaking out again: Feminist epistemology and ontology.* London: Routledge.

Sterling, Robert, and Denise Khouri. 1979. Unemployment indices: The Canadian context. In *Economy, class and social reality,* ed. John Fry. Toronto: Butterworth.

Stinchcombe, Arthur. 1983. The origins of sociology as a discipline. *Ars Sociologica* 27: 1–11.

Suchman, Lucy A. 1987. *Plans and situated actions: The problem of human-machine communication.* Cambridge: Cambridge University Press.

Sullivan, Anne Mansfield. 1909. Passages from the reports and letters of [Helen Keller's] teacher. Included in a supplementary account to Helen Keller's *The story of my life,* prepared by John Albert Macy. New York: Grosset and Dunlap.

Therborn, Göran. 1984. Classes and states: Welfare state developments, 1881–1981. *Studies in Political Economy: A Socialist Review* 14: 7–14.

Turner, Susan M. 1995. Rendering the site developable: Textual organization in the planning process. In *Experience, knowledge, and ruling relations: Explorations in the social organization of knowledge,* ed. Marie Campbell and Ann Manicom, 234–48. Toronto: University of Toronto Press.

Turner, Victor. 1969. *The ritual process: Structure and anti-structure.* Chicago: Aldine Press.

Uchitelle, Louis. 1993. How Clinton's economic strategy ended up looking like Bush's: A theory of growth that has never worked is now the sacred text. *New York Times,* 1 Aug., pp. 1, 4.

Veblen, Thorstein. 1957. *The higher learning in America.* New York: Hill and Wang.

– 1967. *Absentee ownership.* Boston: Beacon Press.

Vološinov, V.I. 1973. *Marxism and the philosophy of language.* Trans. I.R. Titunik. New York: Academic Press.

– 1976. *Freudianism: A Marxist critique.* Trans. L. Matejka and I.R. Titunik. Cambridge, Mass.: Harvard University Press.

Walker, Gillian 1991. *Family violence and the women's movement: The conceptual politics of struggle.* Toronto: University of Toronto Press.

– 1995. Violence and the relations of ruling: Lessons from the battered women's movement. In *Experience, knowledge, and ruling relations: Explorations in the social organization of knowledge,* ed. Marie Campbell and Ann Manicom, 65–89. Toronto: University of Toronto Press.

Wallace, Walter L. 1988. Toward a disciplinary matrix in sociology. In *Handbook of sociology,* ed. Neil J. Smelser. Newbury Park, Calif.: Sage.

Wasserstein, Wendy. 1993. I can get it for you retail: Murder, mystery, and romance, in a novel about a high-profile, high-fashion department store. Review of *Carriage Trade,* by Stephen Birmingham. *New York Times Book Review,* 8 Aug., p. 8.

Weber, Max. 1978. *Economy and society.* Ed. Guenther Roth and Claus Wittich. Trans. E. Fischoff. Berkeley: University of California Press.

Weir, Lorna. 1994. PC then and now: Resignifying political correctness. In *Beyond political correctness: The future of the Canadian academy,* ed. Stephen Richer and Lorna Weir. Toronto: University of Toronto Press.

Westwood, Sallie. 1984. *All day, every day: Factory and family in the making of women's lives.* London: Pluto Press.

White, Hayden. 1976. The fictions of factual representation. In *Selected papers from the English Institute,* ed. A. Fletcher, 21–44. New York: Columbia University Press.

Wieder, D. Lawrence. 1974. *Language and social reality: The case of telling the convict code.* The Hague: Mouton.

Willis, Paul. 1977. *Learning to labor: How working-class kids get working-class jobs.* New York: Columbia University Press.

Wilson, Deborah. 1993. Sexual-politics battle rages in university. *Globe and Mail*, 19 April, p. A1.

Wilson, Edward O. 1978. *On human nature.* Cambridge, Mass.: Harvard University Press.

Wilson, William Julius. 1987. *The truly disadvantaged: The inner city, the underclass, and public policy.* Chicago: University of Chicago Press.

Wittgenstein, Ludwig. 1953. *Philosophical investigations.* Oxford: Basil Blackwell.

Yates, JoAnne. 1989. *Control through communication: The rise of system in American management.* Baltimore: Johns Hopkins University Press.

Young, Michael D., and Peter Willmott. 1986. *Family and kinship in East London.* London: Routledge.

Young, Robert. 1981. *Untying the text: A poststructuralist reader.* London: Routledge.

Žižek, Slavoj. 1993. *Tarrying with the negative: Kant, Hegel, and the critique of ideology.* Durham, N.C.: Duke University Press.

– 1994. *The metastases of enjoyment: Six essays on woman and causality.* London: Verso.

Name Index

Subject Index

academy, the: capitalism and, 27; and class, 15–16, 20–4, 26, 202; disciplinary norms of, 26; and discourse, 17, 19–20, 23, 26, 29, 33, 40, 74, 173, 197, 202, 204–5; and epistemology, 26; and feminism, 9, 10, 20–1, 25–7; and the 'main business' of ruling, 39–40; male domination of discourse in, 20, 202; networks of, in the 'chilly climate' controversy, 196, 221; organization of, 28; politics of, 26; racism in, 197, 198, 204, 208, 209–12, 218–19; and requirements of global capitalism, 27; and the 'ruling relations,' 39–40, 174; universalizing discourse and the order of, 197; women in, 17–18, 20–1, 197, 200–1, 226; women students in, 196, 200–2, 204, 206–9, 212–13, 216, 219–22; and women's experience, 20, 203–4, 209, 214–15, 218–19, 222; women's movement within, 16–17, 17–21, 204. See also faculty; freedom; university

accounting, 83–4, 87–90; and class relations in the workplace, 90; as organizer of relations of work, 88; and the social organization of capital, 82, 84–5, 236n7

achievement. See school achievement

'activation': of men in academic world, 201; of texts, 5, 135, 146, 148, 150–1

'active': texts as, 93, 135–6, 145, 146

activism, 18, 29; Afro-Canadian, 182, 184, 189; campus, 21–3; discursive settings of, 26; of faculty, 22; of feminists in the academy, 21, 25–6; Marxism and, 26; and the PC code, 182, 185–9, 190–3; and sociological discourse, 24, 26; of students, 22, 32, 182, 185–9, 190–1; teaching as, 27; women and, 26; of women's movement, 18, 21, 209

actor: disembodied, in Parsons, 57–8, 233n11; and objectification, 139

actualities, 4–7, 45, 60–1, 65, 73, 74–5, 125, 129, 165, 169, 226; and the 'ideal speech situation,' 222; knowing and, 47–8; Marxist theory and, 34, 225–6, 232n5; objectifications of sociology and, 35, 67; organization of local, 80; and politics of the women's movement, 17; procedures for going from, to objectified repre-

women's movement, 4, 17–20, 20–1, 24, 31, 73, 96, 101, 226; women's studies courses and, 18–20
experiential analysis (Reinharz), 63
explanation, 8, 32, 45, 60, 65, 74

facts: and order of discourse, 61. *See also* social facts
faculty, 202, 210, 212; academic freedom of, 21–3, 198; authority of, 222; authority of male, 219–21; interviews with women, 203–4; junior, 196, 203–4, 206, 207, 213, 220; liberal, 22; male, 196–7, 201, 203–5, 207–8, 214–15, 219–22; and PC, 182, 194; repression of, 22–3; women, 196, 201, 203–4
faculty association (U of V), 196, 214
family: African-American, and unemployment, 165–6, 169; African-American women's, experience, 67–8; 'defective,' 161–3, 168, 171; extended, 167; feminist critique of representation of, 160; household and, equated by SNAF, 169; ideology of the single parent, 163; 'intact' (Wilson), 161–4, 165–7; Marxism and theories of, 160; nonintact, 160; nuclear, 159–60, 163; as peripheral to 'main business' of ruling, 38–9; regulation of, and inheritance, 82, 236n2; representations of, 160; single-parent, 163; sociological representation of, 67–8; theory of, and economics, 160; women-headed, 68, 157–8, 160, 162, 165–9, 171, 246n5. *See also* kin relations; Standard North American Family
feelings, 6, 9, 75; freedom and, 155;

reading and, 148–53; and theory, 150
feminism: in the academy, 9–10, 20–1, 25–7; critical consciousness of, 48; exclusion of topics of, by 'main business' of ruling, 37–8; hegemony within, 24; and juridical definitions of 'sexual harassment,' 210–11; and 'main business' of ruling, 37–41; and Marxism, 29, 207; and method of experience, 161; and PC, 194; as personal practice, 47–8; and politics, 18–19, 29; professionalization of, 21; project of, 27; rejection of unitary subject by, 102; and the 'ruling relations,' 21, 47; subverted by the constitutive conventions, 62–7. *See also* 'chilly climate'; women's movement
feminist: consciousness, 46, 48; critique of agentic assumptions of sociology, 148; critique of the 'chilly climate,' 196, 199, 203–5, 217; critique from experience of, 17; critique of gender order by 'chilly climate' Report, 220; critique and 'juridical discourse,' 198; critique and the 'main business' of ruling, 43; critique of political economy, 29, 37, 43–4; critique of representation of the family, 160; critique rewritten by Letter, 196, 199; critique of scientific epistemology, 105; critique of sociology's objectifying practices, 62–3, 67; dialogue with established disciplines, 26; discourse, 104, 197, 203–5, 207, 218; epistemology, 29, 101; method, 31, 161, 232n5; philosophers, 69; political economists, 38; 'postmodern-,

hegemony, 79, 101, 130; within feminism, 24; interpretive, of sociology, 62; of 'juridical discourse,' 196; white masculine, and the PC code, 194; within the women's movement, 17, 24

heteroglossia, 136, 177; and sociology, 133, 137, 138, 145

Hispanic: neighbourhood and census categories, 166–7; women in the academy, 20–1. *See also* Chicana/o studies

household, 74, 91; African-American, 68, 168; composition of, and census categories, 166; equated with family by SNAF, 169; organization, 167; and political economy, 37; SNAF conception of, 159, 171

housewife, 73. *See also* women's work

Human Relations Area Files (HRAF), 159, 161

humanities, 20, 202, 204–5

hunter-gatherers, 159–60, 170

hybrid sentences/utterances, 137, 141, 147, 187, 207

hyper-reality: reproduction of texts as, 86–7; ruling relations as, 84–91. *See also* simulation

'ideal speech situation' (Habermas), 221–2

'ideological codes,' 11, 158–9; devices and, 175–6; discourse and, 157; as generator of procedures, 175; as ideological intervention, 172; and intentionality of writer or reader, 170; and interpretation, 159, 176; as 'master-frames,' 175–6; as organizers, 175, 177; and PC, 172, 176–7, 178–9, 193; problematic of, 157–8;

and reading, 174–5, 177; and the regulation of public discourse, 172–7; and relations of discourse, 157; and representation, 160; reproduction of the organization of, in texts, 163, 175; as schema, 159, 177. *See also* 'political correctness'; 'political correctness code'; Standard North American Family

ideology, 7, 49, 65, 75, 89, 92, 140, 154, 157, 231n18; and language, 98; and PC, 191–2; and public discourse, 172–6; right-wing, 178, 192; of the school system, 161; of the single-parent family, 163; and the subject (Althusser), 78; and subordination of women, 93

illocutionary force. *See* 'performative'

immigrants, 166

imperialism, 18, 42, 105, 178, 182

indexicality, 95, 125–7, 129–30, 233n13; 'circle of' (Garfinkel), 125–6

'individuated consciousness' (Lacan), 106, 107–9, 118–19, 127

individuated subject, 104–9, 114–15, 118, 127, 240n13

inquiry: knower of, 5, 75; method of, 4–5, 5–8, 48, 73, 74–5, 94–5, 97, 156, 176, 232n5; and post-structuralism/postmodernism, 103–4, 109; social scientific, 4; and sociology, 5, 12, 44, 96–8, 103; and theorizing, 103; and truth, 97, 127–8; from women's standpoint, 94, 225–6; and 'writing the social,' 130

'insider's sociology' (Smith), 49, 225

'institutional ethnography,' 228

'institutional processes' (Smith), 153

'institutionalism' (Scott), 225

reading, 190–1; of post-Parsonian
sociology, 58; qualitative, 5, 63, 138;
quantitative, 5, 58, 61; of 'reading
the social,' 52; of representation, 59; of sampling, 58; social science's, of writing and objectification, 30, 31; of standardization of
texts and utterances, 145; survey,
88, 106; of textual analysis, 144, 199,
218; of writing and reading texts,
54–5; of writing and sociological
theory, 54–5; of 'writing the social,'
11–12, 30–1, 52, 129–30
middle class: gender relations of, 91;
ideology and the, male subject, 92;
male reader, 92; and the ruling relations, 92–3; women excluded from
education, 92–3; women and 'mothering discourse,' 162. See also bourgeoisie
'middle range' theory (Merton), 58
mind: and categories, 7; theory of
(Mead), 109, 240n14, 241n20,
241nn22–3
mode of production, 37–8, 77
modernism: and problem of the subject, 10, 24, 98. See also unitary subject
monologic (Bakhtin), 139, 155, 244n3;
as device in sociology, 139, 141, 145,
152, 153; PC code as, regime, 186
mothering, 6, 47, 73, 93, 157, 161–5,
168, 170, 190–1. See also children;
school; schooling
'mothering discourse' (Griffith and
Smith), 162–5; and interviewing,
164–5; and schemata, 162; as SNAF-
ordered, 162–3
movement: labour, 40; PC represented as, 192–3; PC, in universities, 26,

184–5; social, 136, 172. See also
women's movement
Moynihan Report, 170
multiculturalism, 174, 193

Nabisco. See RJR/Nabisco
naming: and constitution of objects
through social action, 114–22, 126,
127–8; and difference, 121; and
experience, 121; and Helen Keller,
116–17, 121; and 'inter-individual
territory,' 117; and knowledge, 115,
119; and maps, 126; objects as
three-way relation, 116–17; and
recognition, 118; social 'grammar'
of, 117; as social organization of
relations, 116; and the subject,
117
narrative: CBC documentary as,
180–1; PC code and, 184, 190, 191,
193; practices of sociology, 57–8, 62;
of the reporter, 185; SNAF-
governed, 167
National Center for Health Statistics
(U.S.), 166
'new authoritarianism' (Fekete), 216
New Republic, 192
New York Stock Exchange, 90
New York Times, 175, 193
New York Times Book Review, 193
New York University, 190–1
news. See mass media/communication
Newsweek, 190, 193
'nominalization,' 59–60, 107–8. See also
devices
novel: compared to sociological writing, 137–8, 155; dialogic of, 227; representation in, 137; and 'spheres of
activity,' 143; stylistics of, 139; theory
of (Bakhtin), 11, 133, 136–7, 143,

Department of Political Science
(U of V)
politics: of academy, 26; conceptual
practice of discourse of, 4; and feminism, 18–19, 21, 29; of the women's
movement, 17, 31
positivism, 46–7, 55, 61, 63, 214, 232n5
'postmodern-feminist theory' (Fraser
and Nicholson), 101
post-structuralism/postmodernism,
76, 98, 96–130, 227, 239n4; as alternative, 99–104; and capture of the
subject, 80, 120; critique of representation by, 85, 97–8, 99–103, 109,
128; and discourse, 24, 80, 85, 97,
99–101, 102–3, 109, 112, 127, 225;
and experience, 24; feminist, theory, 24, 101, 106–7; inquiry and,
103–4, 109; and knowledge, 99, 100–
1, 103–4, 106, 108–9; and objectification, 130, 225; and the problem of
the subject, 10, 24, 109, 127, 225;
reproducible reference precluded
in, 103, 225; and the social, 107; subject as effect of discourse in, 85, 101,
120, 127; truth claims rejected by,
99–100, 127
'power/knowledge' (Foucault), 33, 34,
94, 100, 105, 108, 173–4, 196
practice, 49, 118, 124, 154–5; accounting, 90; actual, 102, 176; alienated,
48; child's, of constituting an object,
117; conceptual, 4, 41; everyday,
203–5, 223, 225; feminism as personal, 47–8; feminist critique of sociology's objectifying, 62–3, 67; local,
of discourse, 134, 226; local, and
gender organization, 199; local, of
interpretation, 153; local, of
research, 145, 158; local, of sociol-

ogy, 133, 135, 145; local, of universities, 204; local, of writing and
reading, 141; narrative, of sociology,
57–8, 62; objectifying, and 'juridical
discourse,' 198; objectifying, in
sociological discourse, 58; of objectivity, 33, 212; and ontology, 75;
ordinary sociological, of objectification, 59–62; PC as, of interpretation,
176; and PC code, 185, 190, 193; of
pickpockets, 144; racist, 189, 194;
reading as, 50–5, 80, 141, 153, 199;
of recognition, 129; of referring,
116–18, 122, 127, 129; representational, 130; repression as textual,
195; research, 145, 158, 170; and ruling, 158; and the 'ruling relations,'
158; of school mothers, 164–5; of
science, 87, 123–4; sexist, 189, 194;
sociological, 58; sociology as local,
133, 135, 145; and T-discourse, 158;
textual, 55, 87, 123, 177; and theory,
7, 49, 75, 176; thought as actual
socially organized, 49; of women's
movement, 18; writing as, 50, 52–3,
100, 141
primary speech genre. See speech
genre
principle: freedom of speech as,
185–6, 191–2; of rational discourse,
204, 221–3
problematic, 25–8, 48–9, 214; of every-
day/everynight, 7, 25, 44–5, 154,
225; everyday world as (Smith), 161,
232n5; of a feminist sociology, 226;
of 'ideological codes,' 157–8; of
knowledge, 76, 104–5
proletariat, 34. See also working class
proxy: reader as text's, 148, 150–3
'psychiatrized,' 149

Truly Disadvantaged, The (Wilson), 161
truth: claims rejected by post-structur-
    alists/postmodernists, 99–100, 127;
    difference and, 128; as effect of dis-
    course, 100–1; and epistemology,
    101; and the 'ideal speech situa-
    tion,' 221; and inquiry, 97, 127–8;
    and 'juridical discourse,' 212–13; as
    local achievement, 127–8; precondi-
    tions of, 128; as social act, 128;
    sociological theory and, 101; univer-
    sity's commitment to, and writing
    sociology, 222–3; and 'writing the
    social,' 130
typification: language of, 159, 234n14
tyranny: from enlightenment to,
    theme in CBC radio documentary,
    180–1, 184, 186, 188, 190–2

unemployment, 165–6, 169
unions. *See* trade union movement
unitary consciousness, 98
unitary standpoint, 153
unitary subject, 104–9, 241n23; devices
    for creating, 104–5; of philosophy,
    104–5; rejected by feminism, 102;
    rejected by post-structuralism/post-
    modernism, 98, 104, 127; women as,
    105
universal: standpoint, 145; subject,
    202, 239n9
universities, 9, 12, 15, 26–7, 84, 157,
    174, 177, 182, 204, 217, 230n6;
    administration of, 21, 23, 135, 192,
    199, 201, 207; claims to objectivity
    by, 219, 222–3; commitment of, to
    truth, 222–3; and the Enlighten-
    ment, 27; gender order of, 196,
    200–2, 204–5, 219; gender organiza-
    tion of, 196, 204–5, 219, 220–2; inter-

sections of gender with regimes of,
    and discourse, 199–203; and 'juridi-
    cal discourse,' 198; knowledge of
    and for women in, 20, 29, 200; mas-
    culine regime in 202; masculinist
    history of, 200–1; 'new authoritari-
    anism' in, 216; and PC, 26, 172, 179,
    180, 184–5, 192, 194; politicization
    of campuses, 21; politics of, 26;
    repression in, 21–4, 26–7; reproduc-
    tion of, as regime, 217; sexism in,
    195, 197, 207–8, 209–12, 215,
    218–19; sexual harassment in,
    184, 203–4, 206, 208, 210–13,
    215–16, 249n7; and state control, 15.
    See also academy; 'chilly climate';
    'political correctness'; women;
    women students
University of British Columbia (UBC),
    29, 198. *See also* Department of Polit-
    ical Science
University of California, Berkeley
    (UCB), 47, 190; free speech move-
    ment at, 23
University of California, Los Angeles
    (UCLA), 22
University of Michigan, 175
University of Toronto (U of T),
    182–3
University of Victoria (U of V), 195,
    204–5. *See also* Department of Polit-
    ical Science
utterance, 113, 120, 122, 134, 136, 139,
    140, 141–5, 147, 179, 187

Varsity (U of T), 182–3, 189
voice appropriation, 153, 155–6, 199

welfare: and the African-American
    family, 165; SNAF and, legislation,

women's research centre (Vancouver), 25, 29–30, 40

women's standpoint, 3–4, 5, 7, 40, 45, 75–6, 91–5; inquiry from, 94, 225–6; located in bodily sites, 75–6; and the ruling relations, 10, 226; sociology from, 9, 25, 46–8, 73–6, 93–4, 96–8, 103, 120

women's studies programs, 202; courses and experience, 18–20; discourses of, 21; and displacement of white women, 20; marginalization of, 202; at the University of British Columbia, 29

women's work, 41, 73, 74, 91–2, 200; in the academy, 18, 24, 27; and children's schooling, 60, 157, 161, 170; researching, as mothers, 161–5; and the ruling relations, 32, 37–8; in textile plant, 89; unwaged, 161. *See also* parents; women's employment; work

work: accounting as organizer of relations of, 88; discipline, 88–9, 93; of mothering, 47, 161–5; reorganization of, and knowledge, 90; of school mothers, 164–5. *See also* women's work

workers: Iranian, 151–3; striking, 141, 155. *See also* proletariat; working class

working class: domesticity and, women, 40; gendered nature of, 40; isolated from the intelligentsia, 15,

26; male domination of, organization, 40; as object of study, 36; parents and children's school achievement, 62; women and welfare, 40–1. *See also* proletariat; workers

writing, 27, 54, 75; as actual, activity, 135–6; as dialogic, 120–1, 136–7; and 'ideological codes,' 159, 170, 175, 177; and interpretation as intertextual practices, 100; practices of, 50, 52–3, 100, 141; as social organization, 142; social science's method of, and objectification, 30–1; sociological, compared to novel, 137–8, 155; sociological conventions of, society into texts, 93; and sociology, 25–8, 44–5, 97, 133, 137, 170, 222–3, 225; and 'transliterating' experience, 51–2. *See also* 'writing the social'

'writing the social,' 4–12, 25–6, 52, 54; as analysis of the ruling relations, 8, 11, 227–8; and constitutional theories of sociology, 54; and epistemology, 25–6; and inquiry, 130; and 'investigations,' 8; method of, 11–12, 52, 129–30; primacy of theory rejected by method of, 129–30; and recognition, 130; and truth, 130. *See also* writing

Yale University. *See* Human Relations Area Files